THE ITALIAN STORY

Books by Geoffrey Trease

SNARED NIGHTINGALE
SO WILD THE HEART

THE
ITALIAN STORY

From the Etruscans to Modern Times

GEOFFREY TREASE

VANGUARD PRESS

New York

Library of Congress Catalogue Card Number: 64-16262

Copyright, ©, mcmlxiii, by Geoffrey Trease

No portion of this book may be reproduced
in any form without the written permission
of the publisher, except by a reviewer who
may wish to quote brief passages in connection with a review for a newspaper,
magazine, or broadcast.

Manufactured in the United States of America

Contents

Illustrations

FOR
CHRISTOPHER
AND
AMORET SCOTT

Introduction

THIS BOOK, as often happens, has been born out of love and frustration.

The love is for Italy, her people and landscape, history and culture. This emotion, frequently amounting to lifelong infatuation, is one to which the British and Americans have always been peculiarly susceptible.

The frustration springs from the difficulty of finding, for the general reader, a simple source for that background historical knowledge without which he may sometimes feel lost and excluded. It is the frustration he experiences when, for instance, he pauses overnight in an Italian town, opens his guide-book, and reads:

Perugia was one of the twelve confederate cities of Etruria, but was conquered by Rome 310 B.C. At the fall of the Western Empire it was devastated by the Goths under Totila, and afterwards suffered the usual vicissitudes of Italian towns till its union with the Papacy under Julius II and Paul III. In 1708 the town was captured by the Duke of Savoy, in 1849 by the Austrians, and in 1860 by the Piedmontese.

Happy, and well-informed, is the traveller who can confidently answer all the questions which leap to mind from such a paragraph. Rare, too, for the age has passed when every gentleman knew his Gibbon and every young lady toyed with the study of Italian. Gone is the Victorian public in which Browning could assume a familiarity with the minor personalities of the Renaissance and for which Garibaldi was a newspaper idol. Today other educational pressures restrict Italian studies to a small minority. German, Spanish and now Russian have displaced the language, as Science has largely ousted Classics. It is now possible, indeed usual, for even the highly-educated person to know nothing of Italy except such unrelated scraps of information as we all pick up by chance. It is regrettable, but he cannot be expected to apologize. In the modern world there are just too many things to learn.

Yet Italy is all around us, blessedly inescapable. In a public art gallery or great country house we are continually reminded of our cultural inheritance. So too in theatre, opera-house and library. Though we need not pretend that we cannot enjoy *Romeo and Juliet* without studying the historical background (did Shakespeare?), there are vast tracts of literature, English and foreign, where such knowledge multiplies our pleasure. From Chaucer, through the Elizabethans, Milton, Byron, Shelley, Keats, Tennyson, Browning, our poetry glows with Italian influence, sparkles with allusion. Our prose similarly. Italy is everywhere in our novels, travel sketches, memoirs and biographies. And when we read foreign literature, turning from Gissing to Goethe, from Lawrence to Stendhal, we may well find ourselves in Italy again.

We feel this though we have never seen the country; yet in fact, though there are no more milords making the Grand Tour and Florence is no longer colonized by genteel expatriates, more of us visit Italy than ever before. We may be seen in our thousands, brows knitted over guide-book, wondering just what were 'the twelve confederate cities of Etruria' or even, to be honest, whether 'Totila' could conceivably be a dictation error for 'Attila'. It is affectation to pretend that we ought to know, but we are teased by our own ignorance.

Why has Sicily finer Greek temples than Greece — two of them far larger than the Parthenon? How can we simply, without studying to degree-level, sort out the Medicis and Borgias, Viscontis and Sforzas, at least enough to make sense of what we see and hear? What were the Austrians (or French or Spaniards) doing in Italy at this time? How did it happen that Naples had a British ambassador, Lady Hamilton's unfortunate husband? That a Genoese discovered America? That, while Sicily is dotted with Greek temples, Greece is dotted with Venetian forts? Some of these questions are less important than others, but it is frustrating not to know the answers.

Over many years the present writer sought vainly for some

simple non-academic book which would provide such answers and present in sweeping outlines a clear perspective of the territory. He was forced in the end to write it for himself. It is offered now with due diffidence to any who do not feel that they already know it all.

1. Greeks and Etruscans

FOR ONE thing we may be thankful: however confused the
outline of Italian history, the outline of Italian geography is
clean-cut, familiar from childhood, unforgettable. No map
is easier to carry in the mind's eye. The long riding boot, kicking a three-cornered hat, was brought to our notice in our
most absorbent years. Even now we can touch in a few major
features with our eyes shut. We can see the snowy semicircle
of the huddled Alps, sealing off the peninsula. The Apennines
we may remember more vaguely, but we have a notion of
them wriggling down the country like a caterpillar. The one
big plain, Lombardy, is in the only possible place, where the
Alps have finished and the Apennines have not begun. And
the one big river, the Po, flows over it eastwards to the
Adriatic.

A childish simplification, which most of us could elaborate
from our reading or travel, but it will do.

If we think back three or four thousand years, it will still
do. Details, of course, are different. We have to wipe from our
mental picture every human modification of the landscape,
whether ruined aqueduct or modern autostrada. The maize
and rice, too, are innovations of yesterday, the oranges and
lemons date only from the Middle Ages, the prickly pear
from the Spanish occupation; even the ancient olives and
vines have not always patterned the slopes with grove and
terrace. Before 1000 B.C. Italy was largely virgin woodland,
dotted with Bronze Age settlements, scored with trackways
one day to become the roads to Rome.

The outline, however, was roughly the one we know. Here
and there, true, the sea ran a mile or two further inland,
where another three thousand years of silting have widened
the alluvial plain. The mountains were a few feet higher,
more forested, less eroded. Vesuvius and Etna smouldered in
craters of unfamiliar shape; other volcanoes, now forgotten,

1

grumbled in Tuscany. Lakes glittered where crops now grow, and many a stream followed a line which would fox the peasant of today. To us such small discrepancies rarely matter. Our simple geographical image fits all periods. Yellow Tiber ran much the same for Horatius as for us, and the leaves in Vallombrosa were already as thick as Milton was to find them.

Until about 1000 B.C. the country which was destined to be so consistently a leader of civilization was relatively backward among the Mediterranean cultures. There was contact with Greece even in 1500, but the Bronze Age in Italy produced no Mycenaean glories. The chief early monuments are the Sardinian *nuraghi*, strange cone-shaped towers of unmortared blocks, about thirty feet in diameter and up to fifty feet high when built. But who raised them, and who dotted the island with standing stones, are questions for the specialist. The mainland has nothing comparable. There are hut-circles and rock cemeteries, left by people of what archaeologists can only call, lamely, the Apennine culture. Further north in the lowlands, notably in Emilia, another group (the 'Terramare culture') built pile-dwellings inside a defensive ditch. Both groups used bronze and made black pottery.

During the second millennium these early inhabitants were dispossessed by invaders, themselves hounded on by pressures in their former homelands. So much is debatable that any dogmatic over-simplified account — who they were, what they were like, which way they came — would be misleading. This much is known: the newcomers, though of various tribes, belonged mainly to our own Indo-European language-group; they could smelt iron and, although not much interested in exploiting the metals of Italy, they did introduce the Iron Age; and they burnt their dead instead of burying them. For the rest, they behaved like most similar invaders, killing or enslaving or driving the natives into the hills, after which (like the Anglo-Saxons in Britain) they warred incessantly among themselves. In Sicily, for instance, the aboriginal Sicani were squeezed into the western corner by Siculi who had crossed the straits, no doubt encouraged in their emigration by stronger rivals who wanted their mainland territory. So too in the hills of Liguria the non-Indo-Europeans survived.

By about 1000 B.C., then, the country was divided between the new tribes, with pockets of pure aboriginal stock here and there, and a good deal more of it enslaved, with the certainty of inter-breeding and eventual absorption. We need not trouble with all the tribal names, the language groupings and sub-groupings. Some have a familiar ring, being immortalized by some special association — the Sabines perhaps, because the so-called 'rape' of their women has been a theme popular with artists, or the Volscians, so vital to the plot of *Coriolanus*. Their neighbours, the Latins, were to have their name perpetuated in a wider context, though it was to be several centuries before they showed any signs of prominence. Still more obscure was a tribe in the far South, the Itali, who (like Amerigo Vespucci) were to give their name to a wider region than they ever knew.

These tribes were cultivators and stock-breeders, little interested in seafaring or fisheries. They developed neither mining nor manufacture beyond their own needs, and did not build big towns. Even at this stage we detect some of the factors which were to influence the basic Roman character and give Latin literature certain features which distinguish it from that of the globe-trotting Greeks.

But it is over early to speak of literature, for as yet no one in Italy can write. There are no precise dates, no documents. This is still prehistory. The archaeologist can fill museums with cinerary urns and other relics from the important Iron-Age culture we call 'Villanovan' (after the town near Bologna) but it is not until the eighth century that the historian can tell us of people and events.

.   .   .   .

The Romans, who liked things definite (and, for prestige, centred on themselves), dated all history from their city's traditional foundation by Romulus, by modern reckoning 753 B.C. The recent excavation of weapons and other articles suggests that several of the seven hills were inhabited before 1500. On the other hand, the unification of these villages into a town did not happen until about 575, when the first forum or market-place was laid out. We should beware, however, of dismissing the legendary version entirely — even the she-wolf story probably preserves some transmogrified significance. The Lupercal festival, kept up from the earliest days to the late fifth century A.D., takes its name from *lupus*, a wolf. The

Luperci, or 'Wolf Priests', raced round the Palatine Hill, wearing only loin-cloths and flicking goat-skin straps at the women who stood in their path. The nature of this fertility-rite is underlined by Shakespeare:

> *Forget not, in your speed, Antonius,*
> *To touch Calpurnia; for our elders say,*
> *The barren, touched in this holy chase,*
> *Shake off their sterile curse.*

Whatever facts are embedded in such folklore and in the later propaganda of the Augustan writers, it is wiser if we want a definite starting date to choose 757, the year now most favoured for the foundation of a very different city, Cumae, on the coast near Naples.

Cumae too is a name evocative of legend, home of the Sibyl, a somewhat Rider-Haggard-type wise woman, already seven hundred years old when she conducted Aeneas on a tour of the Underworld. But Cumae has historical claims as the first Greek colony on the Italian mainland. It was from Cumae, if indirectly, that the Romans were in an exact sense to 'learn their letters'.

This colony was one of scores which the virile Greeks sowed broadcast round the Mediterranean during the next two centuries. From the Caucasus almost to Gibraltar the coasts were beaded with them, each comprising a single port and as much hinterland as it could dominate. Some, like Marseilles, survive. Some, like Odessa, perished and were refounded by other peoples. In Italy the greatest is Cumae's offshoot, Naples. 'Neapolitan' recalls the original name, Neapolis, 'Newtown'. Others founded within the space of fifty years are Syracuse, Reggio, Catania and Taranto. Many more were planted in the same period, more still in later years, yet more in several other Mediterranean lands simultaneously. Such was the marvellous dynamic of Greek expansion.

Why did it happen? How was it organized?

The causes were various. First, as with bee-swarms, there was overcrowding at home. Emigration, as now, was a recognized part of the Greek economy. A new colony was a civic enterprise, not an individual escape. But individualism contributed much to the other causes.

There was the Greek temperament, inquisitive, volatile, alert for change of scene and commercial opportunity. Today, travelling through the poverty-stricken lands of Southern Italy and Sicily, we may not see many attractions for a settler. We must remember how different it was before deforestation, erosion, and malaria. Sicily shimmered with cornfields which were, for an immigrant from stony Greece, the ancient equivalent of the North American prairie provinces. The analogy can be pushed further: in time the Greek colonies, too, outstripped their mother-country in wealth and power, so that Southern Italy was called 'Greater Greece'.

Farmland was not the sole objective. However fertile the inland valleys, the Greeks liked to keep one foot on the beach. Born sailors and traders, they had an eye for harbour facilities. They shared with the Elizabethans a certain inability to distinguish clearly between piracy and private enterprise. Any strong point from which they could levy tolls and protection-money on other traders was not long left unoccupied. Nor were they alone in this. They had Carthaginian and Etruscan competitors. The Western Mediterranean was a battle-ground for rival imperialisms, like the East Indies in the seventeenth century.

Greek colonies were quite independent of their mother-cities. The glaring gap in the Greek genius was its inability to evolve a unifying political system for a wide geographical area. The Greeks shared a language, culture and religion; they respected the same oracles and pilgrim shrines; they associated in festivals like the Olympian Games; but except for short-lived leagues and alliances no two states ever seemed able to share a government. It was almost a Greek instinct not to trust a fellow Greek further than one could see him — the state frontier roughly coincided with the mountainous horizon — and, having learnt by painful experience at home, the Greeks did not attempt the hopeless task of controlling colonies hundreds of miles away. Though the expedition went forth as a public venture, with an officially nominated 'founder' and sacred fire to sanctify its altars, the colony was autonomous from the start and kept only ties of sentiment with the mother-city.

So every few years during this period a fresh convoy could be seen creeping, with ant-like purpose, across blue waters

calmed by the advent of the sailing season. Some were broad-
beamed merchantmen, others war-galleys, probably of the
new design pioneered by the Corinthians about the time they
founded Syracuse — long, low, undecked, with viciously
tapered ram and a single bank of twenty-one oars a side. The
voyage was no *Mayflower* venture into the unknown. Though
some colonies were founded direct from Greece, many were
hived off from previous settlements. Thus Syracuse, herself
established by far-off Corinth, founded three subsequent
colonies of her own in the south-eastern corner of Sicily.

Such colonies became city-states like those at home, with
harbour, market-place and theatre, with fortified acropolis
or 'upper-town', and temples for all the most influential
deities. There was continual intercourse, sometimes friendly,
sometimes less so, with the parent-city and the rest of the
Greek world. Besides the unending to-and-fro of the traders,
men went to Delphi to consult the oracle, to Olympia for the
games, to Athens for the drama festivals, to Epidaurus for
medical treatment. Even the stay-at-homes could look forward to the arrival of new books and celebrity-lecturers. Plato
visited both Sicily and Southern Italy, Herodotus probably
helped to found Thurii. Pythagoras emigrated to Crotone.
At Syracuse a whole galaxy of writers clustered round the
dictator Hieron. There Aeschylus staged his eye-witness
drama of Salamis, *The Persians*, soon after its festival-award
at Athens, and many of Pindar's odes were commissioned. The
choric poet Bacchylides was there, and his uncle Simonides,
who wrote the Spartans' epitaph at Thermopylae, and Epi-
charmus, whose slick prolific comedies Plato admired. Nor
did the colonies depend solely on immigrants and visitors.
Syracuse produced half a dozen outstanding writers, notably
Theocritus, whose idylls have set an indelible Sicilian stamp
on the pastoral convention, and Sophron, whose prose
comedies led Plato to write in dialogue form. These plays
have vanished, but the title of one (*The Mother-in-Law*)
brings us close to the Syracusans who enjoyed it twenty-four
centuries ago.

Sicily was the nursery of Greek rhetoric. It began with the
law-court 'ghost-writers', as we might call them today. The
citizen was expected to speak for himself and not rely on
counsel, but in practice (since even Greeks varied in fluency)

he often delivered speeches prepared for him by a professional. Gorgias of Leontini extended forensic technique to political and other controversies, so that when he visited Athens on a diplomatic mission, forty-four years before Demosthenes was born, his eloquence staggered the far from inarticulate Athenians.

The title 'Father of Rhetoric', however, was given by Aristotle to an earlier Sicilian, Empedocles. Though Empedocles did not really end his days, as in Matthew Arnold's poem, by jumping into the crater of Etna, he was a sufficiently remarkable person. By birth a rich aristocrat — his grandfather had won the chariot-race at the Olympics — he was a conspicuous figure in Agrigento with his purple robe and golden belt, a garland on his long hair and a file of slaves at his heels. In politics he took after his father, a revolutionary democrat, fortified in his views no doubt by his philosophical beliefs, which included the transmigration of souls. As a surviving fragment of his verse says:

> Before this I have been both boy and girl.
> Bush, and bird too, and mute fish in the main.

Poetry and politics, philosophy and physical science, competed for his attention. He helped to overthrow the governing clique of Agrigento and then, with wisdom and consistency, refused the quasi-royal position which the people offered him. In life he was credited with miracles: his death inspired contradictory legends. It is likely that his disappearance *was* mysterious, less likely that he vanished into a volcano or a blaze of divine glory. Perhaps, as the *Encyclopaedia Britannica* suggests, '*a change in the balance of parties compelled him to leave the city, and he died in the Peloponnese of the results of an accident in 430.*'

Philosophy was the main literary contribution of the southern Italian colonies. Xenophanes crossed from Sicily to Elea and founded the Eleatic school continued by Parmenides and Zeno. Crotone and Taranto also had their philosophers. Poetry flourished less on the mainland, and the chief rival to the song-birds of Sicily, Ibycus of Reggio, spent most of his time in Greece. He wrote passionate lyrics and, whether writing choral odes for girls or boys, responded with equal fervour to the charms of the performers.

This then was the society which developed from the eighth century onwards and flourished independently for a longer period than separates the Pilgrim Fathers from ourselves. It is a society demanding no lengthy description because it was the western extension of one familiar to us in the Greek homeland. Neither materially nor culturally was it inferior.

A map of these ancient Mediterranean colonies reveals significant blanks. There are few Greek cities in Spain, none in Sardinia, only one in Corsica, none on the African coast west of Libya. The western corner of Sicily is strangely empty. The reason is simple: these areas were held by a rival imperialism, that of Carthage, herself the overgrown offspring of Phoenicia. The Greeks did not batter their heads against stone walls.

Another such metaphorical wall crossed Italy to the north of Cumae. Beyond it there was no Greek colony, though Greek traders and craftsmen passed freely. Here lay the country of the Etruscans.

.   .   .   .

It is conventional to write of the 'mysterious' Etruscans. They are held to be mysterious because their origin is debatable, their language is unreadable, and their magnificent tombs suggest a morbid preoccupation with the next world. Presumably, though, they did not themselves feel mysterious and could decipher their own handwriting, while the first thing which emerges from the archaeological evidence of the tombs is their obvious *joie de vivre*, their addiction to banquets and shows, to art, sport and venery in both senses. This art has many Oriental motifs, Egyptian, Syrian and Mesopotamian, supporting the theory that they were immigrants from Asia Minor. That could be the kernel of historical fact enshrined in the legend of Aeneas. But there are other artistic motifs derived from the Greeks, just as their alphabet was adapted from that used by the colonists of Cumae.

It was the Latins who called them 'Etrusci' or 'Tusci', whence 'Tuscany'. Their own name for themselves was 'Rasenna', and the Greek word was 'Tyrrhenoi', which survives in the 'Tyrrhenian' Sea, while the Adriatic is so called from the port they established at Adria.

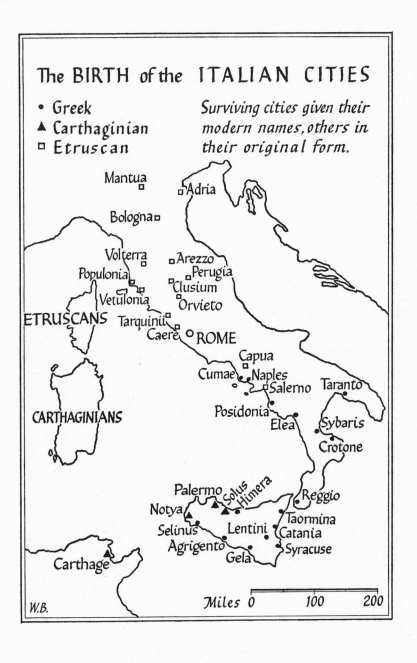

The BIRTH of the ITALIAN CITIES

- Greek
- ▲ Carthaginian
- ▢ Etruscan

Surviving cities given their modern names, others in their original form.

Mantua

Adria

Bologna

Volterra

Arezzo

Populonia

Perugia

Clusium

Vetulonia

Orvieto

ETRUSCANS

Tarquinii

Caere ○ ROME

Capua

Cumae ● Naples

Salerno

Taranto

Posidonia

Elea

Sybaris

CARTHAGINIANS

Crotone

Palermo ▲ Solus Himera

Reggio

Notya ▲

Taormina

Selinus

Lentini Catania

Agrigento

Syracuse

Gela

Carthage ▲

Miles 0   100   200

W.B.

Like the Greeks, they were thrustful merchant venturers, not averse to piracy. They had outposts in Spain, the Balearics, even perhaps in the Canaries. Their exports went as far as Britain and Sweden. Their prosperity was based on mining and metalwork. They were the first to exploit Italy's rich resources of iron and copper, zinc and tin. Tuscany was not particularly fertile and their farms carried more stock than crops. Though they loved horses, hunting and fishing, they were townsmen like the Greeks, in contrast to the country-dwelling Latins and other neighbouring tribes. Unlike the Greeks, however, they built their cities not only along the seaboard at Cerveteri and Piombino, but high in the mountains inland at Orvieto and Chiusi (Lars Porsena's Clusium) and later at Volterra, Perugia and Arezzo.

These cities stood usually on a hill, with another hill close by for burials. The Etruscans were skilful architects, engineers and surveyors: the Romans were to learn much from them. They used arches and barrel-vaulting. One of their gateways still stands at Volterra, relic of a city wall which was five miles round and in places fifty feet high. Wide streets and pavements were laid out to a chequered plan, the bigger houses impressive with loggias, colonnades, and a pillared central hall from which the Romans evolved the atrium. There were built-in water-pipes, fountains and vaulted sewers. In the countryside, canals and irrigation-channels were driven, if necessary, through solid rock.

Small wonder that life for the majority was strenuous. Huge blocks of tufa had to be quarried, transported and built into these miles of cyclopean walls, these acres of road-way and pavement. The miners had to drive perilous little galleries into the mountainside, peck out the ore, and smelt it in crude ovens, after which it was loaded into ships for Athens and other distant destinations. Besides the nameless masters whose work survives in the exquisite bronze chimera at Florence or the terracotta 'Malvolta' head at Rome, there were thousands of journeymen producing swords and scythes or the black *bucchero* pottery which sold from the Sahara to the Thames.

Uppermost of these varied social strata was that elegant ruling class whose dinner-parties and ceremonies the artists immortalized in wall-paintings and sculptures. Husbands and wives reclined at table, silver goblet in hand. The men were long-haired and bearded in the early period; later they cut their hair and shaved. Indoors they were bare-torsoed and kilted like Cretans, laying aside the cloaks (forerunners of the toga) which they wore outside. Beneath the long pleated dresses of the ladies peeped the pointed or curly-toed shoes for which Etruria was famous. Feminine hair-styles passed through all the conceivable mutations of fashion — long, piled up, plaited behind, braided round the temples, framing the face in curls, and the Grecian chignon. The artificial blonde was not unknown, make-up was highly developed, jeweller and goldsmith added sparkle with brooch and bracelet, earring and diadem—and sometimes, when beauty smiled, there was the glint of expert and expensive dentistry. There were flowers in the dining-room, perfume burning on tall stands, and elaborate candelabra in the image of the dancing-girls and boys who entertained the company. The background music of lyre, trumpet and flute provided an additional stimulus to conversation.

To the Greeks (possibly prejudiced by commercial rivalry) the Etruscans were a byword for immorality. The nakedness proper in the gymnasium seemed to them indecent for a servant waiting at table. But what really shocked the Greeks was the presence of women on equal terms at social functions. They alleged that Etruscan women were indiscriminate in their intimacies and uncertain about the paternity of their children. Actually, in some respects, the Etruscan code was quite puritanical, though possibly (like the Ten Commandments in our own society) the more picturesque penalties were not invariably observed in every detail. Homosexuals, for instance, were supposed to be put into a box and thrown into the sea. The strict enforcement of this rule would not (for the Greeks) have offset the daily Etruscan enormity of allowing the ladies to join the gentlemen at dinner.

Religion was important. There was a full establishment of deities, superficially corresponding to those of Olympus. The senior trinity, who sometimes shared a triple temple, were Tinia, Lord of the Thunderbolt, his wife Uni, and Menerva. Maris was god of War, Nethuns of the Sea. Valchans, the smith-god, was understandably favoured in the manufacturing towns, while Turan, goddess of Love, and Fufluns, god of Wine, were nowhere neglected. Turms, who escorted souls to the Underworld, resembled Hermes and Mercury.

Temples were square and massive, only the base of stone, the rest being wood and brick, brilliantly adorned with winged horses, maenads, gorgons, demons, and similar fancies in painted terracotta and other materials. The priesthood wielded considerable political influence, normally conservative. Etruscan religion, unlike Greek, rested on the authority of sacred scriptures which, with augury, allowed subtleties of interpretation and left the layman little scope for disagreement. Even something as obvious as a thunderbolt was ambiguous to the unqualified observer, for no less than nine deities were entitled to hurl one, Tinia having the choice of three types. It was also vital to know which of the sixteen sub-divisions of the sky had been the one selected for the divine manifestation. No less technical queries arose when the internal organs of the sacrificial victims were scrutinized. Even the humblest liver was subdivided like the heavenly vault into areas of divine influence. Young ordinands studied these from bronze models, suitably inscribed and demarcated. This emphasis on augury was perpetuated in Roman religion, as Shakespeare's *Julius Caesar* again reminds us.

Contests of gladiators or wild beasts originated as part of the lavish funeral celebrations for the Etruscan nobility. When they were over, the corpse was conducted to its new habitation in the city of tombs on the next hill—one of those rock-hewn family sepulchres that were, in layout, decor and furnishing, almost a facsimile of the home he had occupied in life. The door was then sealed until the next death, and one more symbol was added to the little cluster outside, each varying in size according to the age of the deceased and in shape, cone or triangle, to indicate the sex.

In the early days each city was ruled by a *lucumo*, or king, attended by lictors bearing the *fasces*, the rods and axes signifying power of chastisement and execution, which the Romans took over and Mussolini revived. The cities were loosely united in a league, which functioned as smoothly as most such associations of sovereign states. Later, when Etruscan power spread north into Lombardy and south to Salerno, there was another league which included Mantua, Parma, Ravenna and Rimini.

Some time about 550 the *lucumo* of Tarquinii saw the possibilities of the Latin settlement which had grown up by the Tiber where a convenient island made it possible to bridge the river. The 'Tarquins' took over Rome, and with them we move on to more familiar ground.

2. The Rise of Rome

THE ETRUSCAN domination of Rome was brief in time, far-reaching in effect. It brought the city inside one of the three competing power-blocs, Etruscan, Greek and Carthaginian, with consequent economic benefits. An Etruscan bridge spanned the Tiber, Etruscan temples rose on the Capitoline and Aventine hills, Etruscan pavements and drains proclaimed a new standard of material comfort. Whether all the kings were outsiders or some were local puppets, they lived in Etruscan style, robed in the early form of toga, guarded by lictors bearing the *fasces*, heedful of omens, sacrificing to Tinia and Maris. In this half-century many features of Roman life acquired a permanent Etruscan cast.

To the conquerors themselves, however, Rome was just one brick in a glorious spell of empire-building. This sixth century B.C. saw them overrun Northern Italy and establish their second federation, developing old towns like Bologna and founding new ones. In a similar advance southwards they outflanked the Greek strongholds of Cumae and Naples, reached the sea again on the beautiful bay of Salerno, and constructed there a new port of their own. Salerno was the limit of their expansion. Immediately afterwards, and while the Tarquins were still consolidating their position in Rome, their nation received the blow which started its decline. That decline was long indeed, spread over two and a half centuries, but the Tarquins were among the first to feel its effects.

It was the Greeks who struck the blow, with the violence of a threatened victim. As we have seen, the Western Mediterranean was the operating area for a triangle of forces, ruthless in rivalry. If the Carthaginians caught foreign traders in their African colonies, they eliminated the competition by dropping them into the sea, adequately weighted with stones. The Greeks and Etruscans were scarcely more amiable. All three peoples were, of course, sophisticated enough to permit

14

exchanges which favoured their own interests. Greek craftsmen lived in many Etruscan towns, the Etruscans exported
to Greece, the Carthaginians allowed trade with Africa, provided that it passed through Carthage and enriched them with
dues and commissions. But under the veneer of diplomatic
courtesy lay tough-grained antipathy. At times cold correct-
ness warmed into war.

The Greeks being the more obvious danger, the Etruscans
made an unsentimental alliance with Carthage. With her
help in 535 they cleared Corsica of the Marseilles Greeks
established there. Corsica remained Etruscan for a hundred
and fifty years, until the Syracusan Greeks reversed the position. The Carthaginians took over the sister-island of Sardinia
as their zone, and held it until the Romans threw them out
three centuries later.

In 524 the Etruscans felt strong enough to mop up the
encircled Greeks of Cumae. They mobilized an unusually
large force against the city, only to be soundly defeated under
its very walls by its dynamic commander, Aristodemus. This
was the high-water limit of Etruscan expansion. The tide
now ebbed, gleefully assisted by the Greeks, who encouraged
the recently subjugated Latin towns to liberate themselves.
The expulsion of the Tarquins from Rome about 510 was
due less to the 'rape of Lucrece' (though we need not necessarily disbelieve the immortal story) than to a general up-
heaval in Central Italy. Similarly the replacement of kings
by a republic of consuls and senators, far from being a novel
concept of the Roman genius, reflected a tendency widespread
at the time to substitute oligarchy for monarchy.

This oligarchy was at first based on noble birth. In Rome an
upper stratum of patricians rested on a bedrock of plebeians.
Gradually, as in other communities, the dividing line was
drawn by wealth rather than gentility. The early centuries of
the republic resound with robust class-struggle, and, as the
plebeians become more demanding and the patricians more
ingenious in rearguard tactics, the constitution becomes as
cluttered with checks and counter-checks as any organism
evolved in our own era. The wonder is not that the Romans
achieved so much but that they got anything done at all.

The former kingly functions were transferred to two consuls, who were elected by the people but (for the first hundred

years and more) had to be patricians. They held office only for twelve months. They were in many respects at the mercy of their own class, whose elders (or 'fathers') made up the Senate. They were also at the mercy of each other, since they officiated for alternate months or even, as generals in war, on alternate days. When occasionally, as was only to be expected, this well-meaning system brought the country in sight of disaster, it could be temporarily superseded by the appointment of one trusted person with unlimited powers but limited time (maximum, six months) in which to clear up the mess. This emergency device, so admirable in origin, has given us our word 'dictator'.

The office of consul, if only as an empty title, outlasted the republic and even the empire which followed it. Caligula nominated his horse for it. As late as A.D. 853 Pope Leo IV conferred it upon a small English boy named Alfred. So tenacious was the tradition started thirteen hundred years before.

There was nothing nominal about the consulship in the 'brave days of old'. As Rome grew, the overworked partners had to delegate more and more of their routine responsibilities. Lesser magistrates were elected to run specific departments. 'Quaestors' kept the public accounts; 'censors' assessed the tax-liability of each citizen; 'praetors' presided over the law-courts; 'aediles' handled the day-to-day running of the city and stage-managed the festivals. These junior ministries formed a training-ground for future consuls, and the ambitious politician was expected to serve in one or more of them.

Entirely different were the two 'tribunes of the people' (later ten), who had to be plebeians, chosen by plebeians, having no executive power but wielding a veto — the original 'veto', from the Latin word, 'I forbid' — against any measure too flagrantly hostile to the masses. The tribunes date from 494 B.C. when the plebeians, recognizing their own strength, threatened literally to walk out of the new republic unless they were given some representation. The tribunes were thus not ministers but official leaders of the opposition.

This brief account necessarily telescopes the political evolution of many generations. It was a long time before the initials S.P.Q.R. (*Senatus Populusque Romanus,* 'The Senate and

the Roman People', even today displayed on the city's buses)
acquired the majestic implications they conveyed to Cicero
and his contemporaries. The first years of the new republic
were probably accompanied by economic recession, the price
of withdrawing from the Etruscan network. Rome's development was checked. But she never sank back completely to her
pre-Etruscan level, and the astute Carthaginians still thought
it worth while to sign a trade agreement with her almost
before Tarquin's fugitive steps had faded in the distance.
There was, as we have seen, little sentiment in the Car-
thaginian-Etruscan alliance.

Contact grew also with the Greeks. In 493, for instance,
two artists were commissioned to decorate a new temple of
Ceres near the Circus Maximus. A Greek verse inscription,
which they took care to incorporate, indicated where the
handiwork of Damophilus gave place to that of Gorgasus.
Whatever the extent of Hellenic influence, there was no
question of Rome's merely having changed masters: the
infant republic was free. Indeed, in its earliest years, it was
at odds with Cumae, whose hero Aristodemus had embarked
on the familiar Greek progression through the stages of
patriotic saviour and revolutionary demagogue to that of
detested dictator. In 509 he was offering refuge to the emigré
Tarquin and arresting Roman merchant-ships on the pretext
that he did not recognize the republican government. Fit-
tingly, the race which had invented the gymnasium was adept
at the diplomatic somersault.

This, we must remember, was their supreme century, in
the West as well as in the East. The year of Salamis, 480, was
to see an equally decisive victory over a non-European invader
in Sicily. So, for a spell, we must change the scene — such
transitions will be frequent but inevitable in tracing the
history of Italy — and, leaving Rome as a tiny autonomous
state hemmed in by dangerous neighbours, turn to Sicily,
where great movements were under way.

.   .   .   .

Though the Greeks are rightly credited with inventing
democracy, we easily forget how often they were ruled by
individuals — self-made strong men, whom we should call
'dictators', though the Romans did not, and whom the Greeks

themselves called 'tyrants', though we in turn should not, since they were not always tyrannical in our sense and were sometimes positively benevolent. It will be convenient to call them dictators, if we do not overload the term with modern prejudice.

One such was Hippocrates of Gela, an ancient colony founded by Crete and Rhodes on the south coast of Sicily. It was famous for horse-breeding and its gentry were noted cavalrymen. This Hippocrates was the first to dream of unifying all the other Greek cities in the island and clearing out the Carthaginians, but early in this design, while attempting to tidy up some unhelpful Siculi, he was himself eliminated.

His ideas were adopted by his energetic cavalry-commander, Gelon. So was his political leadership — for his sons were too young to claim it and in any case the individualistic Greeks had little use for the hereditary principle. Gelon consolidated his position by making an alliance with Theron, the new dictator of near-by Agrigento, and cemented it with a double wedding: he took Theron's daughter, Demarete, as his own bride, and Theron himself, being most conveniently free, married the daughter of Gelon's brother Polyzalus. With these links, and a shrewd appreciation of mutual advantages, there were reasonable hopes of a lasting friendship.

Gelon's next move was to exploit the acute class dissensions in the immensely opulent city of Syracuse, and by helping its nobility against their democratic opponents take possession of the place without a blow. As it was a better base for his grand design, he moved his government there, leaving his brother Hieron to rule in Gela. He then proceeded to increase the supremacy of Syracuse by wholesale transfers of population and the construction of those impregnable fortifications against which, seventy years later, the Athenian expedition was to batter with such tragic futility. Thus far, Gelon appears as a ruthless despot, despising the masses, whom he transplanted at will or even sold into slavery. Yet this portrait would be one-sided. Once, at the height of his power, he was able at least to go through the motions of offering to abdicate, although, not unexpectedly, he was retained by popular demand. Even if we discount this gesture we may note that Gelon, unlike most Greek dictators, died in office and of natural causes; and that he left so respected a memory that

Etruscan soldiers with the goddess of Victory. A painted plaque from
a grave at Cerveteri, late 6th century BC, contemporary with the
Etruscan domination of Rome.

'One of the most exquisite of the Greek art-forms': a Syracusan coin portraying the local nymph, Arethusa.

The Capitoline she-wolf, in the Palazzo dei Conservatori in Rome, an Etruscan masterpiece of the 5th century BC.

'The exquisite bronze chimaera at Florence' (in the Archaeological Museum), 5th century BC, illustrating the Etruscan fondness for mythical monsters.

when, a hundred and fifty years afterwards, every other dictator's monument was condemned to the scrap-heap, his bronze statue alone was preserved by order.

While Gelon was settling into Syracuse, his father-in-law Theron similarly took over Himera, on the north coast. In this case it was not a local democracy which was overthrown, but another dictator, a satellite of the Carthaginians. It is time to say a word about these people, who loom so large in the ancient history of Italy, although unlike other intruders they left few lasting traces. It is said that the Romans took from them the word of greeting, *Ave*, and the less amiable practice of crucifixion, though they did not, like the Carthaginians, extend it to unsuccessful generals. But the real importance of Carthage in Italian history lies in the political and economic changes provoked by the successive wars fought against her.

She was a Phoenician colony, established on the Tunisian coast opposite the western tip of Sicily about fifty years before the earliest Greek settlements. Originally a halfway house between Tyre and the tin-mines of Spain, she built up an independent maritime empire, with her own colonies and trading-posts, a powerful fleet and large mercenary armies.

'Mercenary' is the key word. The Carthaginians were traders first and last. Their colonizations and conquests, even their justly famed explorations along the West African coast and across the Sahara, are scarcely tinged with that patriotism, scientific curiosity, or sheer love of adventure which have usually coloured even the most materialistic enterprises of other nations. Though they peered beyond the furthest horizon in quest of profit, they were congenitally short-sighted. Avid for quick returns, they sold raw materials to their rivals which they later had to buy back in manufactured form. Their mentality was that of the bazaar, with the astute but limiting individualism which builds up businesses and undermines empires in the one operation.

This lack of imagination is reflected in their negligible artistic and literary achievement. Their highest flight was a treatise on agriculture by Mago, a general who had been fortunate enough to survive into happy retirement. Even the Romans admired this book and had it translated. Perhaps the most original idea the Carthaginians ever had was a form of token currency to facilitate trading, but even this was a clumsy device (a leather bag, sealed and alleged to contain an object of a certain value) and it sprang from their reluctance to mint their silver into a beautiful and convenient coinage as the Greeks did.

Their government was an oligarchy of noble and wealthy families, whose one desire was to perpetuate an agreeable and profitable system for themselves. Wars were expensive necessities, which other races could be hired to fight. Fortunately, the aristocracy produced occasional individuals willing and able to take command, but (except when the ruling clique was badly frightened by an emergency) such leaders often had to fight their own government before they could get supplies to fight the enemy.

The fall of Himera's pro-Carthaginian dictator, and the grand design of the Gelon-Theron partnership, could not be ignored even by the most myopic of the Carthaginian senators. In the very year that Xerxes was mobilizing his Asian hosts for the invasion of the Greek homeland, another expedition was being prepared in North Africa to launch a death-blow at the Greek colonies in Sicily.

Gelon knew this. It was embarrassing at such a moment to receive an appeal from Greece for help against the Persians. Too deft a diplomat to refuse outright, he made one condition, that he should be given the supreme command. This being unacceptable to Spartans and Athenians, Gelon was regretfully unable to be present at Thermopylae and Salamis.

That same year, 480, the Carthaginian armada crossed the narrow seas from Africa and, after losing some vessels in a storm, regrouped at one of their own colonies, Panormus (now Palermo), not far from Theron's newly acquired stronghold of Himera, which they forthwith besieged. Their commander was Hamilcar, this name being confusingly popular with Carthaginian generals, including Hannibal's father long afterwards. This earlier Hamilcar had an army of more than a hundred thousand men, mainly infantry, recruited from all round the Western Mediterranean, Africans, Ligurians, Spaniards, Corsicans, Sardinians, as well as the Carthaginian colonists in Sicily. He was even hoping for some Greek assistance. The ex-ruler of Himera had taken refuge with his father-in-law, the dictator of Reggio, who, having his own reasons for disliking the Gelon-Theron partnership, was more than willing to help against it. The Greeks of Selinus also — a westerly colony uncomfortably near the Carthaginian corner of Sicily — had thought it prudent to offer Hamilcar some of the cavalry he badly needed. This transaction was to have disproportionate consequences.

Hamilcar's siege of Himera followed the pattern of the *Iliad*. His beached galleys were protected by a stockade and another fortified camp was built further inland for his soldiers. Homer, however, provided no parallel for Theron's ally, Gelon, who acted decisively before the Carthaginians could add any Greeks to their variegated host. He hurried across Sicily with an army little more than half the size of Hamilcar's, but including five thousand cavalry, cut through the besiegers' lines, and dug himself in on the opposite side of the River Himeras.

It might have been stalemate, but for a stroke of luck. Gelon's patrols intercepted dispatches revealing that Hamilcar expected the Greek cavalry from Selinus on a certain day. Gelon took care that these should not arrive and that a force of his own should keep the appointment. To Hamilcar's sentries one Greek horseman looked very much like another in the dawn-light. The cavalry trotted through the gates of the sea-camp and then turned on the petrified guards. One of their first acts was to race with fire-brands to the drawn-up vessels, robbing the Carthaginians of all chance of escape. As the black smoke wreathed up against the sunrise, Gelon's infantry moved against the inland camp. There were hours of muddled, murderous combat. Hamilcar was cut down before the sacrificial altar: the Carthaginians themselves perpetuated a story that he committed suicide in the flames. In the evening their survivors surrendered, having huddled into a position which they found too late to be waterless.

The Carthaginian power in Sicily was smashed for two generations. A vast indemnity was exacted. Much of it was spent on new temples and the general glorification of Syracuse and Agrigento, the prisoners being made to labour on the various projects. It is said that the terms would have been harsher if Demarete had not pleaded with her husband and father, and that in gratitude the Carthaginians presented her with a gold diadem. This she sold. Part of the proceeds went in religious offerings and part was used for the minting of some outsize silver commemorative coins. One side showed the customary four-horse chariot of Syracuse, with a running lion added beneath to symbolize the triumph over Africa, and on the other was her own portrait, nominally that of the local nymph, Arethusa. Viewing her beauty, immortalized in one of the most exquisite of the Greek art-forms, few would doubt that her influence with Gelon was a factor to be considered.

Gelon did not long enjoy his glory. He died two years later. The political control he left to his brother Hieron, but the military command and his attractive widow he expressly bequeathed to his brother Polyzalus. This distribution was about as successful as most similar arrangements. Soon Polyzalus found it healthier to remove himself to Agrigento, where Theron, already his son-in-law, had now rather confusingly become his father-in-law as well. A rift developed between Syracuse and Agrigento which, though it did not lead to actual hostilities, weakened the original alliance. Polyzalus is now remembered (if at all) as the donor of the famous charioteer statue still displayed at Delphi. Hieron continued Gelon's work, extending Syracusan power and making his court a brilliant centre for writers and artists. In 474, when the Etruscans made a second attack on Cumae, this time by sea, it was Hieron's navy which sailed northwards to defeat them in the Bay of Naples. An inscribed helmet in the British Museum commemorates this victory. So does Pindar's first Pythian Ode.

Hieron died in 467 and was succeeded by another brother, Thrasybulus. Theron had died a little earlier, leaving a son, Thrasydaeus, to rule Agrigento, which he had beautified with a remarkable row of temples, still one of the outstanding relics of the Hellenic world. Neither of the new dictators had the qualities needed to maintain his position, and both were violently replaced by what passed in the fifth century B.C. for democracy.

Sicilian history continued rich in glories and complications, the latter including even a spirited resurgence of the earlier Siculi inhabitants, which subsided when their one remarkable leader Ducentius was defeated by the Syracusans and —

with no less remarkable clemency — merely exiled. In the Peloponnesian War Syracuse favoured Sparta, and 413 saw the catastrophic annihilation of the Athenian expedition sent against her.

This demonstration of Greek disunity encouraged Carthage to seek revenge for Himera. Hamilcar's grandson Hannibal (again not the most famous bearer of that name) led an invasion in 409 which in a few years overran most of Sicily. Agrigento fell after an eight-month siege. Her honey-gold temples still show the red burns of Carthaginian fire. Only Syracuse kept her freedom. Here the crisis produced a new dictator, Dionysius, a civil service clerk of unexpected imagination and initiative. He sought to bring back the glories of Hieron's court, and Plato was only one of the eminent men he collected round him. Otherwise, the great days of Greek Sicily were over, and the island remained in thrall to the Carthaginians until the Romans grew strong enough to eject them.

. . . .

For a long time, however, Rome had other preoccupations.

While Carthage was conquering Sicily, a comparable tide of foreign invaders flooded the North Italian plain and overwhelmed the Etruscan cities there. This was a tribal movement rather than a concerted military campaign. The newcomers came over the Alps from Switzerland and South Germany. Their mobile columns ranged ahead, their laden wagons rumbled behind. They had come to stay. As they made a major contribution to the human stock of the peninsula, they deserve description.

The Romans called them Gauls. They were tall Celts, moustached and muscular, blue-eyed, blond, their long hair swept back like a horse's mane. They wore trousers (to the Romans a mark of barbarism), sleeved shirts, and flamboyant cloaks of red, green and purple, sometimes striped, fringed or braided, clasped with splendid brooches of coral or enamel. For the Gauls loved jewellery. Their rings and bracelets, their belts of silver and gold, showed a high level of artistic development, which despite Etruscan, Greek and Scythian influences was distinctive and original. The Gauls had traded with the Mediterranean peoples for a long time. Now, goaded by pressures from other peoples behind them, they formed up their wagon-trains and trekked southwards.

They were terrifying in their impact upon the now decadent Etruscans. A free race of highlanders, speaking a language akin to Welsh and Gaelic, with the Celtic tribal system of kings, lords and warrior-retainers, they had a tradition of fidelity and fighting to the death. They were not mercenaries to change masters, or citizens to be subverted by political ideology.

Their standard weapons were a long-pointed sword, a couple of throwing spears, and a broad-bladed dagger. Chiefs sometimes fought from a light two-horse chariot which they had learnt how to build from the Etruscans. Otherwise, like the Vikings, they used horses more for covering distances than for mounted combat. They had an unattractive habit of hanging the severed heads of their enemies from their bridles, but this may have been prompted by sincere religious conviction rather than vulgar ostentation. A similar ritual motive is ascribed to the special shock-troops, the Gaesatae, whose battle-dress was confined to golden bangles and neck-rings.

Raiding parties penetrated to the far South, even landing in Sicily. Rome's turn came in 390, about ten years after their first emergence from the Alpine foothills. A horde of thirty thousand Gauls, under a leader named (or possibly titled) Brennus, poured over the Apennines and advanced upon the city.

Against them the young republic mustered ten thousand men, the mass levy (or *legio*) of its able-bodied population. The *legio* had not yet evolved into the highly-trained complex organism which we know as the 'legion'. It was a small citizen army of brave, dogged amateur soldiers, whose hearts were in the land they farmed. They had no dreams of world conquest. That came later, almost accidentally with the habit of self-defence and the constant recession of the frontier.

About five thousand Latin allies joined them on this occasion. They met the Gauls on the banks of the Allia, a tributary of the Tiber, eleven miles north of Rome. The wild Celtic warriors surged round them, pressed them back remorselessly to the river's edge, and obliterated them. It looked like the end of Rome. A small garrison held out on the Capitoline Hill, but the rest of the population were given refuge in the allied town of Veii. The city itself was plundered and burnt. When the Gauls tired of besieging the Capitol, they agreed to go away on payment of a bankrupting danegeld, one thousand pounds' weight of gold. Was there any sense, many surviving Romans wondered, in rebuilding on the ash-strewn foundations? Why not stay in Veii and amalgamate with their allies? They were persuaded otherwise by an experienced leader, Camillus, elected dictator during the crisis. As he held that office five times in his long career, we can imagine that it was a desperate period for Rome.

Henceforth, the Gauls were just another of her perennial adversaries. Intermittent wars continued with them, as with the Samnites and other neighbouring peoples. It was not until as late at 225 that a crushing defeat at Telamon, on the Tuscan coast, drove the Gauls back behind the Apennines. There, in what we call Northern Italy but the Romans called Cisalpine Gaul ('Gaul-this-side-of-the-Alps'), the invaders settled as a peaceable element in the population. Milan was a Celtic foundation. So was Verona. Her famous poet, Catullus, may well have had Celtic blood. His poems gave Latin a new word for 'kiss', *basium*, which was probably of Celtic derivation. Long before Catullus, of course, Cisalpine Gaul had been brought under Roman rule, following another victory in 192 at Bologna.

.   .   .   .

The Gauls, by smashing the Etruscan leagues, had removed one of Rome's traditional enemies. Southwards, the Romans still faced their native Italian rivals and the Greek colonists.

These last never developed the strength of their Sicilian cousins. When Rome clashed with Taranto in 281, that city appealed to King Pyrrhus of Epirus, an adventurer who dreamed of imitating in the West the eastern achievements of Alexander. He brought over the Macedonian phalanx, a fighting formation as novel to the Romans as the armoured elephants he also employed. He won two battles but suffered so many casualties that we still speak of a 'Pyrrhic victory'. In the third, at Benevento, the Romans were successful, and Pyrrhus retired to the Balkans in quest of easier opponents. Deprived of their champion, the Italian Greeks thought it prudent to become satellites of Rome.

This, it will be noted, occurred long before the Romans had finished their struggle with the Gauls, but we have already seen that, in the Italian story, a slavish adherence to chronological order will muddle rather than clarify the mind. The petty wars of the Romans are, as many schoolboys have found, tiresome, intricate and interminable. Here we can only pick out the main threads — Etruscan, Gallic, Greek, and so forth — the constant interweaving of which makes the actual pattern of these centuries.

Instead of detailing campaigns we might ask ourselves the general question: *how did the Romans do it?* Why, at the finish, were they the people who united Italy, rather than the Etruscans, Greeks, Gauls, or any one of half a dozen other native tribes? Fundamentally that question has never been satisfactorily answered. We can only underline certain factors which contributed to their success.

National generalizations are rightly suspect. But, though we may no longer believe in a 'typical Roman', full of traditional 'Roman virtues', there is no doubt that the Romans developed certain characteristics which distinguished them from their rivals. Their farming origins, their attachment to their lands, gave them a stable patriotism. However violent the class-struggle, the state came first in their loyalties. Disgruntled leaders did not go over to the enemy, and never — as often happened in Greek cities — did patricians or plebeians call in foreign aid against the opposition party. There was a basic respect for the law rather than for ideology. Men might be ready enough to alter or interpret the law to party advantage, but it was not disregarded. This enabled the state to survive the most appalling disasters. Nothing illustrates the Roman's attitude better than the contrast between his constitutionally appointed 'dictators' and the Greek's self-made 'tyrants'.

Along with his patriotism, the Roman had a toleration for other nations and their ideas, and a remarkable flair for assimilation. The Greek, though prepared to do business with anybody (including political and treasonable business if it suited him), never lost the arrogant conviction that all foreigners were barbarians. The Roman had no such prejudice. He was prepared, in theory, to exchange reciprocal rights with his neighbours, and, though in practice he did not always do so without a bitter struggle, Roman citizenship *was* gradually extended until (as the famous case of St. Paul reminds us) it was available to the civilized population in three continents. This attitude helped immensely in the unification of the peninsula. The Romans conquered where they had to, but often the new territories joined them as allies. Roman colonies were planted at strategic points, but they were outposts of Rome, not independent offshoots. Practical rather than theoretical, the Romans did not in the least mind a political patchwork of ex-enemies and ex-allies, satellites and ex-soldier colonists. What they wanted was a workable organization.

Broadmindedness would hardly have united Italy if the Romans had not also been able, in the long run, to outfight even the most bellicose of their neighbours. They did this because to a courage equalled by their enemies they added a special capacity for discipline, which enabled them to perfect the legion as a unique military instrument. Previously the Macedonians had invented the phalanx, an infantry formation with which Alexander had cut a triumphal way to the frontiers of India and which had shattered even the Roman ranks when Pyrrhus first used it against them. The legion was the answer to the phalanx. It had weight and impetus but it also had speed and flexibility, adapting itself better to different terrains and shifting situations. Modified from time to time, it was not perfected until about 100 B.C., by which date it was not only a superb fighting organization but excellent at marching and fortification. The Roman general could rely on his men starting at the hour ordered, tramping doggedly all day at regulation speed under a load which might have discouraged a pack-mule, and being ready to fight a battle or dig a trench before supper. In strategy no less than in tactics the legion gave him an incomparable advantage.

Only one more factor can be mentioned here: the road. This played an important part in the holding of new territory, the economical use of troops, and the peaceful development of the country. The first of the great highways, the Appian Way, was begun by Appius Claudius in 312 and eventually ran on through Taranto to Brindisi. The next was the Flaminian Way, the great north road to Rimini. By about 200 B.C. Italy had several such arteries. They all led to Rome.

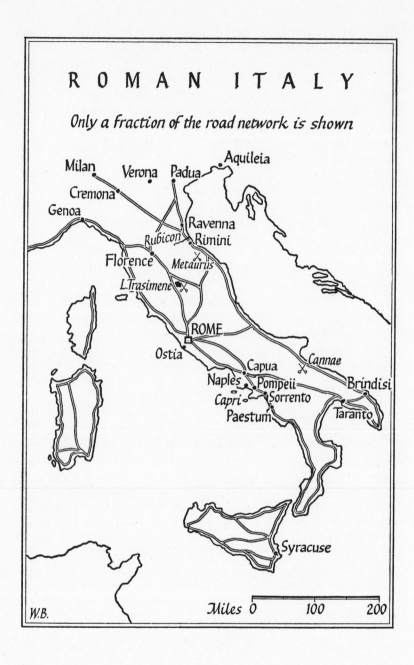

ROMAN ITALY

Only a fraction of the road network is shown

Milan
Verona
Padua
Aquileia
Cremona
Genoa
Rubicon
Ravenna
Rimini
Florence
Metaurus
L.Trasimene
ROME
Ostia
Cannae
Capua
Naples
Pompeii
Brindisi
Capri
Sorrento
Paestum
Taranto
Syracuse

W.B.

Miles 0   100   200

3. Hannibal — and After

THE ROMAN unification of Italy was no smooth, orderly process but the result of a lengthy struggle with many set-backs and several mortal crises. Neighbouring peoples did not view the benefits of Roman leadership with the impartial appreciation of the historian. Conquests which had appeared to be safely digested rose again (if the repellent metaphor may be forgiven) when there was any violent convulsion in the body politic. This happened especially in the gloomier hours of the conflict with Carthage, when the African invader stood almost at the gates of Rome.

It is tempting to think of the three Punic Wars (so named from the Latin *Punicus*, 'Phoenician') as a three-act tragedy lasting with intervals from 264 to 146 B.C. But the real drama ends with the strong second act — Hannibal's — and the final scenes are only a lame and belated epilogue.

The First Punic War came quickly after Rome had beaten Pyrrhus and absorbed Southern Italy. It was fought mainly for the control of Sicily which, except for Syracuse, had been ruled by Carthage since about 400. Dragging on from 264 to 241, it illustrates the dogged, resourceful Roman character. It could be won only by sea-power, and the Romans, never sailors from choice, began it with about as much naval tradition as the modern Swiss. They had no fleet. They faced an enemy whose warships were supreme in the Western Mediterranean and whose navigators were superb, braving the Atlantic to sail certainly as far as the Canaries and Senegal and possibly to Britain and Scandinavia.

Undeterred, the Romans built a fleet. They had the help of Greek technicians, but they had to man most of the ships themselves. They trained their own oarsmen, sitting on benches ashore, while the shipwrights pressed on with their work. The Greeks could not provide officers either — and the Romans knew that they could not learn in five minutes how

29

to handle a vessel as they must if they were to win by traditional tactics. It was easier to scrap traditional tactics, such as the ramming at which the Carthaginians excelled. The Romans must reduce the need for skilful navigation and manoeuvre — they must grapple and board, turning decks into battlefields. So they devised the 'crow', a massive gangway like a drawbridge, which was lashed vertically to the mast until the moment came when it could be sent crashing down across the bulwarks of the vessel alongside. It had an iron spike which bit deep into the planking and made it impossible for the other ship to draw away, and it was wide enough for the irresistible Roman swordsmen to surge across two abreast.

First, however, the Roman galley had to get into position. And there were the other problems, day in, day out, of remaining effectively at sea, maintaining supplies and communications, finding or avoiding the enemy. These could not be solved by ingenious gadgets or intensive rowing practice. Inevitably Rome lost an appalling number of ships through bad weather and bad navigation. Her losses throughout the long war exceeded five hundred vessels, each carrying about three hundred crew and a hundred and twenty soldiers. Yet she fought grimly on to final victory. Paradoxically her worst failure was in the North African land operations, when her expeditionary force under Regulus was defeated.

This war turned Rome into a naval power, but it had an even more important result. By winning Sicily she acquired her first overseas territory, the first land which could not just be assimilated but which had to be separately governed. Sicily was the first province, setting a pattern which became a patchwork spread from Tigris to Tyne. The adolescent Republic now contained, unsuspected, the seeds of the Empire to come.

With political change came economic, no less loaded with unpredictable consequence. Sicily had paid Carthage a grain-tribute, nearly half a million bushels per annum. This was diverted to Rome, where it was sufficient — then — to feed the city for six months. From that date the nation of sturdy farmers began to depend increasingly on imported food, and its treasury on provincial tribute. The first Sicilian grain-sacks carried in them the fatal germ of the 'bread and circuses' which were to enervate the citizens.

．　　．　　．　　．　　．　　．　　．　　．

Carthage seemed down and out. Not only had she lost command of the sea but she was now plunged into a three-year struggle with her rebellious mercenaries, without whom she was equally helpless on land. The Romans, with a cynical disregard of treaty-terms, took the chance to seize Corsica and Sardinia, and combined them into a second province. Then they turned to other problems, notably a Gallic rising in the North, which led to their final conquest of the whole Italian peninsula up to the foothills of the Alps.

Meantime, far away in another peninsula, in Spain, a Carthaginian general was planning a war of revenge with all the bitterness of a commander who has seen his country beaten without having suffered defeat himself. Hamilcar Barca had defied the Romans in Sicily, but his own success had been nullified by the surrender of the island. He dreamed only of a return match, and transmitted the obsession to his sons, Hannibal and Hasdrubal.

Hitherto Carthage had used Spain chiefly as a sphere of commercial interest. Now, having lost her other possessions, she authorized the thorough military occupation of the country as far north as the Ebro. Under the pretext of guarding Carthaginian investments, Hamilcar was able to build up the army he needed to destroy Rome. It was the usual blend of mercenaries, desert horsemen from Numidia, expert slingers from the Balearic Islands, Spanish javelin-men, infantry from Liguria and Libya, and Moroccan elephants. This army owed its allegiance to its commander rather than to the Carthaginian government. For years the Barcid family had a free hand, ruling Spain almost as a sovereign state and even conducting their own diplomacy. Carthage was impotent to control them. Conversely, if the Barcids needed backing from home, their requests were received with suspicion. For a long time, though, liberty of action was more vital than official support.

Hamilcar was drowned on active service in 229. His successor and son-in-law was assassinated in 221. The Spanish command passed to Hamilcar's own son, Hannibal, now twenty-six and dedicated from childhood to the sacred mission of revenge. Hannibal possessed those qualities of imagination and vision which were rare almost to the point of non-existence among the narrow-minded senators of Carthage. Fluent in Greek, he had studied the campaigns of Alexander and the tactical manuals of Hellenic military writers. He had friendly contacts with governments in Macedonia, Asia Minor, and every country hostile to Rome. He had secret agents moving among the Gauls and the Italian peoples recently brought under Roman sway.

So, quite soberly, he planned his march across the Alps. It was a bold but calculated gamble, which, while it staggered his opponents, was logical enough. Rome must be defeated, once and for all, by a stab to the heart. The blow could not be dealt by sea, because Carthage had lost her naval supremacy. The land-route, through Catalonia, France and the Alps, was long, but not impossibly so when measured against the marches of Alexander. And all the way, he was assured, he would be welcomed as a liberator by the Gauls, Etruscans, and others.

So, in the early summer of 218, the incredulous inhabitants of Northern Italy saw the Carthaginian army debouching from the Alpine valleys, if not with snow on their boots at least with abundant marks of hardship. The hundred thousand picked troops who had left Spain were halved in number, the forty or fifty elephants reduced to a pathetic cluster — and very soon to a single survivor. Nevertheless, Hannibal's gamble seemed to be succeeding.

Rome had a potential force of a quarter of a million fighting men, and another half-million allies. But troops are useless in the wrong place. One of her armies was in Sicily. Another, under the brothers Scipio, had gone to attack the Carthaginians in Spain. This expedition, travelling partly by ship and partly by coast-road along the Riviera, had tried to stop Hannibal in the Rhône valley. When Hannibal had slipped past, one brother had proceeded on his mission to Spain while the other had doubled back to take command of the home forces, a mere couple of legions immediately available. With these he barred Hannibal's path on the River Ticinus, only to be swept aside. He was himself seriously wounded, his life being saved by his sixteen-year-old son, later to become famous as Scipio Africanus. Thus, in his opening cavalry affray on Italian soil, Hannibal's purpose was first thwarted by the young Roman destined to become his most formidable opponent. Hannibal lived to compare Africanus with his own model, Alexander, and a later authority, B. H. Liddell Hart, has suggested that he may have been 'greater than Napoleon'.

Glory lay far in the future, however. The young Scipio's first military experiences were daunting in the extreme. That December he saw the Romans go down again in defeat on the Trebia—a disaster the more bitter since it was due to his father's advice being disregarded by the other consul. The Gauls of the Po Valley were meantime rising to join Hannibal, as planned, though (as is the way with the liberated) their enthusiasm cooled after entertaining their deliverers for a few months.

In the following year Scipio senior went to join his brother in Spain, as originally planned, where they campaigned against Hannibal's brother Hasdrubal until they perished in 209. Probably Scipio junior went with his father, and was spared participation in the next Italian catastrophe, at Lake Trasimene. Hannibal had moved out of his winter quarters and crossed the Apennines, a march unexpectedly arduous after his Alpine experiences. The unhealthy marshes of the Arno took further toll of his men. He himself lost the sight of an eye. But Rome lay ahead, and there was only one more Roman army to be dealt with. This was commanded by the consul Flaminius, a man of plebeian stock (unlike the patrician Scipios) whose name is immortalized as the builder of the Flaminian Way. Hannibal slipped past him at Arezzo. Flaminius broke camp and hurried down his own road in pursuit. Near Perugia, in a defile above Lake Trasimene, Hannibal turned and waited calmly like a beast in ambush for its hunter. He fell upon Flaminius out of the morning mists. The consul and fifteen thousand of his men were butchered or drowned, a similar number was taken prisoner. Only the Roman nationals were severely treated. Other Italians were sent home unharmed, duly indoctrinated with the idea of Carthaginian liberation.

So far, despite hardships and casualties, Hannibal's march had gone according to plan. Now, when it remained only to storm Rome, the plan broke down. Hannibal must have known all along the impossibility of bringing siege-artillery overland. Perhaps he had banked on getting it from the Greek cities of the South or by sea from Carthage; or, most likely of all, on Rome's surrender without the necessity of a formal siege. Certainly he had underestimated the stubborn courage of the Romans, just as he had overestimated the help he was to get from their subjects and unwilling allies in the peninsula.

For fourteen long years he ranged up and down Italy like a caged tiger, at once invincible and impotent. When the Romans were foolish enough to face him in the open, his genius struck them down, as at Cannae in Apulia where the eighteen-year-old Scipio had another searing experience — he saw another consul perish with sixty-six thousand of his men. But when the Romans were sensible, they harassed the invader with evasive tactics laid down by their commander Fabius, thereby creating an adjective which we still find useful. Foolish or sensible, they never considered the possibility of final defeat. When, in 211, Hannibal pitched camp at the gates of Rome, the land on which it stood was put up for auction and fetched the full market price.

Meanwhile, far away in Spain, the Roman effort began to look a little less misdirected. At first Hasdrubal had held his ground. The two elder Scipios had been defeated and killed. Now the young one offered to lead a new expedition to avenge them. Though he was below the legal age, a young man still in his early twenties, the future Africanus had such charm and such infectious confidence that he was unanimously voted the command. Within a few years he had justified the choice by taking Cartagena, defeating Hasdrubal, and sweeping the Carthaginians out of Spain. Taking a leaf out of Hannibal's book, he cultivated the friendship of the 'liberated' Spaniards and even made trouble for Carthage on her home ground by intrigues with her Numidian allies.

His work in Spain might have been harder if Hasdrubal had fought to the last ditch, but he was already under orders to join Hannibal in Italy, where, it was hoped, reinforcements might finally overcome Roman resistance. Hasdrubal got no further than the River Metaurus, south of Rimini. Some days later his blood-streaked head was lobbed over the palisade of his brother's camp, a wordless dispatch which

Dancing girls from the mosaic floors of the imperial villa at Piazza Armerina, Sicily, thought to have been the home of Diocletian's western colleague, Maximian.

The Romans in peace and war.
Shopping at the draper's, a marble relief of the time of Julius Caesar, now
in the Uffizi at Florence.

Legionaries about AD 100, depicted on Trajan's Column.

extinguished hope of victory. 'I see the fate of Carthage,' said Hannibal. The youngest of the brothers, Mago, was driven out of Cadiz by Scipio and managed to ship his men across to Liguria, but he was unable to give any effective help.

The game was up. Hannibal held on in Italy for several more years, penned in the hilly peninsula of Calabria. Scipio got him out in the end — by landing in Africa himself and attacking Carthage. The home government appealed to Hannibal. He left Italy, still unbeaten, and for the first time met Scipio — and defeat — at the Battle of Zama. Thus, in 202, ended the Second Punic War. Hannibal, a realist, urged his government to make peace. His own reward was soon exile, due as much to his countrymen's jealousy as to the demands of Rome. Finally, after being harried ignobly through the friendly but frightened anti-Roman capitals of Asia Minor, he was driven to suicide. It is pleasant to know that the triumphant Scipio, now hailed as 'Africanus', favoured a mild policy towards the defeated and modestly re-fused most of the public honours pressed upon him.

.   .   .   .

The Republic was now really an expanding empire. The details are no part of the strictly Italian story, but the general development must be sketched. One sighs for the quick technique of television. Failing it, picture an outline map of the Mediterranean countries, and watch the dark stain of empire creep over one white area after another. Spain, North Africa, Macedonia, Dalmatia, Greece, Syria, France, Egypt — by Julius Caesar's time Rome is somehow mistress of them all.

It happens variously. Sometimes the spreading stain falters and even for a while recedes. Not all the new provinces were conquered. Even when they were, the Romans often took them reluctantly, concerned mainly to secure peace for their existing possessions or to fill some political vacuum. Like the British, they collected much of their empire by invitation and legacy. Thus Attalus, the last king of Pergamum (in modern Turkey), bequeathed both his kingdom and his personal treasure to the Roman people. And Rome, answering an appeal to free Greece from the Macedonians, seems to have made a sincere effort to reconstitute her as an independent state, only to be frustrated by the familiar Greek inability to agree on a form of government. Against these examples we must set others of cynical diplomacy and crude coercion. The Romans were the usual human mixture of schemers and dreamers, enterprising exploiters, corrupt politicians, and honest (if unimaginative) public servants. Sometimes one element triumphed, sometimes another. The Senate was never at any time a united body, with a conscious step-by-step programme for acquiring the assets of the known world, though sometimes the picture looks a little like that, viewed in the light of history.

How did this imperial expansion affect the common man?

Shortly after the Second Punic War a senator brought home from Africa a slave-boy to whom he gave a thorough education and a name, Terence, immortal in theatrical annals. This is mentioned not because it is, in itself, of major historical importance but because Terence personifies, in a convenient mnemonic way, three general tendencies which were now to modify the life and culture of the peninsula. First, he was an alien slave who replaced a free Italian worker: the other great comic playwright, Plautus, who died soon after Terence's arrival, had started as a stage handyman from Umbria. Second, a slavish origin did not stop Terence from developing his genius or from mixing in cultivated society. Third, as he admitted, his plays imitated the Greek comedy of manners: the fashion, not only in the theatre but in almost everything, was Greek.

Let us examine the tendencies which Terence happens to illustrate.

Slavery. Before Hannibal, the land had been cultivated by small farmers with one or two slaves or often none at all. Then followed the fifteen-year nightmare, during which the armies marched and counter-marched, the countryside was ravaged and depopulated, and the farmers either perished in disastrous battles or rotted as city-bound refugees. Peace came to an Italy of weeds and ruins, of farms not worth going back to and farms with no family to claim them. The continuity had been broken for too long. Things could never be the same again.

The only quick way to revive agriculture was to use the prisoners of war. Slave-labour became, for the first time, cheap and plentiful. Subsequent wars produced fresh supplies, until the prisoners represented one of the most considerable economic rewards of victory. Later still, when war ceased to produce enough suitable labour, slavery had become indispensable, and the flow had to be kept up by piracy, by kidnapping, and eventually by breeding.

The small family farms began to be merged into large estates, run by a slave-gang of perhaps fifty, under a foreman who was himself a slave. The owner might be a patrician or a wealthy capitalist. The very face of the land changed. As the overseas corn tribute took the profit out of arable farming, the new masters turned to stock. The vine and olive, too, began to assume their modern importance in the landscape. Being slow to produce returns, they had not always suited the struggling peasant, but owners with capital could afford to wait. In some respects the slave-run estates, like the English enclosures, contributed to progress; but in purely human terms, by destroying the free peasantry, they were equally pernicious.

Not only on the farm was the free man displaced. Slaves were employed on building roads and aqueducts, in trade, manufacture, the skilled professions, and the public services. In every sphere the free man competed at a disadvantage, and the social consequences were extensive. Manual work came to be regarded as fit only for slaves, and, as free men had less and less practical experience, there was neither opportunity nor incentive for technical progress.

As Terence's case reminds us, slavery had its own gradings, and conditions varied almost as widely as in the parallel society of the free. In law the slave was an expendable commodity. He could be worked to death, beaten, tortured, and —for diverse misdeeds—put down. 'You have as many enemies as you have slaves,' Cato warned his fellow senators. 'That is due to the cruel treatment we give them, as though they were not men but animals.' Why then did not this vast slave-population rebel? It did, more than once. For seven terrible years from 139 B.C. a motley army of two hundred thousand slaves kept Sicily in chaos. In 73 B.C. there was the famous revolt of the Thracian gladiator, Spartacus, who defeated several armies but fell in a heroic attempt to fight his way to liberty beyond the Alps. Such risings provoked the usual reprisals of frightened men—the road from Rome to

Capua became, on one occasion, a ghastly avenue of six thousand crucified slaves. A similar attitude decreed that, if a slave murdered his master, all the other slaves in the household should be executed. This happened to a staff of four hundred as late as A.D. 61, though by that date it was sufficiently unusual to cause an outcry.

It is a relief to remember that masters differed as much in ancient Italy as they did on the Russian estates or the American plantations of the nineteenth century. Slaves were often kindly, even affectionately, treated. The law was winked at: they might earn money and hold property, even slaves of their own. They could often buy their freedom. They might be given it in their master's lifetime or under his will.

Out in the world, their training and experience gave them advantages over the free-born. They gained many key positions in public administration, they piled up fortunes in business. They met with no worse snobbery than usually confronts the self-made man. Horace, son of an ex-slave, became the personal friend of Maecenas and was offered — but declined — the post of private secretary to the Emperor Augustus. His career was no more of a struggle than Cicero's, for Cicero, though born of a respectable country family, was essentially a *novus homo*, 'a new man', outside the patrician clique. However flagrant the faults of Roman society, it was flexible. Merit could usually bend the bars of class. Though this was more true as the centuries passed and the old senatorial dominance withered away, the success of Terence as a fashionable playwright shows that even in the second century B.C. a slave might wear garlands instead of chains.

Finally, Terence illustrates the Greek influence.

There had always been a good deal of this, filtering from the Greek communities of the South. The trickle became a stream when those communities were incorporated into the Roman system and when Sicily was made a province. When the legions went to Greece proper, Macedonia, and the hellenized coast of Asia Minor, the stream became a flood. Greek art was looted or copied, Greek authors were taken as models, educated Greek slaves were in demand as secretaries and doctors. The Olympian attributes were attached, however incongruously, to the Roman deities who seemed superficially to correspond, and a bright mantle of Greek mythology was thrown over the more sombre side of the old Italian religion. Higher education became Greek education. Cicero, Caesar and Horace went to Athens or Rhodes as to an ancient Oxford or Cambridge. They spoke and wrote Greek as fluently as Latin. We recall Shakespeare's lines: *'Did Cicero say anything?' 'Ay, he spoke Greek.'*

Hellenic influence was often resisted. Terence himself did not really manage to transplant the comedy of manners to a country which preferred the less subtle pleasures of circus and arena. All too frequently Greek vices, not virtues, were imitated. But from about 200 B.C. the Greek element in Roman culture is pervasive in so many fields that it can hardly be overestimated.

.   .   .   .

What sort of city was the Rome which now queened it, unchallenged, over the Mediterranean world?

Though it had defied Hannibal, it had not escaped other misfortunes since its rebuilding after the Gauls. It suffered a great fire in 213, an earthquake in 192. But despite setbacks the city had grown steadily into a vast wall-girt warren of twisting lanes. Ironically, while the Romans built thousands of miles of splendid straight roads to converge upon the capital, they were quite unable to cope with the resultant congestion. Even after Nero's much-publicized town-planning and all the other imperial improvements, wheeled traffic still had to be banned during daylight.

Rome before Christ, republican Rome, showed few signs of planning at all. We must subtract from our mental picture most of the grandiose monuments such as the Colosseum and the various triumphal arches. These came later. The city was still almost all on the east bank of the Tiber, and there was open country where the Vatican now stands. The first stone bridge was built only in 142, and six more were added by the time of Augustus. Four great aqueducts, the oldest dating from 313, marched into the city on massive arches, bringing pure water from the hills of the Campagna. The rich householder had water laid on, paying a rate based on the diameter of the supply pipe, though it was not unknown for the mains to be tapped illegally and supplies obtained through unofficial channels.

The most conspicuous public buildings were the temples and the 'basilicas', at this period law-courts and commercial exchanges. The chief temple, in which the consuls took their oath of office and victorious generals gave thanks, was the Capitol, a square shrine dedicated Etruscan-fashion to the trinity of Jupiter, Juno and Minerva. The Forum, a paved open space, was the setting for mass-meetings, with the Senate House near by. Other fora were used mainly as markets for cattle and produce. Colonnades gave shade and shelter to promenading citizens, but the wholesale provision of these, as of public baths and parks, belongs to later, more luxurious ages. So too with other recreational facilities. The idea of a permanent theatre building was long resisted, and the first was erected by Pompey only in 55 B.C. A few years later Caesar enlarged the rough-and-ready race-ground of the Circus Maximus and the first amphitheatre was constructed.

Thus, in the main, republican Rome was a motley conglomeration of mean dwellings, marked here and there by the increasingly palatial mansions of the rich. Augustus later claimed to have found a city of brick and left one of marble, but in fact there was even more demand for bricks after his time than before. The early Romans had favoured blocks of tufa from the extinct volcanoes of the Alban Hills, and in later republican times they quarried the travertine, a hard limestone found just outside the city.

So 'the eternal city' crept over its little hills and first put on the mantle of greatness. This was the town, full of contradictions, where Terence could electrify an audience with his superb line, 'I count naught human alien to myself', while the newly imported slaves lined up, chalk-marked and naked for the purchaser's inspection, not a mile away.

4. The Strong Men

THIS ROME was riven with class-conflict. Power rested, theoretically, with 'the Senate and the Roman People'; but the demarcation between those two, that is between the Senate and the Assembly, was continually in dispute. There were, as usual in ancient republics, two natural groupings (they were not so formally organized as to deserve the name of 'parties')—the upper-class minority, the oligarchs or aristocrats, known in Latin as the optimates, and the democrats, whom (from their behaviour) we should hardly recognize as such. The true 'workers', being predominantly slaves, were of course unrepresented. The Senate tended to align itself with the optimates, but there was no uniformity in this, and, as senators were not supposed to demean themselves with trade, the wealthiest citizens were not to be found in its ranks so much as in the civic stratum next below it, the Order of Knights. So, too, though consuls traditionally worked with the Senate, and their official opponents, the tribunes, were the champions of the Assembly, it was sometimes possible to find tribunes acting as senatorial pawns and consuls second to none as revolutionary demagogues. The Roman constitution, with its passion for checks and counter-checks, and its vagueness in defining the respective powers of Senate and Assembly, provided every possible facility for political fratricide.

All this would have been awkward enough in a city-state or in a single country like Italy, which had its own struggle with the central government to obtain increased civic rights for the non-Latin inhabitants. It was still more awkward now that an empire had been acquired, almost by accident, with provinces proliferating to all points of the compass and demanding administration from a body originally designed for merely local requirements. Who was to govern Spain, North Africa, Asia Minor? The best solution seemed to be to send out experienced ex-consuls with the new rank of 'proconsul'. But who, remote in Rome, was to govern these governors? Inevitably they wielded tremendous power and were, during their term of office, virtually uncontrollable. Some, like the notorious Verres in Sicily, used that power simply to milk the territory placed at their mercy. Others, like Caesar in Gaul, triumphant generals with devoted armies at their call, saw even wider scope. As the conquests and annexations multiplied, the political stresses were extended further and further from Senate House and Forum, until a distant provincial governorship was viewed not as a retirement from the party struggle but as a vital preliminary move to a revolutionary coup.

We now enter the age of the strong men. Without unduly favouring the 'great man' conception of history, we shall get the clearest picture of this period if we glance briefly at about half a dozen outstanding politicians.

First the brothers, Tiberius and Gaius Gracchus. Their father, a distinguished proconsul, died when they were children. Their mother, Cornelia, a daughter of Scipio Africanus and a woman of remarkable character and culture, refused another marriage proposal from the King of Egypt so that she could concentrate on the bringing up of her boys. Added to the Roman family tradition of public service was the full treatment of the new Greek education, with all its seductive idealism. The boys needed only the emotional stimulus of personal experience to turn them into the familiar historical type of aristocratic revolutionary.

Tiberius was first awakened when, as a young officer travelling overland to Spain, he saw the slave-gangs in all the fields of Italy and was appalled by the absence of free peasants. Later, the Senate's unjust treatment of his commander increased his revulsion against the ruling clique. For half a century that clique had run the state. It was not even the full Senate of three hundred, but a dominant inner circle, controlling by patronage a host of supporters not only in the capital but in key positions in the provinces.

The young idealist launched a frontal attack on this citadel of privilege. He stood for the tribuneship, promising land reform. 'Even the beasts have their dens,' he thundered to ecstatic crowds, 'but the men who fight and die for their country have only the air they breathe! You are exhorted to fight for hearth and home. You have neither. You fight only to keep the rich in luxury! '

Voters were organized in thirty-five electoral ' tribes ', rather like constituencies except that they were not based on geography. Eventually, as new areas of Italy were granted Roman citizenship, their inhabitants were enrolled in the existing thirty-five tribes, so that each register was a mixture of the far and near. As the ballot was held in the capital — and there was a specific ban on market-days, when it would have been convenient at least for countryfolk in the immediate locality — the single block-vote for each tribe was in practice determined by that small minority of its members who were able to take part. This vastly simplified the task of electioneering and reduced the financial burden of bribery.

Tiberius was elected. But the original conception of the office was a negative one — to protect the people by veto, not to pioneer legislation — and when he brought in his land-reform schemes the senatorial clique ingeniously arranged for one of his fellow-tribunes to clap on the veto. A constitutional crisis followed. *Was* such a veto all-powerful? The insidious Greek notion was spreading that the really important factor was the democratic will. Despite misgivings in some quarters, Tiberius got this interpretation accepted.

A year, however, was too short to put through his policy. He stood for re-election, which was unusual and perhaps illegal. This split his supporters, and violence flared up on election day. Tiberius was beaten to death in front of the Capitol, and his body thrown into the river with three hundred others. His Land Commission survived. Eventually, more than half a million acres were redistributed to about fifty thousand small farmers. Something had been achieved, but it was impossible to reverse the general trend of Italian agriculture.

One of the land commissioners was Gaius Gracchus. Warned by his elder brother's fate, but the more determined rather than deterred, he prepared carefully for the next round. He knew he would need every possible ally, and few candidates for the American presidency can have courted such a variety of sectional interests. An ambitious public-works programme was to attract the capitalists who would receive the contracts, while the proletarians were to be bribed with imported corn at half cost price. As a further attraction to the financial interests, the right to collect taxes in the Asian provinces was to be auctioned to the highest bidder; and any subsequent public inquiry into alleged extortion was to be conducted not by the Senate but by the Order of Knights, the very class from which the exploiters were drawn. Full Roman citizenship was to be granted to all other Latins, and the modified 'Latin rights' to all other Italians. New colonies were to be established in Italy and one on the site of Carthage, derelict since its vindictive destruction after the Third Punic War.

With this patchwork programme of good and bad (of which the bad, the tax-farming and the corn-dole, had the more permanent effect on the nation) Gaius gained the tribuneship in 123 and 122. Clearly no veto was going to stop him. The optimates thought of a better plan — to run a rival demagogue against him at the next election, who should outbid him in promises, however impracticable, and exploit every weakness in his incongruous alliance. The plan worked. Gaius lost the election, rioting broke out, and the Senate was given an excuse to declare martial law. Gaius rallied his party on the Aventine Hill, there was more fighting, and they were beaten. He fled across the Tiber and then, alone in a grove, knowing that the game was up, committed suicide. Over three thousand democrats were liquidated in the brief reign of terror which ensued.

Twice the optimates had proved their ability to crush a dangerous reformer, but not to undo his work completely or to find their own solutions. Two years later the list of new tribunes included the name of Marius, next of the landmark figures in the final century of the Republic's history.

Marius was a complete contrast to the Gracchi brothers — a rough soldier of peasant origins, contemptuous of Greek education, as deficient in political theory as he was effective in military practice. He married well (his wife later had a nephew, Julius Caesar) and this social asset, backing his own abilities, gave him the chance to reach the highest rank. First he successfully wound up one of those drawn-out wars in North Africa, the graveyard of so many reputations down the ages. Then, when Italy was threatened by a barbarian horde of Cimbri and Teutoni from the North, he beat them soundly and was hailed as a national saviour. Besides fighting qualities he had a genius for army organization. He gave the legion a flexible new form which was retained throughout the centuries of Roman greatness — ten cohorts, like battalions, each with six companies of a hundred men under a centurion. He based their weapon-training on the professional expertise of the gladiators. He had their javelins made so that the head was displaced if it struck an impenetrable surface, and the missile could not immediately be hurled back by the enemy. Army-service, formerly restricted to men with a certain property-qualification, he threw open to the proletariat, thus altering the class complexion of the forces. He was the first Roman general who could count on his soldiers backing him, if necessary, against the government. He was not the last.

After such military triumphs, political power came easily. He was elected consul six times in eight years, though he was an incoherent speaker and had to use ghost-writers. He had no clear programme, except to fulfil a personal ambition and be consul for a seventh term. He soon suffered the common fate of wartime heroes who try to shine in post-war politics. His popularity dwindled, and the optimates elbowed him into what they hoped would be permanent retirement.

A younger man, Sulla, who had served on his staff in North Africa, was more to their taste. Sulla was one of themselves, of old family, in reduced circumstances. These had delayed his entry into public life, but it was eventually made possible by two convenient legacies, one from his stepmother, one from a mistress. He further retrieved his social status by marrying a consul's widow. He was also better company than Marius. He was never serious from dinner-time onwards, his blotchy face was aptly compared with a flour-dusted mulberry, and his own choice of a Greek nickname was Epaphroditus, 'Love's Favourite'. His convivial habits did not prevent his being a successful general and a ruthless politician.

His incompatibility with Marius was soon apparent, but for years a clash was avoided by Sulla's turning to Asia Minor as his sphere of activity. In 91, however, there was a revolt of the Italian peoples, notably the Samnites, who were still denied the citizenship promised them by Gaius Gracchus.

The emergency made Marius and Sulla reluctant comrades again. Sulla was conspicuously more successful than his senior. He was elected consul for 88 and given a vitally important command in the East, where Mithridates, King of Pontus, had just overrun the Roman territories and massacred eighty thousand Romans and Italians settled there.

Marius, now nearly seventy and drinking far too much, felt that the command should have been his. He had triumphed in Africa and Europe. He wanted to crown his career with a great victory in Asia and that seventh consulship which had become a superstitious obsession. He put up a tribune, Sulpicius, to rush a bill through the Assembly, cancelling Sulla's appointment and awarding it to himself.

This manoeuvre understandably strengthened Sulla's feeling that government was better left to a responsible and gentlemanly body like the Senate. But this was no time for constitutional discussions. He galloped off to his camp at Nola, where the army for Asia was mustering, and re-entered Rome at the head of his legions. Marius, Sulpicius, and their supporters were proclaimed outlaws. Sulpicius was soon hunted down and executed, but Marius, after hiding in the swamps of Minturnae, got away to North Africa.

Considering his age and condition, Sulla probably thought him finished. Certainly he was a less immediate danger than Mithridates, whose armies had now invaded Greece. Sulla therefore crossed the Adriatic, retook Athens, and after three years of hard fighting and hard bargaining got Mithridates to evacuate all the Roman territories.

Meantime, cheered by the knowledge that his rival was so far away and so busy, Marius slipped back to Rome, led the democrats in bloodthirsty reprisals against the optimates, and, without putting the citizens to the trouble of a formal election, made himself consul for the seventh time. He then felt presumably that he could die happy. Die at least he did, a few weeks later.

Sulla did not hurry home. He had his army, and he had learnt what was to remain the central political truth in Roman history, that power now was where the legions were. He completed his mission in Asia and returned at leisure. Appointed dictator, the first for over a century, he proceeded with cold-blooded ferocity to wipe out the opposition. He invented the formula of 'proscription'. Long lists of 'public enemies' were displayed in the Forum, with substantial rewards for anyone who killed them. Five thousand were liquidated in this way. On Sulla's side many a new family-fortune was based on the acquisition of confiscated properties.

Monstrous though his methods were, Sulla had a constructive policy. He felt that the real power should return to the Senate, but a healthier Senate, continually refreshed by recruitment from below. The party strife of recent years had reduced its numbers to a hundred and fifty, so he had ample scope. Believing in the value of experience, he decreed that each year the twenty quaestors who had just served in the treasury should be promoted to senatorial rank. The minimum age for each public office was to be strictly enforced, so that no one could reach the consulship before he was forty-two. The obstructive powers of the tribunes were curtailed.

The greatest paradox in Sulla's career was its end. In 79 B.C. he resigned his dictatorship without any fuss, retired into private life — and lived. Not for long, as it happened; but death, when it came, came naturally. Before that, he had enjoyed his brief retirement to the full, living on his Campanian estate with the young divorcee, Valeria, who had become his wife, hunting, fishing, entertaining stage people, and writing his memoirs. Even schoolboys may regret that these are among the lost books of Latin literature.

.   .   .   .

Sulla's well-meant reforms were about as efficacious as one square meal given to a castaway who is then abandoned on the same desert island. When Sulla was gone, there was no party organization to carry on the rescue-work. Without leadership, the new senators were no better than the old. The effective power slipped gradually into the hands of three men, whose uneasy and mutually suspicious partnership is remembered as the First Triumvirate.

They began as a pair, Crassus and Pompey. Both had started as supporters of Sulla; but whereas Crassus had offended his leader and been quietly excluded from political promotion, Pompey had stayed in favour. Crassus, ambitious and frustrated, turned naturally to the democrats. Pompey, much more of a soldier and much less of a politician, did so only much later, and reluctantly, when the Senate snubbed him and refused what he felt were the just claims of his legionaries.

The two men disliked each other, but necessity yoked them. Crassus, though fairly successful as a military commander, was primarily an inspired financial operator, versatile and indefatigable. No enterprise was too large, none too small. Rome, though much subject to fires, had at this time no public brigade: Crassus raised a private corps of five hundred which he rushed to every outbreak. Before, however, a ladder was raised or a bucket emptied, he negotiated with the neighbouring landlords. If they agreed to sell (at the sort of price appropriate to an imminently threatened building), the brigade went into action. If not, it returned to base. In this manner, aided by the naturally high fire-risks of the overcrowded city (and, it is not unthinkable, by an occasional well-calculated act of arson or false alarm), Crassus soon owned a considerable area of Rome. Even so, he did not think it beneath his dignity to give personal supervision to another of his lucrative sidelines, a training-school which turned cheaply bought, unskilled slaves into the high-grade servants most in demand. It was said that Crassus himself took some of the classes.

For this millionaire money was only a means to an end— political power. He lent liberally, an effective way if not of making friends at least of influencing people. Dozens of senators were in his debt and formed a useful nucleus of support in that otherwise hostile body. The masses were wooed by less subtle methods, such as a street-banquet with ten thousand tables. He had the knack of fitting names to faces. He never ignored the humblest salutation. He would act for all sorts of people in law-suits, making up for his lack of brilliance by the care with which he prepared his case. It is hard to imagine when Crassus slept. Certainly these multifarious activities left no time for thinking out a coherent political programme. Power became an end in itself.

Pompey was less enterprising. He was really too honest, too humane, for this ruthless age. He held at various times immense powers by land and sea, but when he had finished the task in hand he was naïve enough to surrender them and expect to be treated on his merits. He was a home-loving, family man: only the first of his four marriages ended in divorce, which in the current state of Roman society hardly counted. Given a straightforward assignment, he carried it out brilliantly. Thus, in an incredibly short space of time, he cleared the Mediterranean of the pirate-fleets which had brought merchant-shipping almost to a standstill, and — no less incredibly — settled the pirates in colonies and reformed many of them. He defeated Sulla's old enemy, Mithridates, and pacified Asia Minor. On a third occasion, faced with a critical failure of the corn-imports, he made so sensible a reorganization that these periodical shortages did not recur.

As the loyal servant of a stable government, Pompey would have been invaluable. Lacking such a government, he was drawn into politics against his natural disposition, to win ratification for measures he had been forced to take in Asia and to secure justice for his troops. He had, too, his share of vanity, and, like many another general disgusted with politicians, felt an excusable confidence that he could do better himself.

During Pompey's absence in the East Crassus acquired a useful lieutenant. This young man, a nephew of Marius by marriage, had been lucky to survive Sulla's purge. Though a patrician, he inclined to the democrats and had a talent for directing those thuggish gangs which in Rome were the nearest thing to a party organization. Abstemious at table, he had a keen appetite for other pleasures and was notoriously extravagant. Crassus lent him all the money he wanted, judging him valuable as an assistant, even as a junior partner, who would never get out of hand. When Pompey came home, Crassus introduced his protégé as a skilful party-manager. Thus the Triumvirate was completed by the inclusion of Julius Caesar.

Caesar was then, in 60 B.C., forty-two, tall and well-built, with a broad face and alert brown eyes. He was something of a dandy and took pains to conceal his thinning hair. Thus far, his career had been conventional: travel, a course of rhetoric at Rhodes, military service which showed no promise of future genius, the usual junior ministries and ceremonial religious offices. He had lost his first wife and just divorced his second on flimsy evidence, on the arrogant argument that 'Caesar's wife must be above suspicion'. His own morality was never in doubt. Later, his soldiers had an affectionate marching song with the refrain:

> *Lock up your wives, O citizens!*
> *Here comes the bald old lecher!*

Crassus and Caesar both envied Pompey his military achievements. Political manipulation, however adept, was not enough. It needed the backing of legions. Both pondered how to get them.

Caesar found the answer in Gaul. As his share of the triumvirate deal he took the next consulship, with a colleague so ineffective that he virtually ruled alone and men joked that the two consuls were Julius and Caesar. His term ended, he received the usual provincial governorship; but it was arranged that he should hold it for a longer period than normal, and that it should cover not only Near Gaul (the Lombardy plain, still not reckoned as 'Italy') but also Further Gaul, or Provence. Thus he gained time and space for his schemes.

Over the next nine years Caesar fought the independent Gallic tribes and pushed back the frontier until he held all modern France and Belgium. He even made two big demonstrations in Britain, not with any idea of conquering the islanders but to frighten them out of helping their Celtic cousins in Gaul. Late as he had started in his serious military career, he proved himself a brilliant commander. Nor was he less brilliant in the writing of his war-memoirs, whose deceptively simple and objective style masked for many readers the propagandist content. The Roman book-trade was highly organized, with slaves transcribing numerous copies from the author's manuscript and public readings a fashionable amusement. Even without printing, a work like Caesar's could circulate rapidly among those whose opinion mattered.

One trait which was firmly implanted in the minds of later readers was his 'clemency', and it is true that he knew how to be merciful when it suited his plans. Less often remembered is the remorseless savagery he showed at other times, whether to the captured Gallic hero, Vercingetorix, or to the German tribes peacefully withdrawing across the Rhine under an agreement. Of these he massacred 430,000 men, women and children. The figure is his own.

Crassus now realized that he was the only triumvir without a following of devoted veterans. To remedy this, he dealt himself a governorship in Syria, whence, after looting the Temple at Jerusalem, he mounted an ambitious expedition against the Parthians. While Caesar was conducting his carefully limited operations near London, his sexagenarian partner was advancing ever further into the sands of Mesopotamia. Crassus was not a bad general, merely unlucky. He was the first Roman commander to meet the deadly horsed archers of Parthia — and against them the legionaries were as helpless as Redcoats against Red Indians. Their throwing-spears were outranged by the arrows, it was waste of breath for heavy infantry to charge light cavalry, and they had not enough mounted auxiliaries to do the work for them. Crassus led them bravely but was treacherously stabbed during truce negotiations. His head was sent to the Parthian king who, at the moment of its delivery, was watching a performance of Euripides' *Bacchae*. The actor playing Agave, who has to dance round with the severed head of Pentheus, had the quick wit to substitute the proconsul's head for the stage-property normally used, and earned a substantial present from his delighted patron.

Had Crassus lived, how long would the Triumvirate have survived? Caesar's only child, Julia, had married Pompey — but she too died, breaking the personal link between them. As Caesar's long term in Gaul drew to a close, men wondered what would happen when the two remaining partners, equals now in military reputation, came face to face again in Rome.

One must of course avoid the over-simplification which comes from later knowledge. The contemporary observer saw not only a possible duel between two individuals. He saw a political stage crowded and infinitely complex, on which many different things might happen. Pompey and Caesar were not isolated figures. There was Cicero, the humane intellectual, eloquent, vain, fatally soft at core. There was Cato, honest, brave, ostentatiously and uncompromisingly tenacious of tradition. Cassius, an able soldier who had saved the remnants of Crassus' army after the Parthian debacle. His friend Brutus, the earnest young student of philosophy. Marcus Antonius, the unstable sensualist, dependable only in his support of Caesar. And dozens of others, diverse in their degrees of courage, corruption and conceit, none quite negligible, each contributing something to the balance of forces.

In parenthesis, though, it is refreshing to remember that not all memorable Romans were absorbed in the bloody business of politics. While Caesar was slaughtering Gauls and Germans and Britons and forging the military weapon which would win him Rome, Catullus was pouring out white-hot love-lyrics, and Lucretius was fusing poetry, rationalism and the atomic theory, demolishing superstition in ruggedly noble hexameters:

Fast fly the spirit's fears, and the walls of the world recede.

Virgil, having finished school in Milan and Cremona, was perfecting his Greek at Naples, and Horace was trotting to his lessons with Orbilius in Rome, taking his place, ex-slave's son though he was, with the children of millionaires and senators.

Meanwhile, after months of manoeuvre, the political crisis came. Caesar wished, when his governorship ended, to return as consul-elect for the ensuing year. His enemies insisted that he must come home as a private citizen and appear in person as a candidate. They and he knew that under existing conditions such an act would be suicidal. His enemies were in the ascendant. Pompey had at last been drawn into the optimate party to which by natural temperament and origin he belonged. And Pompey, though officially governor of Spain, was running that province through a deputy. He remained in Rome, ready to check his rival.

Bluff was met by counter-bluff, hypocritical legal objections were bandied to and fro, insincere offers exchanged. Caesar came south with one legion to Ravenna, where he was still just, but only just, inside the boundaries of his province. The Senate voted for his recall and replacement. Marcus Antonius applied his tribune's veto, but was overruled. He fled to his leader. Caesar knew it was now or never. He marched to the Rubicon, the small river separating Near Gaul from Italy proper. It was illegal for any commander to lead his troops out of his own province into Italy. 'We can still draw back,' he told his officers, 'but once over that little bridge we must fight it out.' He knew his men. They followed him forward, across the Rubicon.

There was no more hesitation, only the speed of the launched thunderbolt. Small as his immediate force was, he knew that Pompey and the Senate had even less. In the two deep-winter months of January and February, he swept over the Apennines, occupied Rome, and nearly caught Pompey at Brindisi before he escaped overseas.

Master of Italy, Caesar faced dangers to east and west. Pompey was raising an army in Greece, many Romans were flitting away to join him. In Spain, Pompey's lieutenants had seven legions ready to march. Again Caesar acted with decision. In a hurricane six-week campaign he pulverized the Pompeian legions in Catalonia. Early the next year he shipped his troops across the Adriatic and, though outnumbered, impudently besieged Pompey in Durazzo. Pompey broke out and chased him into Thessaly. At Pharsalus the hard-bitten veterans from Gaul routed the numerous but less-disciplined Pompeians. Pompey fled to Egypt, now the last independent Mediterranean state, hoping to hire her large army of mainly Italian mercenaries. His approach greatly embarrassed the advisers of the ten-year-old Egyptian king. To refuse help would antagonize Pompey; to give it would antagonize Caesar; and one of the rivals — 'but *which* of the two was not quite clear' — would shortly be master of the world. They did the logical thing, and had Pompey stabbed to death as he stepped ashore.

The Civil War dragged on for several months. Caesar, now officially dictator, spent only a few months in Rome. He had to fight in Asia, Africa and Spain, where Pompey's two sons, underrated as mere boys, made him fight (he admitted) not only for victory but for his life. But it was in Egypt that he spent much of this period, involved in those court intrigues to which Shaw's *Caesar and Cleopatra* is not perhaps the student's most reliable guide. The beautiful princess soon replaced her brother on the throne of the Pharaohs and bore a son whom she named Caesarion. Caesar's responsibility for both developments was generally regarded as considerable. When he returned to Rome she went too and openly lived with him.

It was July, 45 B.C., before Caesar could turn his mind fully to the constructive use of the power he had won. His dictatorship was legally extended, first for ten years, then for life. The gang-warfare of rival politicians was to be scotched in future by the stationing of troops in the capital. Provincial governors were to be answerable to himself. There was to be a cut in the numbers entitled to the corn-dole. Emigration was to be encouraged to colonies abroad. A healthier political life was to be stimulated through local government and the promotion of eminent Gauls and Spaniards to the Senate, a body whose numbers he increased even as he diminished its real powers.

At fifty-seven Caesar's mental and physical energies were both vital and versatile. He found leisure to write his version of the Civil War and to reform the calendar, which over the centuries had got hopelessly out of step with nature. The name July is yet another of his memorials. He was preparing an expedition against the Parthians which he proposed to lead in person. Did he persuade himself that he still had unlimited time for all the work ahead? He had only just begun to groom his eighteen-year-old great-nephew Octavian as his eventual successor. He had no legitimate descendant, for his only daughter's child had already followed her to the grave.

So the year 45 passed into 44. In March, only six months after his return to Rome and two months after his proclamation as life-dictator, he was struck down by Cassius and other conspirators at the foot of Pompey's statue in the Senate House. Thus, like Pompey and Crassus before him, the last of the partners fell to the assassins.

5. The Great Emperors

SHAKESPEARE HAS familiarized us with the confused aftermath of Caesar's assassination: the unplanned muddlings of the elated conspirators, their flight to Greece, their defeat by Antony and Octavian at Philippi; the victors' uneasy partnership with the 'slight unmeritable' Lepidus in the Second Triumvirate; and the bloody purge of those who opposed or did not support them with sufficient enthusiasm, a purge which cost even Cicero his head. *Antony and Cleopatra* continues the tale. Lepidus relegated to the background, his partners divide the world. Antony, underrating the cold deceptive youth, relaxes exquisitely in Egypt. Roused to realities, he sails with Cleopatra and her fleet to fight Octavian at Actium, off the west coast of Greece. When she takes flight, he ignominiously follows, and finally, knowing that the game is up, they both commit suicide.

This was in 30 B.C. It was another three years — seventeen since Caesar's murder — before power was again fully concentrated in one pair of hands and the Roman Empire had begun. Even then, the Romans would not have admitted that they had an 'emperor' in our sense. *Imperator, imperium,* evade exact translation. Octavian, now styled 'Augustus', claimed actually to be 'restoring the Republic'. His technique was to keep the old forms, consuls, senators and suchlike, while transforming their functions unnoticed. The Romans, like the British, distrusted innovations and theoretical schemes, and enjoyed contemplating their past through rose-tinted spectacles. Augustus dared not call himself king or even dictator, but he could safely behave like either if he maintained an apparent concern for precedent. At first he served as consul, with a duly elected colleague; later he let both consulships be held by others. All his powers were voted to him by the Senate, and he regarded himself simply as *princeps*, or 'first citizen', a description given to both Pompey and Caesar in their time.

He wanted the reality of power, not the show. He kept control of the outer provinces and thus of the armies, leaving the Senate to govern the nearer regions where few troops were stationed. Italy itself was nominally a senatorial territory, but its garrison was the new Praetorian Guard of about nine thousand highly-paid and specially privileged men, owing direct allegiance to Augustus. They, and the Prefect commanding them, came in time to occupy a key position, able to make and unmake emperors as they pleased. Augustus, however, had them (like everything else) well under control.

The Senate appointed public officials, but on his recommendation, so that all posts were filled by his nominees. The Assembly withered away: he was granted the 'tribunician power' for life, which made him in theory the watchdog of the common man. After a century of civil disturbance the new authoritarian system was accepted with scarcely a murmur, and predominantly with a sense of relief.

Augustus created an administrative service which was efficient and reasonably honest. The corrupt old method of tax-farming was gradually superseded. Economic surveys were made and (as the Bible reminds us) a population-census. Departments were set up for highways and public works, the corn supply and the upkeep of temples. Rome was given police and a city fire-brigade. There was much building there and elsewhere. Augustus luckily had ample funds. He had kept Cleopatra's treasure for himself and personally drew the annual revenues of Egypt as the heir to the Ptolemies.

His ideas went far beyond mere practical reforms. He sought to weld the people together with a new, slightly self-conscious patriotism. The Muses were mobilized. Horace had to turn sometimes from the more congenial topics of wine and girls to the solemn theme of imperial destiny. Virgil, singer of quiet rustic joys, had to provide a Latin *Iliad*, linking Rome with Troy and equipping Augustus with a semi-divine pedigree. Virgil was needlessly dissatisfied with the result and asked, on his death-bed, that the manuscript should be burnt. We have Augustus himself to thank for preserving the *Aeneid*. Propertius, the excitable love-poet from Assisi, poked fun at the new school of sponsored writing, but was induced to contribute to it after his final disenchantment with Cynthia. So were Tibullus and even Ovid, most erotic of them all. Meantime, as a prose equivalent to the *Aeneid*, Livy wrote his history of Rome from its dubious origins down to his own period, producing (over forty years) enough to fill twenty-five modern volumes.

Marriage reforms also engaged the versatile emperor's attention, and, in the existing state of Roman morals, not a moment too soon. As pagans the Romans had no sense of sin, but they were not without standards of decency. Promiscuity was generally deplored, though prostitution was accepted as a safeguard for respectable women and a safety-valve for young men: it has been estimated that the female population of Rome at this time was 17 per cent less than the male. Homosexuality was not illegal, but it was called, rather unfairly, 'the Greek vice'.

Divorce was by consent. Abortion and birth-control made many unions childless. The wives avoided parenthood so that they could be free, the husbands to reduce their expenses. A man with children by one marriage often chose not to remarry but to live with a mistress, rather than risk a second legitimate family, and he could do so without social stigma. The net result was an alarming slump in the birth-rate of the upper classes, which Augustus, with his ideas of national regeneration, could not tolerate.

He therefore brought in laws to punish adultery, penalize celibacy, and subsidize parenthood. Divorce he did not discourage, if the parties used their freedom to remarry. As Seneca remarked some time later, 'The most illustrious ladies now reckon the year not by the names of the consuls but by those of their husbands.' Ingenious bachelors tried to evade taxation by announcing their engagement, breaking it off, announcing another, and so on, indefinitely. Augustus countered this by making breach of promise an offence against the state.

In all these daunting tasks he had several advantages. The weariness of the people, the longing for peace and order, reduced opposition. And there was the sheer length of time granted to him: he lived to seventy-five and so, from 27 B.C., enjoyed forty-one years of unchallenged authority. He was lucky too in the ability and loyalty of his chief assistants, men like Agrippa, his school-friend and later his son-in-law, a brilliant admiral, general and civil administrator, whose lasting memorial is the Pantheon, and Maecenas, who as patron of Horace and Virgil stimulated the literary movement the emperor desired.

Augustus thought himself less lucky in his choice of a successor. As we shall see, very few emperors were followed by their sons. Many had none. Others, like Augustus himself, were fated to see their children and even their grandchildren die before them. But the Romans were never obsessed by the hereditary principle, and the 'adopted son' was a common phenomenon, not only in imperial families. He might be older than his 'father', who might be a bachelor. There was at first no limiting rule whatever, except that the 'father' must not be a eunuch. Augustus outlived all the potential successors he would have preferred — nephew, grandsons, son-in-law Agrippa — and had to choose, rather grudgingly, his stepson Tiberius. For Rome it was perhaps a happier selection than he realized.

.   .   .   .

Tiberius accepted his empire with an equal lack of enthusiasm. He was a reserved, moody man of fifty-two, painfully conscious that he had no flair for personal relations. Administration he understood, and finance, but not people. His instinct was to ask himself what Augustus would have done in a similar situation, and act accordingly. By following that principle conscientiously for twenty-five years, he consolidated the new order.

Such worthy qualities seldom win the cheers of the populace. Tiberius spent little on further amenities for Rome, a city which he disliked and feared rather as Louis XIV did Paris. He pruned the spending on gladiators and was thought mean, though in times of catastrophe he was prompt and generous with relief. Like Augustus, he had no wish to enlarge the overgrown empire by further adventures on the frontier. His aim was efficient, honest government for the existing provinces.

In his loneliness he acquired an evil genius. Sejanus, a man of Etruscan origin, was commander of the Praetorians, the first to use that position for political ends. Tiberius trusted him completely. Once, travelling through Campania, they stopped to eat at a country house, known as the Grotto because its dining-room was a natural cave. A sudden fall of rock crushed some of the slaves, but Sejanus shielded Tiberius with his own body. Whether Sejanus saved his life or (as some think) staged the whole incident, Tiberius allowed him ever-increasing influence.

It was then, after seven distasteful years in Rome mastering the intricacies of government, that Tiberius left the capital for ever and withdrew to his villa on Capri. It was alleged that his motive was to enjoy in seclusion all those indescribable orgies which Suetonius describes with such gusto in his biography. This legend, still used to titillate the modern tourist, is inherently unlikely. Tiberius was simple, almost ascetic, in his personal habits and lived to seventy-seven without troubling the doctors. He had several times earlier in his life gone into retirement, which suited his nature. Even at Capri he attended diligently to his dispatch-boxes. Though the island household may not in every respect have resembled Victorian Balmoral, his distant ministers were probably far less inconvenienced than Mr. Gladstone.

Capri was not only pleasanter than Rome, it was safer. No emperor, however popular, was without enemies: a man like Tiberius inevitably provoked conspiracies. His reign saw a rash of informers and treason-trials. It is fair to remember that Rome had no state prosecutor and without the action of individual citizens no case would have reached the courts.

Sejanus took care of things in Rome. Too well. With his Praetorians now concentrated there in permanent barracks, he felt himself unassailable. He began to see the imperial succession as his, and toyed with the notion of accelerating matters. He seduced Tiberius' daughter-in-law and poisoned her husband. Tiberius did not learn this until much later. Before that, he discovered enough to realize that Sejanus must go.

But how? Tiberius went to work with characteristic caution and efficiency. His young great-nephew Gaius — his own choice for the succession — was brought safely to Capri. A squadron of warships stood by, in case a swift safe departure to the East should become advisable. He then sent a trusted officer, Macro, to Rome with a sealed commission to take over the Praetorian Guard and a lengthy dispatch to be read to the Senate.

The plan went well. The unsuspecting Sejanus attended the session and listened indulgently to this strangely rambling epistle from his elderly master. The sting was in the final paragraphs — a sudden venomous denunciation of Sejanus which stupefied the hearers. All, that is, except the consul, who, forewarned by Macro, ordered his lictors to arrest Sejanus. The deposed prefect was tried, sentenced and executed that day. Swift couriers took the news to Naples and an agreed signal told Tiberius, anxiously watching from a high cliff on his island, that all was well.

There is a regrettable story that when he was dying, some years later, this same Macro shortened the process with a pillow. If so, Macro was no doubt only showing an official's natural concern about his professional future and a desire to stand well with the next emperor. It was difficult to survive in public life without occasionally removing other people. Macro himself was driven to suicide soon afterwards.

Gaius, the new emperor, was known as Caligula, an affectionate nickname ('Bootikins') inspired by the miniature army boots he wore as a child. He was an epileptic and had a severe mental breakdown during his mercifully short reign of three or four years. We need not believe all the scabrous stories about him — 'It was his habit to commit incest with each of his three sisters in turn,' remarks Suetonius blandly — but we cannot doubt that he was a murderous monstrosity. He was himself murdered by some Praetorian officers in his thirtieth year. Despite all his scandalous doings he was far more popular than Tiberius with the masses, for he was a lavish spender on games and shows.

He was succeeded — most reluctantly — by his uncle Claudius, an individual of antiquarian tastes but considerable administrative talents. He was hiding behind a curtain when Caligula's assassins pulled him out and proclaimed him emperor. His oft-quoted timidity is excusable if we recall the fate of his predecessors, successors, and relatives. He was in fact, after thirteen years, poisoned by his second wife, Agrippina, so that his stepson Nero could take the throne and in due course murder her too. But history is not all daggers, mushrooms, and ingeniously collapsing boats: in those few years Britain and other new provinces were added to the Empire, citizenship was extended to many people outside Italy, Rome gained two fine aqueducts, Ostia was given better port facilities, a great drainage scheme created new farmlands in Central Italy, and the civil service was still further improved.

Thanks to that service, the day-to-day government always continued with comparative smoothness. An emperor might be a fool or a psychopath, he might devote himself to trivialities or absent himself for years in distant regions, he might be one of two or three rival claimants, but for the next century or two the imperial machinery could be relied upon to run itself without major catastrophes. Thus Rome survived the fourteen-year fooleries of Nero and the anarchic 'year of the four emperors', A.D. 69, when four rivals contended for the succession.

Of Nero it is chiefly remembered, with periodical reminders from the sensational cinema, that he burnt Rome to facilitate his town-planning and then blamed the Christians, using them as human torches or throwing them to the lions. The first of these statements is about as true as the suggestion that he played the as-yet-uninvented fiddle during the fire, but both legends are in keeping with his character. His artistic aspirations give his reign a touch of comic relief, though in sadistic horror it equals that of Caligula. When Nero toured Greece, all competitive festivals had to be staged in turn, irrespective of their normal dates, and the judges diplomatically awarded him all the first prizes, totalling eighteen hundred and eight, even in the contests for which he had not entered. Nero accepted them with naïve pleasure. At least his absurdities — his platform appearances as a singer, for instance — occupied time which he might otherwise have spent on more murderous amusements. Meanwhile the ordinary life of Italy went on, equally undisturbed by the roar of the arena lions and the warblings of the imperial amateur.

On his death, however, the peninsula became again for a brief moment the stage for decisive historical events. Galba, proclaimed emperor by the legions in Spain, had scarcely established himself in Rome when he was struck down in the Forum by partisans of his rival Otho. In Germany the legions favoured their own general, Vitellius, who quickly won the support of the other western and North African armies, although those of the Danube and Euphrates declared for Otho. Vitellius sent his troops through the Alps in a three-pronged advance. Otho tried to stop them in the Po Valley, was beaten near Cremona, and preferred a dignified suicide to a continuation of the struggle. Vitellius swept on to Rome, but his triumph was short. The armies of the East now persuaded Vespasian, the commander in Judea, to take a hand, and the Danubian legions, having lost Otho, switched their support to him. Being nearer, they were first in Italy, where they defeated the supporters of Vitellius in a second battle near Cremona. There followed a four-day sack of the city, in which fifty thousand people were massacred. Similar atrocities occurred in Rome two months later after bitter street-fighting between the rival legions from the Danube and the Rhine. The soldiers, it should be remembered, were by now neither Romans nor even Italians, but primarily natives of their respective provinces. Vitellius tried to save his life by abdication but was seized and executed. So ended the 'year of the four emperors', and Italy relapsed thankfully into the quietude she had learnt to appreciate since the end of the Republic a century before.

.   .   .   .

We come now to a happier period, A.D. 70 to 180, in which the monotonous pattern of intrigue and homicide changes to one of benevolence and order. Of eight emperors only one, Domitian, died by violence. Even in his case, the worst excesses were crowded into the last three years, and their memory has obscured his earlier achievement as an administrator. The characters of the other seven emperors are in the main attractive.

Vespasian hailed from Rieti and marked the break with the two old Roman families, the Julians and the Claudians, who had so far monopolized the purple. He had the countryman's instinct for economy, welcome after Nero's extravagance, and the countryman's bluff humour. When the Stoic philosophers attacked his government on theoretical republican grounds, he cleared them out of Rome but did not pursue them with his vengeance. 'I'm not going to kill dogs for barking at me,' he said. He had no illusions about the flattery heaped on a man in his position, least of all the 'divine honours' sometimes accorded posthumously to a popular emperor. His death-bed joke is famous: 'I think I'm in process of becoming a god.'

His two sons complete the brief Flavian dynasty. Titus, 'the darling of mankind', was remembered wistfully as a Prince Charming, handsome and generous to all. True, it was he who, in the Jewish revolt, had destroyed the Temple and the whole city of Jerusalem, but this did not affect his popularity elsewhere. In Italy he was the man who energetically pro-moted relief-work when Pompeii was blotted out and who, when Rome suffered yet another great fire, sold some of his own furniture for charity; who completed the Flavian Amphi-theatre, which we call the Colosseum, and built the magnifi-cent public baths near by; who had nobody executed, and counted any day wasted on which he had done no kind act. All too soon he was succeeded by his brother, Domitian, who (as just indicated) was rather less amiable.

Before long, however, the shadow lifts again. The stop-gap reign of Nerva, an elderly senatorial figure-head, was marked only by the state's taking over and developing the welfare schemes known as *alimenta*. Under these, small farmers obtained mortgages at a modest five per cent, paid not to the treasury but to their own local authority, which redistributed the money in the form of child-maintenance grants to poor parents. It was a highly-organized system with a head office in Rome, and operated in every town of any size throughout Italy. It is interesting as an anticipation of modern ideas and as an example of co-operation between central and municipal government.

That the next two emperors were of Spanish birth under-lines the broadening basis of the Empire. Trajan was born near Seville. Strong-faced, with straight-cut hair over a wide but low forehead, he looked the conqueror he was. Though his constructive contribution was great and his supervision of administrative detail almost excessive, he was pre-eminently the aggressive soldier whose victories are commemorated in the spiral bas-reliefs of the famous column built to contain his ashes. Trajan, like all the emperors after him, was per-petually concerned with the problem of the barbarians beyond the frontier. There was nothing new about that problem. From the days of Brennus Rome had lived with it, and not a century had passed without its crisis. Trajan's answer was to go out and smash the barbarians on their own territory, to roll back the threat beyond the eastward horizon. That was his motive, not mere glory, when he annexed Mesopotamia, Armenia, and the Dacian lands across the Danube. Now at its zenith in 117 A.D. the Empire touched the Persian Gulf and the Caspian.

Being childless, Trajan chose as his successor his young cousin Hadrian. In appearance, interests, and policy the new emperor was remarkably different. Whereas Trajan had cared little for art or literature, Hadrian was a somewhat uncritical enthusiast. His devotion to Greek culture won him the nickname of 'the Greekling', and there was an Hellenic suggestion in the beard which he was the first of a series of emperors to wear—though its purpose was possibly to hide a scar. He was an indefatigable traveller, determined to see every province for himself, so that of his twenty-one years' reign he spent barely half in Italy. His answer to the barbarian problem was different. He believed in defensible frontiers, as we can still see from the wall he personally planned in Britain, and he evacuated Armenia and Mesopotamia. Despite his broader interests, he was no less a soldier than Trajan. He was a strict disciplinarian, as tireless in his inspection of military training as in his surveillance of the civilian departments. Both emperors are perhaps equally to blame for multiplying those central controls which were later to stifle the Empire with its own bureaucracy. Whether Trajan had the right answer to the barbarian problem, and whether Hadrian was disastrously wrong in reversing his policy, would take longer to argue.

Hadrian's tours were not just a duty but a personal delight. He had a keen love of natural scenery—he climbed Etna when he was fifty—and an unflagging appetite for art treasures, famous buildings, and curiosities of every kind. His travels over, he built himself a villa at Tivoli, the extent of which (as now excavated) suggests not so much a country retreat as an ambitious lay-out for a university. But he was not destined to enjoy the seclusion of that moated library which is so attractive a feature of the scheme. His last years were over-shadowed by painful illness, probably tuberculosis accompanied by dropsy, which made him harsh, irritable, and unpopular. Soon he was laid to rest in the vast drum-like mausoleum beside the Tiber (now the Castel Sant' Angelo), the most striking of the buildings he had added to Rome.

His successor, Antoninus Pius, was of Gallic origin and appropriately one of the outstanding relics of his reign is the Pont du Gard. Another is the Antonine Wall between Forth and Clyde, with which he tried to shorten the defence-line against the Scots. Otherwise he did not worry unduly about the barbarians and scarcely moved outside Italy, regarding Hadrian's continual inspections as a waste of money. His personal interest was the overhaul of the legal code which Hadrian had begun and which, perfected in the next century, made Roman law the worthy model for the modern world. His reforms were always directed to equity and humanity. He established the principle that the accused must be treated as innocent until proved guilty, and he greatly reduced the use of torture.

Antoninus was kindly, informal, devoted to his wife and daughters, never happier than when enjoying the simple country life. Typically, when he lay dying and was asked by the captain of the guard to choose the next day's password, he answered: 'Equanimity'. An affectionate word-portrait of him is contained in the *Meditations* of Marcus Aurelius, his son-in-law and successor.

Marcus Aurelius, though born in Rome, was another emperor of Spanish origin. Antoninus, conscientious in this as in everything, adopted him early and gave him the title of 'Caesar' now customarily bestowed on the heir, the ruler himself being 'Augustus'. Marcus Aurelius thus had the unusual asset of long preparation. His *Meditations* (written in Greek and genuinely intended more for the writer's own edification than for others') open with a recital of acknowledgements to Antoninus, various relatives, and all the tutors for whose influence he was grateful.

A philosopher by instinct and training, Marcus Aurelius represented, at its very best, the Stoicism which was the finest alternative the pagan world could offer to the Christian religion now spreading through society. His judgement was based on moral principle rather than political expediency. He somewhat unwisely insisted on making his younger brother, Verus, co-emperor with equal honours, an act which did no good but luckily did not produce the evil it might easily have done. It would, though, be a mistake to picture the author of the *Meditations* playing ducks and drakes with the Empire. He carried on the government very much on the lines already established. He had little choice, for desperate emergencies soon demanded his attention.

First there was trouble in Parthia, a legion wiped out, the Asiatic frontier overrun. The situation was restored, but the returning troops and prisoners brought plague to Italy, which raged as lethally as the Black Death in Boccaccio's time. Next came a stirring of the tribes in Central and Eastern Europe, a tidal wave swamping the defences. Again the legions gave way: they had seen little action since Trajan, done no rigorous training since Hadrian. The invaders, the Marcomanni and others, surged through the Julian Alps and swept down to the head of the Adriatic.

Marcus Aurelius showed himself an energetic soldier as well as a reflective philosopher. In twelve years of tough campaigning he pushed back the barbarian tide. Reviving Trajan's theory of aggressive defence, he planned to avert a recurrence by shifting the imperial boundary eastwards to the Elbe and absorbing Central Europe. He was in sight of achieving this when he caught a fever and died at Vienna in 180 A.D., at the age of fifty-nine. With him ended what Gibbon called in an oft-quoted passage *'the period in the history of the world during which the condition of the human race was most happy and prosperous'*.

   .   .   .   .

It is easy to invest this period with undeserved glamour. Extant ruins suggest a life lived exclusively against a backdrop of arches and colonnades. Museum showcases give the impression that every meal was served on exquisite silver plate. Films portray each meal as a banquet, if not an orgy, with undraped slave-girls showering rose-petals and well-developed youths posing as live candelabra. It is even supposed that all Romans enjoyed central heating, whereas in fact, the hypocaust was a late and limited development, the

ordinary room never having more than a charcoal brazier
to mitigate the cold.

True, Rome *was* a magnificent background, hard to exag-
gerate if we remember that today's weathered masonry shone
then with marble facings and polished bronze. Almost every
emperor added some breath-taking monument. But just as
their personalities and policies add up to only one kind of
history, so there are other backgrounds to be visualized,
against which the anonymous masses acted out their lives.

Rome was now a city of about a million people, and even
more cosmopolitan than most capitals. Besides being a magnet
to ambitious provincials, she contained a high percentage of
freed slaves and their progeny. Tombstones show only one
Italian name in four. As only registered citizens qualified for
the corn-dole, the majority had to work, if not very hard, to
gain a living. Every wealthy man had his queue of early morning callers, his 'clients' or hangers-on, who hoped for another
little dole in cash or kind.

In some ways the luxury of the upper classes cannot be
overestimated. They drew on the rarities of the whole world,
far beyond the frontiers. Rome's river-mouth port of Ostia
drew in argosies from every direction. Cadiz was a week's sail
distant, Alexandria rather longer — and from Alexandria a
short overland crossing was the link with the Red Sea, where,
in the season, there were almost daily arrivals from India or
Malaya or Zanzibar. Chinese merchandise came across Central
Asia by caravan. Not only Rome, not only Italy, but the whole
Empire had an adverse trade balance. Gold and silver drained
eastwards, until a debasement of the currency was unavoid-
able.

This luxury was not for the masses. The average Roman
lived simply, not to say uncomfortably, in a crowded tene-
ment. People complained (as the inhabitants of a capital
always will) that an attic cost as much as a decent provincial
house, and that they had to dress beyond their means. When
we think of the mansions on the Palatine we should remember also the *insulae* or island-blocks, towering seventy feet
above the airless street, with no piped water above ground-
level and sometimes no sanitation of their own. Fortunately
the Romans were pioneers of the public convenience. With
its pleasing decor, its semicircle of marble seats divided only

by dolphin arm-rests, and its altar to the goddess of health and happiness, it was something of a local community-centre where (as one of Martial's poems informs us) men could meet, gossip and exchange dinner-invitations.

Still more of a social rendezvous were the *thermae*, the vast public baths, which besides holding hundreds of bathers at a time had lounges, gymnasia and even art galleries. Mixed bathing was usual until Hadrian was forced to bring in restrictions.

The book-lover was served by twenty-five public libraries, stocked with Greek as well as Latin manuscripts. The mood of the contemporary writer was predominantly satirical or scandalized. In Nero's reign Petronius had written his lively picaresque novel, *Satyricon*. Juvenal and Martial, a little later, flayed the follies of the Roman scene in their verses. Suetonius, aided by his official position as archivist to Hadrian, exposed the peculiar habits attributed to earlier emperors safely dead, and Tacitus chronicled recent reigns with equal disapproval but more regard for evidence. There was a copious critical and technical literature in both languages — travel-books, medical and scientific treatises, collections of letters — by such authors as Strabo, Ptolemy, Galen, Quintilian and Pliny. It was, in short, a highly sophisticated and slightly jaded period, with a well-developed book trade. Authors grumbled as always. Martial laments: ' *Britain is said to hum my verses. What use is that? My purse feels no difference.*' And there were the usual intellectual snobs, who, complained Seneca, ' *possess books not to read but to decorate their dining-rooms.*'

What did these men believe in, beyond the materialism of day-to-day existence? Not in the Olympians. Despite all the temples to Jupiter, Mars, Venus and the rest, those deities were not real in people's minds. Their worship had always been, at best, a business-like procedure of vows and sacrifices — 'I give that Thou mayest give' — remote from personal morality. Ethical guidance was sought from the philosophers, emotional satisfaction from the mystic cults.

The lectures of Epictetus, a crippled ex-slave from Phrygia, did much to popularize Stoicism. Marcus Aurelius gives us an insight into the thinking of the cultured minority at its most serious. Christianity was slowly beginning to penetrate the upper classes, but it was still primarily a cult for the lower orders, its teachings unknown or misunderstood, just another eccentric foreign superstition, not meriting discussion by the Stoic intelligentsia. The capital was full of such imported sects. The government was tolerant and intervened only when their practices became anti-social. Besides Jews and Christians there were devotees of Oriental superstitions, such as the cult of Mithras, God of Light, especially popular with soldiers, of Isis, with its promise of everlasting life, and of Cybele, the Great Mother, whose clergy so impressively demonstrated their sincerity by self-castration. All this was very exotic, and serves usefully to remind us that Rome was by far the least Italian city in Italy. It is high time to turn our eyes to the rest of the country.

Italy held a privileged position in the Empire: she paid no direct taxes. Except for this advantage, her economic life was more balanced and natural than that of Rome. There was no great population of subsidized idlers. People worked on the land. As the supply of slaves diminished, more and more small farms were let to free men. Northern and Central Italy were fully cultivated. The South was an emptier country-side, given up to lonely shepherds. There was plenty of industry. The red-glazed pottery of Arezzo went all over the Empire, Rimini shipped tiles across the Adriatic, Carrara marble found its way to Britain. Milan was already a manufacturing centre, Capua was famous for metalwork, Rome made glass. On the whole, though, Italy found it increasingly difficult to compete with the lower production-costs in Gaul and other provinces. The cheap textiles of Flanders, for instance, could undersell those of Italy even in her home market.

The population by Trajan's time was about twenty million. It fell after the great plague in the reign of Marcus Aurelius. It was largely urban, Italy being thickly dotted with towns, linked by excellent, if narrow, roads. A well-organized post-horse system facilitated correspondence and allowed travellers to average fifty miles a day. A news bulletin, the *Acta Diurna,* was displayed in the Forum and gave at least an official summary of what was happening in the world. Towns had their own magistrates, senates and public corporations; elections were fought and there could be, at this local level, a genuine political activity which compared favourably with that of Rome. Florence, Milan, Verona, Parma, Taranto, with sixty or seventy other centres, had amphitheatres. Many had fine theatres too — the auditorium at Verona rose splendidly above the sweeping curve of the green twinkling river — as well as *thermae* and other amenities. Every corner of Italy contained a miniature Rome.

There was of course variety. Ostia, with its wharves and warehouses, was very different from Pompeii, as the respective excavations demonstrate. Ravenna again, the Adriatic naval base, was an ancient Venice, built on piles amid lagoons which have now silted up, and (says Strabo) *'provided with thoroughfares by means of bridges and ferries'*. The west-coast naval base was Miseno, on the Bay of Naples, and the other main commercial ports were near-by Pozzuoli, Genoa and Brindisi. The Neapolitan coast was lined with smart health-resorts, Baiae being especially notorious for the scandalous doings in its luxurious villas. Julius Caesar had owned a house there, in which Hadrian later died, and Nero had built himself one. Sorrento and Herculaneum were also popular.

Inland there were prosperous trading and industrial centres, notably the old Etruscan cities, and peaceful holiday-resorts in the hills. Baiae had its rival in Tivoli, where genera-tions of rich Romans from Maecenas to Hadrian built elegant country retreats on the cliffs above the murmurous cascades of the Anio. Nor was appreciation of natural beauty confined to a few emperors and poets. One of Pliny's letters, describing the Clitumnus springs near Assisi, emphasizes for us the contrast between the comparative solitude of that lovely spot today and its popularity in the second century. Then, the local people had formed an organization *'to maintain the bathing station and provide lodgings for visitors'*. There was sailing above the bridge, swimming below. There was an *'ancient and venerable temple'* with a statue of Clitumnus *'draped in a crimson-bordered robe'*, with smaller shrines to other river deities. Villas lined the water's edge. And — so little does the tourist alter down the ages — *'there are many inscriptions in different hands,'* Pliny added, *'written on every wall and column.'*

6. The Long Sunset

IF MARCUS AURELIUS had lived a few months longer and consolidated his shorter frontier; or if his son Commodus had been even moderately able and willing to carry on his policy; or if the idealist emperor had been a better judge of imperfect humanity and had picked another heir . . . It is fascinating, but not very profitable, to play with the 'ifs' of history.

Could anything have held off for ever the eventual triumph of the outer barbarians? Could anything have done more than still further lengthen 'the long sunset', as R. C. Sherriff termed the decline of Rome in his play of that title? At any rate, from 180 A.D. we can now see that the long sunset had begun and the shadow of barbarism was creeping across Europe with a terrible inevitability.

Yet for almost three more centuries the Empire went on, confounding ten generations of pessimists. With incredible vitality it bore the wounds of foreign and civil war, the ravages of plague. It was chronically sick with over-centralized bureaucracy, unbalanced trade, debased currency, and general stagnation — political, intellectual, and spiritual. Yet defying probability it staggered on.

It survived rulers of inconceivable viciousness and absurdity. It survived Commodus, a madman who fancied himself as a gladiator, who emptied the treasury and executed thousands of his subjects. It survived the young pervert Elagabalus, who identified himself with the Sun-god and whose five marriages in three years (one to a Vestal Virgin) were but one facet of a sexual versatility amply demonstrated by the time of his murder at eighteen. It survived a sequence of twelve emperors in thirty-six years, and the indignity of an auction, once, when the soldiers awarded the succession to the man who offered them the biggest 'donation' per head.

71

These donations were now an established custom. The armies knew that they, not the Senate, had the real power to decide a disputed claim. Their sole criterion was the bounty offered by the new Augustus. This gave them a vested interest in frequent change, and helps to explain the monotonous cycle of murder and mutiny, a cycle which a prudent emperor might break by supplementary donations, to celebrate (for instance) the completion of five years' rule.

Under these circumstances an emperor might be proclaimed in York or Antioch. He might seldom — in one case never — set foot in Rome. There had already been emperors of Spanish and Gallic extraction, but these had been thoroughly romanized. The centuries of decline produced emperors like Maximinus, a Thracian peasant promoted centurion because of his towering physique, and the North African Septimus Severus, and the three energetic Illyrians, one of whom, Aurelian, gave Rome the twelve-mile wall which still bears his name. The mere building of that wall, about 275 A.D., showed that even the capital was no longer completely safe. The Alemanni had poured over the Brenner more than once in preceding years and advanced dangerously far into Northern Italy before they were ejected.

Even the opulent gesture of the Aurelian Wall could not hide the fact that Rome was no longer the centre of the Empire. That centre was where the emperor had his headquarters, Trier or Arles, Nicaea or Nicomedia. Caracalla gave citizenship to all and sundry, not so much from political broadmindedness as from a wish to multiply the number of taxpayers. Even the Praetorian Guards had now, like the legionaries, lost their Italian exclusiveness. Italy was no longer a specially favoured region. The history of the later Empire is so largely non-Italian that it has no place in this book, and it will be sufficient to pick out those salient events which affected the peninsula itself.

One such was the accession in 284 of a dynamic and masterful Illyrian officer, Diocletian. No Roman emperor was more imperial. The strong bearded face surveyed the world from beneath the first royal crown with which any ruler had ever dared to flout the lingering, meaningless, yet potent tradition of the old Republic. Diocletian's broad band of gold, set with pearls, was the forerunner of all the crowns of Europe,

medieval or modern. His inspiration was Oriental. He carried
it into the resplendent new robes of purple silk and gold
thread which were to distinguish, with appropriate grada-
tions of magnificence, the sovereign and his most exalted
officers. He extended it to the creation of a more formal
etiquette and protocol, more suggestive of Persia than Italy.
But after all (and this is what we must note about him)
Diocletian came from east of the Adriatic and it was to the
East that his eyes most naturally turned. He personifies the
tendency to displace Rome from her old dominance.

Diocletian completely reorganized the Empire. The provinces were redivided into '*dioceses*', each governed by a
vicarius. Only later did these words acquire their ecclesiastical
flavour. Italy was split. The so-called 'Vicar of Italy' had his
capital at Milan and ruled a 'diocese' stretching north from
the Apennines to the Danube. Italy south of the Apennines
came under the 'Vicar in Rome'. Diocletian himself was
far away: his usual headquarters were at Nicomedia (now
Izmit) on the Sea of Marmora. The Empire, he felt, had
become too unwieldy for one man. He devised the system of
the Tetrarchy instead. There were to be two senior emperors,
western and eastern, each styled Augustus. Each should have
a junior colleague, a 'Caesar', who would eventually take
his place and in turn adopt a Caesar. This, thought Diocletian,
should end intrigues and assassinations. Stability would be
achieved.

Stability was his aim. In seeking it he struck hard at
individual liberty. The debased coinage had brought infla-
tion: he restored a high silver content to the denarius and
tried to freeze prices by edict. As taxes would not cover public
expenditure, he imposed a system of requisitions, extracting
free goods and services from the various trade guilds and
corporations. To keep essential industries going, he enacted
the most rigorous direction of labour. Not only must men stay
in their trades but their sons must follow them. Soldiers' sons
joined the army, country families were tied to the land (which
was the beginning of serfdom), and a town boy's occupation
was dictated by heredity, as under the strictest caste system.
Even the post of local councillor became hereditary. There
was no other way to get candidates for this unpopular duty.

For us Diocletian's name is most immediately associated

with his persecution of the Christians. Despite spasms of repression under Nero, Domitian, and some later emperors, they had so far enjoyed much the same mildly contemptuous toleration as other Oriental sects. Pliny, in a letter to Trajan, had referred to their 'wrong-headed and boundless superstition', and Marcus Aurelius to their 'pure wrong-headedness', but they were seldom interfered with so long as they did not become a nuisance. They were probably not popular with their neighbours, for they tended to be exclusive and sometimes to exude a tiresome spiritual superiority. Their confidence in an imminent Second Coming made them uninterested in chariot-racing results and other topics which absorbed the citizen, while the rules of their faith made it hard for them (as for orthodox Jews or Brahmins) to participate in social life. Even their ceremonies and phraseology gave rise to occasional misunderstandings, though probably few people believed the rumour that human sacrifice was a regular feature of the Communion service.

Most Italian towns had by now a Christian community, self-supporting and meeting usually in private houses, the Church property amounting only to a few silver vessels and sacred books. The catacombs were their cemeteries, for, believing literally in the resurrection of the body, Christians rejected the hygienic but pagan practice of cremation. Only on exceptional occasions were the catacombs used either for secret worship or for refuge. Cities with several priests had a bishop, chosen with the help of neighbouring bishops and consecrated by one of them. Fraternal contacts were kept up with other congregations, 'and special deference was paid to the Bishop of Rome, the capital city and St. Peter's own See.

By Diocletian's time Christianity had won converts in high circles throughout the Empire. They included his wife, his daughter, and many of his courtiers. It was these last who provoked his first outburst. The omens were being taken in his presence and the augurers twice failed to discover any marks on the sacrificial livers. They blamed the Christians present, who had nullified the ceremony by crossing themselves and generally blighting the occasion with their silent disapproval. This refusal by Christians to take part in pagan sacrifices had always irked their neighbours. Tolerant themselves, always willing to admit one more god into the pantheon, the Romans could not understand why the Christians made a fuss over a formality.

Diocletian's reaction to this particular incident was that of any impatient disciplinarian. He ordered that all should take part in the regulation ceremonies or be flogged. It is not recorded what happened in the case of his wife and daughter. He then did nothing more for several years until, in 303, he issued the first of several decrees aimed at Christianity throughout the Empire. The army and civil service were to be purged of Christians, churches closed, sacred books destroyed. Many people were imprisoned, tortured, or put to death. But this happened almost entirely in the eastern half of the Empire, Diocletian's particular sphere. In the West (including Italy) his co-emperor Maximian had little enthusiasm for the policy, and did not even publish all the decrees.

Later that year Diocletian went to Rome to confer with his colleague. He was old, tired and ill. He had ruled for nearly twenty years and wished to retire to his native Dalmatia. He asked Maximian also to abdicate, allowing their respective Caesars to step up together. Maximian agreed to this with extreme reluctance, and on 1st May, 305, as Diocletian paraded his troops at Nicomedia and announced his abdication, Maximian made a similar gesture in Milan.

There followed seven years of exquisite confusion. Diocletian retired to his superb palace at Split, cultivated vegetables, and read dispatches about the quarrels and intrigues of the new Augusti and their Caesars. The neat scheme of the Tetrarchy never worked. Maximian wrote, urging his old colleague to emerge from retirement and help to clear up the mess, as he himself was only too eager to do. Diocletian refused. All he would do was preside, as a private individual, at a conference of the bickering emperors. Otherwise he stuck to his gardening in Dalmatia, where he died in 313. By which time a new epoch had opened, the age of Constantine.

.   .   .   .

Constantine was the son of Constantius, Maximian's successor as western Augustus, and of a Bithynian serving-maid, more familiar to us as St. Helena, finder of the reputed Cross. When Constantius died at York in 306, the soldiers promptly saluted his eighteen-year-old son as the new emperor, ignoring the Caesar originally approved by Diocletian. After six years of tangled negotiations and manoeuvres, impossible to unravel here, we find Constantine an active contender for the supreme power, backed by the legions of Gaul and Britain. His rival was Maximian's son, Maxentius, who had the double advantage of commanding bigger forces and being already established in Rome.

The campaign of 312 was superficially just another civil war: actually, it was laden with incalculable consequences for our civilization. As the young Constantine rode southwards with his legions — clean-shaven, strong-featured, steady-eyed, if we may trust the portrait-head at Rome with its suggestion of archaic Greek sculpture — he was pondering more than strategy. Nothing less, indeed, than the Christian faith.

Just what went on in his mind we cannot tell. Clearly he was not so much 'converted' to Christianity as attracted, for only on his death-bed was he baptized. But at this date, like many others in the West where Diocletian's repressive edicts had been largely ignored, he was sympathetic. He was aware that the savage persecutions in some of the eastern regions had achieved nothing. Galerius, Diocletian's successor and a far more zestful persecutor, had just called them off, confessing himself beaten. Galerius' ensuing death, of a painful and protracted illness, was explained by many as the vengeance of the Christian deity. People were beginning to wonder whether such a deity would not be a better friend than an enemy.

Constantine was thus in a receptive mood for the vision he saw during his long march to Rome. Many years later he described it to his biographer, Eusebius, as a monogram shining before him in the afternoon sky, composed of the two Greek letters CH and R, with three words in that language, 'In this conquer'. Scientists have suggested that the monogram was a halo phenomenon caused by ice crystals falling across the sun's rays. Whatever it was, it ended his theological doubts. When his soldiers reached Rome the sacred monogram was already displayed upon their shields.

Before that, there was hard fighting. Constantine came down into Italy over the Mont Cenis. His troops were mainly Britons, Gauls and Germans, all he dared withdraw from the

Rhineland and Scottish frontier. The forces Maxentius sent to stop him were largely cavalry. Diocletian had instituted army reforms, replacing the traditional legionary with the horseman better suited to the new needs of the Empire, but Constantine's army had not been modernized to this extent. In battle, therefore, he told his men to give ground at first and then, as the impetus of the enemy's cavalry slackened, to close in again and envelop them. Outnumbered, Maxentius' troops were routed in this way at Turin and Brescia. A stronger force defied Constantine from the river-girt ramparts of Verona. He slipped some of his men across the Adige and smashed a relieving column, whereupon Verona surrendered. More and more towns opened their gates. That autumn he swept irresistibly down the road to Rome.

Maxentius waited calmly behind the massive Aurelian Walls. He had plenty of troops, ample provisions. Had he sat still, could Constantine have succeeded where Hannibal had failed? But there was an important difference — in the morale of the citizens. The crowd at the races taunted Maxentius, shouting that he would never beat Constantine. Goaded into action, instead of leaving the footsore legionaries to batter vainly against the fortifications or to attempt an impossible blockade of a twelve-mile perimeter, Maxentius led out his garrison across the Milvian Bridge.

Nothing, short of angelic intervention, could have done more to convince Constantine that Heaven was indeed on his side. As the emerging columns extended themselves, he attacked them and rolled them back against the river. Cramped, unable to deploy properly, they fought stubbornly for a time, then crumpled in panic, making for the Milvian Bridge and a supplementary pontoon-bridge beside it. Soon the latter parted in the middle and the rout became a massacre. Maxentius was one of the thousands who perished in the Tiber. The next day, Constantine entered Rome in triumph, and the Empire had acquired its first ruler officially to favour Christianity. The Milvian Bridge linked not only two river-banks but two great historical periods.

For the next eleven years Constantine reigned in uneasy partnership with his eastern colleague, Licinius, a pagan. Thereafter the tetrarchy scheme was sunk without trace and he reigned supreme for fourteen more. Never again, except

for two brief interludes under Julian the Apostate and
Eugenius, was a pagan to wear the imperial purple. Constantine did not, however, impose his personal beliefs upon
his subjects. His Edict of Milan in 313 merely granted Christians freedom of worship and legalized their churches as
public corporations. The Christians, hitherto perhaps a ten
per cent minority in the Empire, naturally gained ground
once their creed was safe and fashionable, but it is perhaps to
the credit of the others that they did not all scramble to join
the winning side. While the emperor was founding the
churches of St. Peter and St. John Lateran, crowds were still
sacrificing to the old gods in the countless temples of the
city, and when he was presiding over the deliberations of the
Church at Nicaea the intelligentsia of the Empire remained
loyal to pagan art and philosophy.

Not until 380 did Christianity become the official state
religion under Theodosius. Other forms of worship were
then banned, but that was not, by a long chalk, the end of the
matter. If the Church showed her ingenuity in taking over
pagan observances and embodying them in her own, the
unconvinced pagan was no less adept at camouflage. Ancient
cults survived underground into the age of medieval witch-
craft, and who would swear that even today the old gods are
entirely without honour?

.   .   .   .

Though Rome now gained some compensating influence
as the seat of the most important Christian bishop, the political centre of gravity continued to shift eastwards. Constantine
followed Diocletian's example by fixing his capital where
Europe and Asia joined, but he chose Byzantium, which he
transformed into 'New Rome' or Constantinople. The formal
division of the Empire into East and West, Greek and Latin,
came two generations later on the death of Theodosius in 395.

And all this time, we must remember, the long sunset was
inexorably proceeding, the twilight of barbarism was imper-
ceptibly thickening beyond the frontier. . . .

We must nevertheless beware of over-dramatizing — of
creating false pictures of hairy hordes emerging suddenly
from No-Man's-Land to overrun the defences. The Goths
and Vandals, for instance, originating from Scandinavia and

Germany respectively, were romanized by long contact and were Christians, though of the Arian heresy, believing that God the Son was the subordinate creation of God the Father. In 375 these Goths, hard pressed by the heathen Huns sweeping westwards from Mongolia, were allowed to settle inside the Danube frontier in return for defending it. More and more the emperors, unable to raise enough troops of their own, came to rely upon such barbarian mercenaries. Their chiefs held the highest commands and were socially acceptable. Alaric the Goth was a general under Theodosius, as was the Vandal Stilicho. Stilicho indeed married the emperor's niece, Serena, a cultured and even scholarly woman.

Not only the army but the civil population was by now heavily diluted with immigrants and ex-prisoners from beyond the Rhine and Danube. The process was not new. Two centuries earlier, Marcus Aurelius had settled numbers of the Marcomanni in Italy. So, while there *were* sudden and dramatic onslaughts, like the barbarians' crossing of the frozen Rhine in 406, the Empire did not so much collapse under a tidal wave as yield to an insidious infiltration spread over many lifetimes.

Theodosius, the last strong emperor in the West, partitioned his realm at death between his two sons. The West went to the eleven-year-old Honorius. Stilicho, the trusted Vandal, was made his guardian. This duty he interpreted most conscientiously, marrying Honorius (at fourteen) to his daughter Maria and, when she died, supplying a second daughter as replacement.

The Gothic general, Alaric, was less satisfied with the new regime. He had seen enough of the Empire to grasp the realities of the situation. To serve the mighty Theodosius was one thing: to serve a feeble boy, a puppet worked by a mere Vandal, was quite another. His soldiers encouraged him. Better, they said, to carve new kingdoms with their own strength than live subject to aliens. Lifting him on a shield, they hailed him King of the Goths.

Alaric's ambition took him eastwards at first, but soon he invaded Italy, only to be defeated by Stilicho in a surprise attack on Easter Sunday, the irreverence of which seems to have shocked the Christian conscience of the Goths. The victory was stirringly described in Virgilian style by the court poet Claudian, an Alexandrian Greek writing in Latin, and a pagan whose work does not even refer to the newly-established Christian religion. So complex was society in this transition period.

Alaric had been thrown back beyond the Alps, but the Western Empire was shaken. A legion was transferred from Britain: that island's separation from Rome was soon to follow. Gaul and Spain were being overrun by Vandals quite unlike the domesticated Stilicho. Passing over into North Africa, they threatened the corn supply.

Alaric's invasion had shown that Milan was dangerously exposed. Honorius, now a timid youth of nineteen, always happy to bury his head in the sand of ecclesiastical business, was easily persuaded to move the imperial court to Ravenna, where the marshes offered protection against land-attack and the harbour a convenient escape by sea. But Stilicho, in advising the move, had other considerations in mind. Ravenna commanded the road south across the Apennines: it was a vital outpost defending Rome. And the harbour allowed ships to arrive as well as depart: Ravenna was a bridge-head for seaborne reinforcements from Byzantium.

In this perilous decade Stilicho might yet have supplied the military leadership so badly needed in the West — as he did when he outmanoeuvred another horde of invading barbarians under Radagaisus and starved them into surrender at Fiesole. Unluckily he roused in Honorius the hostility which ex-regents so often inspire in weak young rulers. After Honorius had been induced to take Stilicho's second daughter as his second wife, he began to wonder, not unreasonably, if his old guardian's influence upon him had not gone beyond the proper limit. There were obscure intrigues and insinuations, the justice of which cannot now be established. Stilicho was deserted by his soldiers, took sanctuary in a church at Ravenna, was unwise enough to come out, and was murdered. There was no one now to stop the Goths. Soon Alaric was back, across the Apennines, and menacing Rome. After twice allowing himself to be bought off with immense ransoms, he actually took possession of the city in 410.

Not since the Gauls, exactly eight hundred years before, had a foreign army forced its way into Rome. The psychological effect was immeasurable. The shock reverberated through all lands. We are told that St. Jerome, in his cell at Bethlehem, broke off his work and exclaimed in a grief-choked voice: 'They have captured the city which once took the whole world captive.'

The material effects were less catastrophic. The 'sack of Rome' lasted only three days. No buildings were destroyed. The Goths, as Christian as any soldier who ever looted a city, respected the churches and sang hymns as they conveyed the holy vessels to safety. The wealthier citizens had prudently taken ship to Sardinia and other islands, and there had been a considerable exodus of humbler folk, but those who had stayed suffered little violence. In a few months the refugees were drifting home and Rome was outwardly back to normal.

Alaric proceeded southwards, intending to cross to Africa, perhaps to settle there. He took with him, as an honoured hostage, a remarkable young woman of about twenty, Galla Placidia, whose mausoleum at Ravenna (if it really was hers) is itself, with its exquisite mosaics softly illuminated by narrow windows of alabaster, one of the most remarkable memorials of the dying Empire. Placidia was the half-sister of Honorius, but she had been living with relatives in Rome.

In Calabria the marauding army faltered to a standstill. Alaric caught fever. He died and was given a strange funeral, a reversion perhaps to the barbarism beneath the skin. The River Busento was diverted and the conqueror laid to rest, with a selection of his plunder, in the bed of the stream. Then the water was turned back into its channel, obliterating the grave, and the digging party slaughtered to obliterate the memory. Alaric's brother-in-law, Ataulfus, was hailed King of the Goths.

Ataulfus had begun with a barbarian's desire to destroy the Empire. After traversing Italy from end to end, he modified his views. He later confessed to a man, who repeated the words to St. Jerome and the historian Orosius: 'I wanted now to be known to posterity as the stranger who used the Gothic sword not to overthrow the Empire but to restore and preserve it.' It was a common barbarian reaction after closer acquaintance with Roman civilization, but in his case there was a special emollient influence, Placidia. A strong mutual affection had sprung up. Ataulfus offered her brother an alliance, to be cemented by marriage. There was opposition at Ravenna, mainly from Honorius' new minister, Constantius, whose eye had fallen speculatively upon the princess. But a Gothic alliance against the other barbarians was too valuable to be refused, and at last in 414, by which time Ataulfus had taken his army and his hostage into Gaul, the marriage took place. A son was born, Theodosius, but he died young.

What seems to have been a love-match as well as a diplomatic arrangement came all too quickly to a tragic end. Ataulfus was assassinated in the palace at Barcelona. For a few days Placidia was treated as a common captive, forced to trudge on foot while the usurper rode behind. Honorius sent an army under Constantius to secure her release, and after suffering considerable hardship she was ransomed. A year later, feeling no doubt that she had little alternative, the twenty-seven-year-old widow married her deliverer amid scenes of imperial pomp at Ravenna. She bore him a daughter, Honoria, and a son, Valentinian.

All was going well for the ambitious minister. Soon he attained his objective: Honorius made him co-emperor. There Constantius' good fortune ended, for he died a few months afterwards. Widowed again, Placidia suffered the embarrassment of incestuous advances from her half-brother. She fled with her children to Constantinople where her young nephew had now succeeded to the Eastern Empire. Soon followed news that Honorius too had died, and that his crown had been assumed by a civil servant named Joannes. This was more than the Eastern emperor could stomach. He sent an army to restore Placidia and her children, recognizing her as Augusta, Empress of the West, and regent for her six-year-old heir Valentinian.

Thus it came about that Placidia, the daughter, sister, wife, mother and aunt of emperors, became herself the effective ruler of the Western Empire for a quarter of a century. With a character forged by extraordinary vicissitudes, she was worth all the men of her family put together, and, not surprisingly, she never really relinquished the controls. This proved a remarkably peaceful period for Italy itself, and she was able to enhance the architectural glories of Ravenna with some noble Byzantine work. She was in her

Classical art adapts itself to Christian themes. The Good Shepherd motif was popular in the transition period (4th century AD). This example is in the Lateran Museum.

Theodoric—'once secure, an enlightened ruler'—
with, above, his grandson, Athalaric and his
daughter Amalasuntha. From an ivory diptych in
the Victoria and Albert Museum.

Theodoric's palace at Ravenna, from a mosaic frieze in St Apollinare Nuovo.

sixties when she died in Rome, where there was a short-lived attempt to re-establish the imperial capital.

The year was 450. The curtain was about to rise on the next act of the drama. Waiting in the wings stood Attila.

.　　.　　.　　.　　.　　.　　.　　.

Attila, 'the Scourge of God', was ruler of the Huns, those Mongol nomads who had evicted the Goths from Hungary two generations earlier and now straddled the continent from the Caspian to the Rhine. Short, swarthy and snub-nosed — the Huns deformed their infants' noses and skulls with tight bandaging — Attila held court in a vast kraal-like palace, in a capital which was itself only an overgrown stockaded camp. The only stone building was a bath-house constructed for him in Roman style, for, while far more truly 'barbarous' than Alaric or Ataulfus, he was not without appreciation of the civilized refinements. Nor was he without a sense of humour.

This was apparent, along with his Oriental taste for devious diplomacy, when he received a ring and proposal of marriage from Honoria. This princess must have inherited much of her mother's independence. Frustrated in an affair with a court official at Ravenna, she reacted by appealing to the one man who snapped his fingers at emperors and empresses. She may have argued that Placidia was the last person to criticize marriage with a barbarian.

Nothing ever came of the romantic proposal, but Attila was too chivalrous — or too canny — to decline it outright. When it suited him, he could claim to be protecting the lawful interests of his bride-to-be; and when (her formidable mother being dead and her deplorable brother in full control) he seized the chance to invade Italy, he could argue with unwinking gravity that he was concerned only with the marriage settlement.

Aquileia, Padua and other cities at the head of the Adriatic went up in flames. The people fled to the lagoons, Valentinian to Rome. Attila would have ridden after him. He was met, however, by a delegation of senators near Lake Garda, headed by Pope Leo, a Tuscan, and one of those strong personalities now more often found in the service of the Church than in that of the Empire. Attila listened amiably and agreed to spare Rome, just as in Gaul, a year previously, he had let Bishop Lupus dissuade him from sacking Troyes. Punning on their names, he remarked that he knew how to conquer men, but that the 'Lion' and the 'Wolf' were too much for him.

Terms settled, he retired across the Alps, hinting that he would soon return if Honoria were not properly treated. The princess herself was left in a state of semi-permanent betrothal which may have been as emotionally frustrating to her as it was politically convenient to Attila. That convenience was clearly diminishing, for in the following year he married another lady, named Ildico, only to die suddenly of a broken blood-vessel in the course of the wedding night.

Two years later Rome *was* sacked, drastically and for four-teen days, not by Attila's heathens but by the Christian Vandals, sailing across from Carthage under their ruthless king, the lame Gaiseric. They first ravaged Ostia, then came up-river to plunder the capital. As heretics they showed Leo less respect than the Huns had paid him, but he persuaded them at least to spare the three most ancient basilicas. After this, there was a permanent decline in the Roman population, the great monuments began to decay, and the court returned to Ravenna.

A shadowy Western Empire lived on for another twenty-one years. The barbarians were now the real masters of Italy, though no fewer than nine puppet emperors followed Valen-tinian, the last one named (with a fine sense of anti-climax) Romulus Augustulus. In 476 it seemed time to end the farce. A barbarian general, Odoacer, took charge. He deposed the boy Romulus, pensioned him off humanely with a luxurious villa in Campania, and punctiliously forwarded all the regalia to the Eastern emperor. It was, he explained, no longer required. The Western Empire was no more. He acknow-ledged the nominal overlordship of Constantinople and would be happy to govern the diocese of Italy with the title of 'Patrician'.

7. Goths and Lombards

IT WAS make-believe, of course, that Odoacer ruled Italy as Constantinople's viceroy. Yet for the moment it suited everybody: the Eastern emperor, because he was in no position to reconquer the West; the barbarians, because they could occupy but could not administer without the local officials; and the inhabitants, because it made their collaboration respectable. It also soothed the religious conscience; for whereas the Empire was orthodox Catholic (those terms remaining equivalent despite occasional disagreements until the eleventh century) Italy's new masters were Arian heretics.

The make-believe wore thin after a few years, when Dalmatia became an area of dispute between Odoacer and his nominal sovereign. The imperial recognition was withdrawn. Authority to depose the 'rebel' was obtained by the enterprising leader of the Ostrogoths, the easterly cousins of those Visigoths who had followed Alaric nearly a hundred years before and who were now settled in Spain and Southern France.

The Ostrogoth leader, Theodoric, had spent ten impressionable years, from seven to seventeen, as a hostage at Constantinople. He had learnt to admire Roman culture without letting it soften him. His commission from the emperor was another piece of make-believe. He wanted land for his people, and his advance through the Julian Alps was a tribal migration. Behind the galloping warriors rumbled the covered wagons.

Odoacer tried to stop him at the River Isonzo, failed, tried again at the Adige, was beaten, and fled to the marsh-moated security of Ravenna. But how secure *was* Ravenna, when its harbour no longer looked out towards a friendly Constantinople? What help could come? If the worst happened, what refuge overseas remained?

Ravenna held out for two and a half years, when almost

every other town had submitted to Theodoric. Desperate with hunger, the garrison tried a sortie. There was a ferocious hand-to-hand struggle in the adjacent pinewood — the now-famous Pineta, Byron's 'immemorial wood', where Dante and Boccaccio were also in their time to find inspiration, and Garibaldi a hiding-place from his Austrian pursuers. Odoacer's men were hurled back into the city, now blockaded by sea as well as by land, and, faced with starvation, he accepted terms so generous that he can hardly have believed in them.

Probably he was planning treachery. Theodoric certainly was. Arriving for a banquet, Odoacer was accosted by two petitioners who knelt before him, each seizing one of his hands in supplication. The appointed assassins then sprang forward, but bungled their work. It was Theodoric himself who cut down his enemy with an appalling butcher's stroke, observing with sardonic amusement that Odoacer seemed to be quite boneless. Subsequently the dead man's wife died in prison and his son was executed.

This savage episode was, improbably, the prelude to over thirty years of undisturbed prosperity such as Italy had not known for centuries. The treacherous barbarian whose murder of Odoacer might well have come from the bloodier pages of the Icelandic sagas was also the man who issued the following directive to the local farmers:

The aqueducts are of special concern to us. We want you forthwith to root out the bushes growing in the channel, which will soon be tall trees requiring an axe and which contaminate the water in the Ravenna aqueduct. Vegetation is the peaceful destroyer of buildings, a battering-ram which overthrows them without ever a trumpet sounding for the siege. Now we shall have baths we can contemplate again with pleasure, water that will clean not stain, water that we can use without needing to wash afresh, and drinking-water whose mere look will not rob us of appetite.

This was no isolated example. Once secure, Theodoric was an enlightened ruler. While repairing aqueducts, improving harbours and reclaiming swamps, he managed to cut taxes. He enforced the law so that it became safe again to keep valuables in unprotected country houses, and the cities no longer had to bar their gates at dusk. He himself remained illiterate and had some qualms about the effect of education on the warrior-class — 'If they fear the teacher's strap now, they will never see sword or spear without a shudder! ' — but he saw its value for other people and encouraged the schools. Perhaps his outstanding achievement was his revival of agriculture: Italy, after centuries of importing corn, produced enough to feed herself and even export a surplus.

All this was made possible by his tolerant handling of the non-Gothic people, at least until his latter years. His men had to have land, like Odoacer's before them, but it seems to have been found without causing undue hardship. Southern Italy received very few settlers at all. The two peoples, Goths and 'Romans', kept their own laws and customs, their separate Arian and Catholic churches. So far as was feasible, they remained two nations sharing a ruler. The tradition of consuls and Senate went on. The administrative apparatus was taken over entire. There was still a Praetorian Prefect, purple-robed and impressive in his state chariot, who fixed taxes, appointed governors, and was the supreme judge of appeal. There was the Master of the Offices, heading the civil service. These two, with several other departmental chiefs, formed an inner advisory council. The old civil service continued to function, graded down to the lowliest clerk and messenger.

Theodoric's own driving power was essential to success, but his officials were more than cogs in a machine. One was Boethius, who attracted the king's notice when he visited Rome and who rose to be the Master of the Offices. A versatile intellectual, as well as a public figure of courageous independence and integrity, Boethius wrote on logic, mathematics and music, his textbook on the last subject being standard reading at Oxford and Cambridge many centuries afterwards. In the closing years of Theodoric's reign, when the king's mind seems to have been clouded with suspicions of one sort or another, Boethius was imprisoned on a charge of treasonable negotiations with Constantinople. It was then that he wrote his famous *Consolation of Philosophy*, which Alfred the Great was one day to translate into Anglo-Saxon and Caxton into English. The cruel execution of Boethius, coupled with other acts of intolerance such as a draft edict handing over all Catholic churches to the Arians, suggests some sort of mental degeneration in Theodoric, and perhaps only his sudden death from dysentery in 526 saved him from ruining much of his earlier achievement.

As it was, the wheels were kept turning for some time longer by Cassiodorus, the remarkable man who succeeded Boethius. A Calabrian, whose father had served Odoacer, Cassiodorus was an enthusiast for co-existence between Roman and barbarian, writing a history of the Goths to prove that they were worthy partners. His other great enthusiasm was the preservation of literature, the pagan classical authors no less than the Early Fathers. He was able to devote himself to this when he retired from office at sixty, founded two monasteries, and set the inmates to copying manuscripts. He was himself an active author at ninety.

Until Theodoric's time, the only monks in Italy had been devotees of the extreme ascetic ideal more suited to the psychology and climate of Egypt or Asia Minor. In his reign, however, appeared the man to whom the West owes its monastic system. Benedict, like Boethius, was born in 480. An Umbrian, he went to study in Rome, where he was appalled by the immorality of his fellow-students and fled to the solitude of the hills. Coming to Subiaco, a lovely spot in the Abruzzi, he spent three years as a hermit in a cave overlooking the ruins of Nero's villa and the lake that emperor had made. His only visitor was a monk from a near-by monastery, but soon he was talked about as a holy man and eventually the local monks (themselves noticeably deficient in holiness) elected him head of their community. This they quickly regretted when he began a campaign of reforms. They tried to poison him, so Benedict sensibly returned to his cave.

His ideas, nevertheless, were gaining ground. More and more followers rallied to him, some from the best families in Rome. He formed small communities, each limited to a dozen, until there were twelve houses under his direction. Such success could hardly fail to irritate the local clergy, and he decided to seek fresh fields. Gathering a party of new candidates, and leaving the first gross of disciples at Subiaco, he wandered southwards until he reached Monte Cassino. There he founded the famous monastery from which the Benedictine

Order was to spread throughout Western Europe. There he received the young Gothic King Totila in 543, and four years later died.

. . . .

Cassiodorus and Benedict, symbolic figures of the sixth century, the one so much in the world, the other so much retired from it, have carried us beyond Theodoric's reign. We now enter a murky period in which Macbeth himself would have felt quite at home.

Theodoric left no son, only a widowed daughter, Amalasuntha, who tried to govern as regent for her little boy, Athalaric. She was a cultured woman, too romanized to please the Goths, who in any case had no precedent for a queen. They criticized the bookish education she gave her son and insisted on making a man of him, with the result that at sixteen he died of drink and other premature pleasures. She then tried to keep effective power by taking a cousin, Theodahad, into nominal partnership, but this underestimated relative promptly allied himself with her enemies and imprisoned her on a rocky islet in Lake Bolsena. There, with his connivance, she was surprised in her bath and strangled.

At this stage Constantinople took a hand. The East had a great emperor again in Justinian, who felt that the moment had come for the recovery of Italy. Posing as the avenger of the murdered queen, he sent an army under his Illyrian general, Belisarius, who had already reconquered North Africa from the Vandals. Belisarius took Sicily and swept up through the South, where there were few Goths to oppose him. Most of his men were cavalry in chain-mail, armed with bow and lance, a formidable combination now favoured by the Eastern Empire. He captured Rome, but the Goths surged back in strength under a vigorous new leader, Vitigis, and besieged him there.

It was then that the aqueducts were deliberately destroyed, creating new marshes outside the city, and that many other ancient buildings were irreparably damaged. There was, for example, an attack on the great bastion of Hadrian's Tomb, from which the defenders hurled statues upon their assailants. At length, having received reinforcements by sea, Belisarius broke out and harried the Goths all the way back to Ravenna. In desperation they offered to accept him as Emperor of the West, if he would desert Justinian. Belisarius pretended interest, though he scrupulously avoided taking an oath, and tricked them into surrender. He sailed back to Constantinople in triumph, taking Vitigis as an honoured captive.

The Goths were not the men to accept a defeat they could blame on treachery. They promptly rose in revolt under the brilliant and aggressive leadership of Totila and recovered control of Italy, except for Ravenna and a few other ports held by Byzantine garrisons. When they first occupied Rome, Totila seriously considered demolishing the walls, expelling the population, and leaving the city an empty shell; but later he reversed this policy, repaired the damaged buildings, and encouraged refugees to return by promoting a lavish programme of public entertainments. Though gladiator-fights had been stopped by Honorius a century and a half before, there were still wild-beast shows (Theodoric had even built new amphitheatres), and the chariot-races were as popular as they were in Constantinople.

Belisarius was sent back to retrieve the situation, but with inadequate forces, since he had unluckily incurred the dislike of Theodora, a beautiful circus-dancer whom Justinian had made his empress. The reconquest of Italy was eventually entrusted to Narses, an Armenian eunuch of seventy-five who had served in the previous campaign and whose vigour in both military and political matters was remarkably preserved. He marched round the head of the Adriatic with thirty-five thousand men and, as Ravenna was still safely held for the Empire, started straight down the Flaminian Way.

There, in a high valley of the Apennines, Totila barred his path. Knowing the chivalrous conventions of these northern barbarians, the wily eunuch invited him to name a convenient day for battle. Totila courteously made the fixture for a week hence, and Narses launched a surprise attack the very next day. Vainly the Goths flung themselves against the bristling lances of the dismounted Byzantine cavalry, while arrows rained upon them from inaccessible archers. At last they broke. Totila was stabbed in the back by one of Narses' barbarian mercenaries, and died shortly afterwards. The survivors fled southwards and for two days made a heroic last stand at the foot of Vesuvius, after which they were granted an honourable safe-conduct beyond the Alps. So, in 553, the last of the Goths withdrew from Italy.

For seventeen years the country had been ravaged from end to end by counter-marching armies. Irremediable ruin had been inflicted on Rome and other cities which had been besieged and besieged again. The Byzantines had perpetrated a massacre in Naples, the Goths in Milan. On both sides there had been atrocities, murders and mutilations.

Occasionally, heroic figures loom through the dust and smoke — Totila in his gilded armour, Belisarius on the grey charger with the conspicuous blaze — and noble words are caught above the squeal of the trumpets, like those with which Belisarius dissuaded Totila from obliterating Rome. But there is more relief in the thought that, contemporary with all the horror, Benedict was quietly working at Monte Cassino, Cassiodorus was editing classics and experimenting with water-clocks, and the pagan poet Maximian was writing nostalgic elegies about the amours of his youth. Anonymous masons and mosaic-workers were creating the glorious churches of San Vitale and Sant' Apollinare in Classe at Ravenna — and all over Italy, no doubt, thousands of people were enjoying private lives, thankful when the armies did not pass their way. We must beware of visualizing a whole age as one sombre battle-scene. Even in the sixth century the Italian sun shone as usual, the peach-blossom unfurled, the grapes ripened, and the mild-eyed ox-teams were commoner on the road than thundering cavalcades.

.   .   .   .

For thirteen years Narses governed Italy from Ravenna. Apart from a brief invasion by Franks and Alemanni, trying unsuccessfully to replace the departed Goths, it was a time of peace if not of prosperity. Taxes were heavy. Narses had to remit substantial funds to Justinian, who had his own troubles in the East. There was expensive reconstruction to be done all over Italy. And Narses, though freed from normal family responsibilities, believed in providing for his own old age. The amazing little eunuch was about ninety-three when a change of emperors and charges of corruption precipitated his reluctant retirement from the public service. He died in

Rome at ninety-five, his well-feathered nest so skilfully concealed that it was not found for several years, when it was used to finance various deserving charities.

Narses would have argued that, in an imperfect world where faithful service was not always rewarded, he had been fully justified in taking something as he went along. He had been a victorious general, an efficient governor. As it turned out, he was the last man really to control Italy as part of the Empire. By the time his leaden coffin was lifted aboard the ship which was to carry it to Constantinople, the Lombards had begun the most drastic and most durable of all the barbarian invasions.

Successive Popes called them 'the unspeakable Lombards'. Popes seldom shrank from forthright generalizations — such as 'the most wicked Neapolitans' and 'the Greeks hateful to God' — and these Lombards were Arian heretics of German stock, beside whom the Goths were gentlemen. Typically, their new king, Alboin, having recently slain a neighbouring barbarian sovereign, had had his skull made into a wine-cup. That he had also forcibly married his victim's daughter would scarcely have excited remark, but when he compelled her to drink out of his cup it was widely felt that he had gone too far. Rosamund herself never forgave him and sought the first opportunity of achieving widowhood. But it was several years before she was able to organize his assassination, and by that time Alboin and his followers had swept through the peninsula from end to end.

The North was quickly overrun except for impregnable Ravenna and Pavia, which fell after a three-year siege and became the Lombard capital, probably because near-by Milan had not recovered from the Goths. This was when the islands of Venice were permanently settled. For generations the mainlanders had been using them as temporary refuges during invasions. When they saw the Lombards, and realized that they had come to stay, the fugitives wisely decided to make the best of life in the lagoons.

Meantime, while Alboin besieged Pavia and carved his kingdom out of the plain we still call Lombardy, two of his followers rode southwards and cut themselves generous slices of territory which became semi-independent duchies. One made his headquarters at Spoleto in Umbria, the other at

Benevento, the ancient Samnite capital, a Campanian hilltop city girdled by higher peaks.

More parasitic than the Goths, the Lombards took a share not of the land itself but of its produce. Farmers in the occupied regions were reduced to an intermediate status, neither slave nor free. There was no talk of co-existence. One of Alboin's successors showed his contempt for the Italians by walking some like dogs, on leash, in view of the beleaguered people of Rome.

That city defied the invaders. So did all the strong coastal places where sea-power enabled the Empire to hold its own. The map now assumes that patchwork look which it will wear, with frequent changes of colour, till modern times. The Empire keeps the islands, Sicily, Sardinia, Corsica. It keeps, for some time, Genoa and the Ligurian coastal strip; a wide area round Rome, a much smaller one round Naples, the mere heel and toe in the far South; over on the Adriatic side, Ravenna and its hinterland, and the bordering but distinct Pentapolis, the country of the 'Five Cities', Rimini, Ancona, Pesaro, Fano and Sinigaglia. This last is tenuously linked with the now-styled 'Duchy of Rome' by the strategic Flaminian Way across the Apennines. Here, where the two imperial territories stretch out to touch each other, the vital road also serves to demarcate where the Lombard king's domain gives place to the duchy of Spoleto.

In theory there are only two sovereign powers controlling these thirteen fragmented regions. The emperor's representative, the Exarch of Ravenna, has general jurisdiction over the other imperial possessions — but here the theory wears thinner and thinner with the years, as men ask what their faraway monarch ever does for them in return for the taxes he demands. Increasingly they look inside their own country for leadership and protection. Rome becomes their rallying-point, the Pope their champion. Sometimes Rome and Ravenna are in open conflict. On the Lombard side, too, Pavia's control of the southern duchies fluctuates with the strength of the king. Once, for a whole decade, Lombardy splinters into three dozen petty dukedoms.

Culturally, the uncouth newcomers were slowly assimilated by their subjects. Few words of their own language, for instance, passed into the speech of Italy. The assimilation was

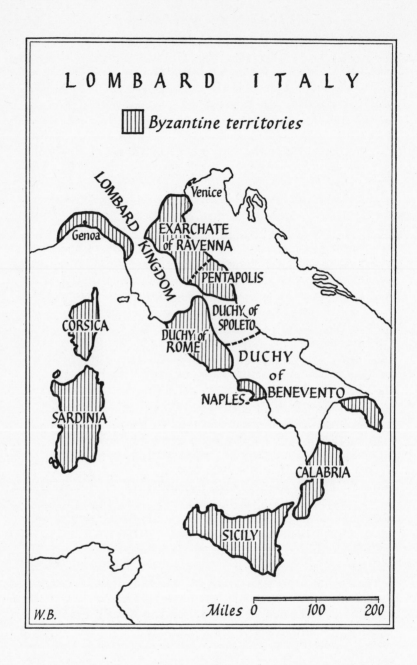

LOMBARD ITALY

Byzantine territories

LOMBARD KINGDOM

Venice

EXARCHATE
of RAVENNA

Genoa

PENTAPOLIS

DUCHY of
SPOLETO

CORSICA

DUCHY of
ROME

DUCHY
of
BENEVENTO

NAPLES

SARDINIA

CALABRIA

SICILY

W.B.

Miles 0   100   200

considerably helped by large-scale conversions to the Catholic faith. This began about 600, and was due in the first instance to the personality of a Lombard queen.

Theodolinda was herself a Catholic, daughter of Garibald, Duke of Bavaria. She was wooed incognito by that same Lombard king, Authari, who walked his leashed captives before the walls of Rome. She saw through his disguise and accepted him. From the day of her marriage in Pavia she enchanted her new people. When Authari died soon afterwards, they were so anxious to keep her that they asked her to choose a second husband to become their king. Theodolinda was thus able to continue her civilizing influence, and, though she converted neither husband from his heresy, she won a great number of Lombards to Catholicism, starting a trend which was completed within a generation or two. The Pope, as a token of his appreciation, sent her one of the nails from the True Cross, which, when beaten into a thin circlet, became the celebrated Iron Crown of the Lombards.

This Pope was Gregory the Great, who, besides so much else, promoted the mission to England. A good-looking man, brown-eyed and tawny-bearded, with delicate tapering fingers, he was — like many of the early bishops — a born patrician. He had been City Prefect of Rome before he felt the call to become a Benedictine monk. Thereupon, perhaps to make up for the destruction of Monte Cassino by the Lombards about that time, he turned his family home on the Caelian Hill into a monastery and endowed six more with his inherited estates in Sicily. His political ability was not allowed to atrophy, however, for he was sent to Constantinople for six years as papal representative. His refusal, even then, to learn Greek illustrates his instinctive dislike for the imperial government, which he felt neglected the interests of Italy.

Back in Rome, he was elected Pope against his will. He petitioned the emperor to refuse ratification, he even considered going into hiding, but he was seized and dragged to the throne of St. Peter.

Once reconciled to his position, he was a keen upholder of papal authority. In the Church at large he asserted Rome's supremacy, and, as the first monk to become Pope, he strengthened the monasteries by making them answerable to him direct instead of to their local bishops. In Italy he made the Papacy a political power. He, not any nominee of the Exarch of Ravenna, was the effective ruler of the duchy of Rome. He, more than the Exarch or even the remote emperor, was the leader to whom the other imperial territories in Italy looked. Gregory, the man on the spot, saw the realities of the situation and knew how necessary it was to work for co-existence with the Lombards. He would not let his flock be sacrificed to impracticable policies concocted in Constanti-nople. When necessary he would go against Ravenna, playing off Exarch against Lombard, so that Italy might live.

Sixty years after Gregory's death one emperor, Constans II, actually appeared in Italy with the optimistic idea of expel-ling the Lombards. He landed at Taranto, failed to capture Benevento, lost half his army at Forino, and was thankful to reach Rome, where he bullied the timorous Pope Vitalian, stripped the Pantheon roof of its copper tiles, and ransacked the city for anything else worth removing. Neither this brief visit nor his subsequent five-year exploitation of Sicily did much to revive enthusiasm for the imperial connection, and there was many a dry eye when the news arrived from Syra-cuse that a servant had brained him in his bath with a copper soap-dish.

How far things had developed, how complex had become the play of forces, was well illustrated in the next century when, in 730, we find the Lombard king, Liutprand, and the Exarch of Ravenna combining to besiege Rome — whose astute old Pope had formed an equally incongruous associa-tion with the Dukes of Spoleto and Benevento. The reasons for these alignments were that Liutprand, a strong man with a dream of unifying and enlarging the Lombard kingdom, had not only taken Bologna and the Pentapolis but had assailed the independence of the two duchies; while the Pope on the other hand was in acrimonious conflict with the emperor over his new iconoclastic policy, which, if accepted in the West, would have destroyed so many treasures of early Christian art.

On this occasion there was another of those memorable face-to-face encounters between Pope and victorious barbarian, and once more the mysterious moral ascendancy of the pontiff prevailed. Liutprand symbolically dedicated his crown and robes at St. Peter's shrine, agreed to the Pope's peace-formula, and imposed it upon the Exarch too.

For all that, and for all their gradual acquisition of culture, the Lombards remained essentially 'unspeakable'. The struggle went on. Hope of any real help from Constantinople had died long ago. The next Pope turned to the Franks, who were, if only slightly, the most civilized of the former Germanic tribes. Now occupying very approximately what had been Gaul, they had adopted a quaint form of monarchy, under which their king was a mere figurehead, only occasionally quitting his country house in an ox-cart to make some ceremonial appearance, while the actual power was held by the 'Mayor of the Palace', a sort of hereditary prime minister. Charles Martel, the first of these mayors to be approached, declined to take on any commitments in Italy, but his son Pepin was more sympathetic. In 750, being absolved by the Pope from his oath of allegiance to his master, Childeric, he made himself king of the Franks.

It was not long before he was called upon to fulfil his own part of the bargain. The Lombards had an aggressive new king, Aistulf, who the very next year took Ravenna, thus extinguishing the Byzantine power in Northern Italy. Turning on Rome, he threatened to destroy the city unless the inhabitants paid him a poll-tax. In this crisis Pope Stephen himself made the long journey to visit Pepin, whom he crowned in person and proclaimed not only King of the Franks but also Patrician of Italy, a title which (whatever it now meant) could traditionally be given only by an Eastern emperor.

The gratified Pepin crossed the Mont Cenis, dictated terms to Aistulf, and went home. As soon as he had disappeared beyond the Alps, the irrepressible Aistulf renewed his demands on Rome. The Pope sent an urgent appeal to Pepin, worded as though from St. Peter himself, to come and deliver 'this my city of Rome'. Pepin returned, defeated Aistulf, and this time made a more durable settlement. The keys of Ravenna and over twenty other towns were surrendered by the Lombards and offered up at the shrine of St. Peter. Despite diplomatic protests none of the liberated territory was restored to the emperor. Rome was left in control of a wide belt of land slanting across the peninsula to the head of the Adriatic.

The Papal States had been created, destined to survive until the age of Garibaldi.

Aistulf's successor, Desiderius, was ingenious in his manoeuvres to rebuild Lombard supremacy. He even contrived during one brief chaotic interlude to get his own nominee unconstitutionally elected Pope. But he met more than his match in Pepin's successor, who happened to be Charlemagne. The Lombards never had a chance against the mighty Frank, who, in forty-six years of incessant fighting, was to conquer an empire stretching from the Elbe and Danube to the Pyrenees.

Desiderius stung Charlemagne by backing rival claimants, Charlemagne's young nephews, to the Frankish crown. Charlemagne cracked down like the hammer from which his grandfather Charles had taken his nickname. He captured Pavia, consigned Desiderius to a Frankish monastery, and assumed the Iron Crown himself, adding 'King of the Lombards' to his titles.

Another and greater title was to come. Twenty-six years afterwards, on Christmas Day, 800, Charlemagne and his sons knelt at Mass in St. Peter's. Later he declared that, if he had known what was to happen, he would never have entered the church. This was probably a diplomatic disclaimer, for Leo III was scarcely the man to spring an unwelcome surprise on his powerful protector. As the service ended, before Charlemagne could rise from his knees, the Pope stepped forward and placed a golden crown upon his head. The vast congregation broke instantly into a demonstration which, if it was spontaneous, must have been a remarkable feat of unrehearsed choral speaking, for we are told that they cried with one voice: 'Long life and victory to Charles the Augustus, crowned by God, the great and pacific emperor!' Charlemagne stood up with admirable composure and was invested with the traditional insignia, long ago returned by Constantinople at the insistence of Theodoric.

Thus was born a new Western Empire, thus Italy formally threw off the last vestige of Byzantine authority, and thus a far-sighted pontiff demonstrated that the coronation of emperors was yet another papal prerogative.

Belvedere Marittimo in Calabria, typical of the compact hill-top town-building dictated by the turbulence of Italian history.

'Pisa's glory endured two centuries . . . ' Her white marble cathedral, begun about 1063, and even its leaning campanile have proved more durable.

'Saracen craftsmen adorned Catholic churches' in Sicily, as in the cloisters of Monreale at Palermo.

Frederick's 'great Apulian stronghold of Lucera'.

8. Re-enter Citizens

IT WAS a splendid scene, that Christmas coronation in St. Peter's. Had the sequel lived up to the promise, had Charlemagne been as successful at empire-building as the first Augustus, Western Europe might have attained the unity towards which she was still stumbling nearly twelve centuries later. There need never have been a separate, antagonistic France and Germany, but a union, enriched by the absorption of Italy.

It did not happen. The ageing emperor's admiration for Italian culture was limited. True, he was impressed by Ravenna, declaring San Vitale to be the most splendid church in the world and ordering a close copy of it to be built at Aachen. To Aachen he removed the marble pillars, pavements and mosaics from the palace of the exarchs, together with the massive equestrian statue commemorating Theodoric, and at Aachen he remained for the rest of his life, seldom travelling far except on hunting expeditions. The government of Italy he delegated to others, and when he died, leaving only a grandson, Louis the Pious, to succeed him, Louis in turn handed over his Italian territories to his own son, Lothar.

Lothar was quite unable to control his Lombard subjects. The country soon splintered, like a sheet of glass, into a number of feudal fragments, large and small, each a law to itself. The Empire as a whole became the battleground of Charlemagne's descendants. We need not trouble ourselves here with the doings of Charles the Bold or Charles the Simple, Louis the Stammerer or Louis the Blind, except to note that the latter's blindness was inflicted on him by a political rival and was but one example of a commonly practised barbarity — Charles the Bold, indeed, blinded his own son, Carloman. So far as Italy was concerned, the last Frankish ruler was Charles the Fat, crowned at Rome in 881

99

but deposed by his dissatisfied nobles at Frankfort six years later.

In fact, Frankish rule had been shadowy since the strong hand of Charlemagne relaxed in death. The nominally Frankish half of Italy extended just south of Rome. It had split into independent domains, the chief being Friuli, Tuscany and Spoleto, while the Papal States kept their own privileged position.

In the South a similar process went on. The Lombard Duchy of Benevento, which had successfully withstood the Franks, lost control of Capua and Salerno. They set up as miniature duchies themselves. Far-off Constantinople was even less able to control her Italian possessions. Naples became again what the first Greek colonists had made her, an autonomous republic. So did Gaeta and Amalfi. It is strange to think that the latter, now a self-consciously picturesque little fishing-port, was once twelve times as large, a naval power rivalling Genoa, the 'Malfi' of Webster's horrific tragedy. Her ships then traded so widely that her maritime law was internationally recognized until the sixteenth century, and it was her navigators who introduced the floating magnet to this part of the Mediterranean, an innovation which has been inflated into a claim that one of them, 'Flavio Gioia', invented the compass in 1302. In reality nothing was invented but the man and his name. This, however, has not deterred the people, with equal patriotism and commercial acumen, from erecting a statue near the beach to their fictitious fellow-citizen.

The proliferation of these independent states sprang from the urgency of the time. Only by their own exertions could they survive, not merely against lawless Lombards and fratricidal Franks but against new enemies, Northmen, Magyars and Saracens. Of these the Northmen, so formidable elsewhere in Europe, were the least menace to Italy. Their solitary incursion was in 862, when Bjorn Ironside landed in Tuscany and plundered Luna under the mistaken impression that it was Rome. More serious was the invasion of the Magyars, nomadic mounted bowmen from the Russian steppes, who swept across Lombardy in 899 and for half a century ravaged the peninsula as far down as Apulia. In 955 their horde suffered a pulverizing defeat in Bavaria, on the stony waste of Lechfeld, after which the remnants were thankful to settle in Hungary and the roads of Italy shuddered under their flying hoofs no more.

The Saracen invasion was quite different: more important, more durable, in many respects beneficent.

The Saracens burst upon the scene as part of the great Arab expansion following Mohammed's death in 632. Their conquest of Egypt gave them a fleet. Soon they threatened the sea-lanes linking Italy with Constantinople. Spreading along the African coast they entered Spain and then France, where they were thrown back by Charlemagne's grandfather in 732. Nearly another hundred years passed before, in 817, they first crossed from Africa into Sicily, invited by a rebellious Byzantine governor in need of allies. When he was murdered, they stayed on, as such guests are apt to do.

The Orient had returned to Sicily, but with graces of which the Carthaginians had been incapable. The Saracens developed Palermo into a rich trading city of three hundred thousand people, and, though the name of Allah was invoked in three hundred mosques, the markets were open to Christian and Jew, and the great harbour bristled with the masts of foreign merchantmen. The palaces of the emirs rivalled Cordova in arabesque magnificence, and new gardens blossomed in colour and fragrance. On the landward side the mountain-girdled plain was now first planted with those lemon and orange groves which still delight the eye. These fruits, novel to Europe, were brought in by the Saracens along with the cotton-plant and sugar-cane.

Within fifty years all Sicily came under their rule, with many compensations for the Christian inhabitants, who were treated tolerantly, taxed lightly, and excused military service. On the mainland the Saracens' influence was less welcome, for, meeting strong opposition, they had little chance to be constructive. They were identified with piracy rather than prosperity.

Naples called them in as allies against Benevento in 837, for there was no permanent demarcation on religious grounds and infidel assistance was not to be despised. Three years later the Saracens occupied Bari and Taranto and set up a small Muslim state. Soon afterwards they turned against Naples and unsuccessfully besieged the city. In 846 they burnt the suburbs of Rome, notably the Borgo or 'borough', so

called because it was the home of a numerous Anglo-Saxon
colony. The memory of this horror — the very tombs of the
Apostles had been defiled by the Saracens — was still fresh
when a small boy, the future Alfred the Great, arrived on
pilgrimage with his father. He was kindly received by Pope
Leo IV, who ceremonially if rather meaninglessly invested
him with the dignities of a Roman consul. It was this Leo
who, combining the naval strength of Naples, Amalfi, and
Gaeta, had organized the destruction of the Saracen fleet at
Ostia, and had thereafter set the prisoners to work building
the 'Leonine Walls' round the Vatican as an insurance
against further attacks. Though a shadow of its ancient
self, the ninth-century city left an ineffaceable imprint
on the English boy's mind, which inspired him throughout
his own lifelong struggle against invasion.

For many more years the Saracens were a force to be
reckoned with on the mainland, but they were never comfortable enough to develop the sort of culture they created in
Sicily. The fortune of war had too much ebb and flow. The
Byzantines threw them out of Bari and Taranto, but failed
to recover Sicily, while at various other times the Saracens
invaded Calabria, besieged Naples again, stormed Genoa
from the sea, made alliances with Naples and Benevento, and
made persistent raids into the Roman Campagna from a
strongly fortified camp on the River Garigliano.

The obliteration of this base in 915, by the Pope and the
Marquis of Spoleto, with a Byzantine fleet blockading the
river-mouth, was a turning-point in the history of the Saracens on the mainland. It ended the first (and worst) eighty
years. The century which followed had many bad moments,
especially when the Magyars also were ravaging Italy, but the
cities were learning that self-help led logically to mutual help.
In 1002 the Venetians prevented the recapture of Bari by the
Saracens, in 1005 the Pisans won a battle in the Straits of
Messina, in 1016 Pisans and Genoese united to save Sardinia
from the Muslims in Spain. That was the second turning-
point, a hundred and one years after the victory on the
Garigliano. Only in Sicily did the Saracens remain masters.

.   .   .   .

It is time now to glance at the developing cities, such as

Venice, growing up amid her reedy lagoons, Genoa at the head of her gulf, walled off by a hinterland of arid hills, the busy port of Pisa, then much closer to the sea, Naples, Salerno, and the many inland towns.

In the Frankish North, Charlemagne appointed a count to be his representative in each city. But the roads, posts and civil service of ancient Rome were no longer available for centralized control. The men on the spot were virtually independent and in time showed a tendency to make their office hereditary. Later Frankish rulers tried to counter this by uniting the role of count and bishop. Italian bishops had a tradition of political leadership and in theory at least they were debarred from legitimate paternity. Clerical celibacy was still, however, a highly debatable issue in the ninth and tenth centuries, and, what with the inordinate interest often taken by bishops and even Popes in their nephews, the combination of spiritual and temporal leadership did not invariably check the drift towards hereditary government. Nevertheless, emperors and kings found it safer in general to delegate power to churchmen than to warriors.

Whoever the nominal overlord, some Frank beyond the Alps or Byzantine on the Bosphorus, the actual running of a city's affairs devolved upon its inhabitants. When the watchman on his tower sighted the lateen sails of the Saracen galleys or the Magyar horsemen coming over the hill, the people's only hope lay in their own ships, their own militia, their own strong walls which they had sweated to build against such an emergency. They elected the best man they had to command that militia and the imperial approval of his election became more and more a formality. He was their leader, their *dux*, *doge*, or 'duke'. Though these dukes too eventually became hereditary, they began as popular leaders chosen from below, not aristocrats ennobled by remote royalty.

There was no set pattern in the several cities. There was no Doge of Genoa until 1339. At this earlier period the Genoese were organized in seven companies, each supplying a quota of warships, each headed by a consul. Elsewhere, as in Naples, the dukes often added the old Roman titles, *consul* and *magister militum*, to their new ones. Naples of course was in the still Byzantine part of Italy. Her duke was originally nominated by the Exarch of Ravenna and later, when Ravenna was lost, by the Eastern emperor himself. He came under the authority of the Byzantine governor in Sicily, until the Saracens reduced that authority to a shadow. By then the independence of Naples was an established fact. The duke ruled, with an advisory council of 'Notables', landlords, ship-owners and business-men. By about 950 Duke Giovanni III had his own ambassadors at Constantinople. We may still be grateful for some of their activities: they sent their master transcripts of numerous Greek books which might otherwise have been lost to us through the later Turkish destruction.

Venice was always a law to herself. Her first doge was elected as far back as 697, when a dozen communities scattered among the islets of the lagoon united for mutual protection. The doges ruled, with one break of five years, for the next eleven centuries. Except that the people's assembly had to vote for peace or war, the early doges had absolute power. They controlled defence and foreign policy, levied taxes, appointed officials, and could veto even the choice of bishops. Such arbitrary power inevitably provoked plots and rebellions, especially since it was, throughout the first three centuries, the preserve of only four different families.

Venice was neither Frankish nor Byzantine. She began by helping Charlemagne. Twenty-four of her galleys rowed up the river to help him in his siege of the last Lombard king at Pavia. But soon she incurred his disfavour. Neither he nor the Pope liked the Venetian traffic in slaves, especially girls from Russia and the Caucasus. This, with other less altruistic reasons, prompted the Franks to attack Venice in 810. In six months of dogged fighting they were quite unable to overcome the Venetians, who evacuated their less defensible villages and concentrated their people in the district now known as the Rialto. After this successful defiance of the Franks, Venice went from strength to strength, but the population, instead of dispersing again all over the lagoon, showed an understandable preference for developing the space nearest to the Rialto. The first Doge's Palace was built on its present site in 814, and next to it, in 829, the first church of San Marco, to enshrine the body of the patron saint, which had been stolen from Alexandria and ingeniously smuggled through the Saracen customs there by describing it as pork.

Both palace and church were soon burnt down and then rebuilt, not for the last time.

For a period Venice, like Naples, paid lip-service to the Eastern emperor, who was further away than the Franks and even less able to exact obedience. The Venetians were adept at playing off one great power against another. Soon they could afford to throw off even the pretence of obedience. Their aggressive seamen extended their influence across the Adriatic. The doge took the additional title of 'Doge of Dalmatia' and a ceremony was instituted which developed into the symbolic 'marriage with the sea'. The Lion of St. Mark was spreading his wings, the great age of the Most Serene Republic had begun.

In all the Italian cities the same impulse for self-help was drawing the people together not only for defence and government but for trade, church-building and charitable enterprise. Merchants and craftsmen had formed corporations in ancient times. Some such organizations may have survived throughout the Dark Ages. Certainly, at this date, Rome and Ravenna had associations of shoemakers, blacksmiths, and other craftsmen, precursors of the medieval guilds. Economic life was vigorous. There was a brisk, competitive exchange of commodities by ship, river-boat and mule-train. Oil and wine, salt and spices, horses and hides, woollens and linen, were in constant transit. The Church, with its ever-accumulating endowments from the truly pious and the merely apprehensive, was itself actively in business. It owned houses, shops, farms, woodlands, and salt-pans, chartered boats to transport the produce of its estates, held markets and fairs. Another stimulus came from the Saracens, with whom the Christians spent far more time trading than making war. Italy was a half-way house between Europe and the Islamic world which stretched through Persia to the boundaries of India. Religious scruples cracked under the pressures of that commercial advantage.

The citizens probably reasoned that it was better to serve God by building churches with part of the profits. It was certainly a busy period for church-building. Masons and stone-carvers wandered through Italy and beyond her borders, plying their crafts with the traditional knowledge passed down from Roman times. Each city had, or obtained, its saint. The Venetians were by no means the only body-snatchers. Civic pride everywhere demanded the acquisition, by fair means or foul, of some saintly remains or sacred relic, and then the erection of a worthy church, round-arched, small-windowed, Romanesque.

Hospitals and guest-houses were usually maintained by the local bishop, but the townspeople often added to them. Lucca had no fewer than four hospitals in the ninth century, Siena had a privately endowed one, Milan possessed a home for foundlings. Salerno boasted the first medical school in Europe, a secular institution staffed by married laymen and even women, for we hear of a Constanza and a Stephana among the instructors. Through Salerno's contact with the Saracens Europe was introduced to the study of pharmacy as a distinct science. Law and music were taught in other centres. A somewhat shadowy Benedictine, Guido of Arezzo, is credited with the invention of musical notation. There were grammar schools in most of the main towns.

There must have been a traffic in ideas as well as in material goods, for, undaunted by distance, discomfort and danger, a surprising proportion of the people seems to have been intermittently on the move. There were wandering scholars and renegade churchmen, not always easy to distinguish; itinerant building workers and (it is guessed) strolling players, who kept a crude dramatic tradition alive through centuries which are blank in our theatrical records; and always there were pilgrims, in numbers which embarrassed the Church authorities. In the eighth century Boniface forbade nuns and other women to make the Rome pilgrimage, and hinted to men that such enterprises did not necessarily guarantee spiritual edification. 'There is not a town in France or Italy,' he told them, 'where there is not an English whore.' But the pilgrims went forward undeterred.

We may begin now, much as we miss the pictorial evidence of later ages, to sketch in our mind's eye a rough outline of these dynamic little towns as they were about the year 1000. The houses huddle close inside massive walls. Round a piazza, which is still not so much an architectural feature as a utilitarian market-place, stand a Romanesque church, a cloistered Benedictine monastery, a hostel, a grammar school, a ducal palace. If it is a port we add quays, a mole, and some carvel-built ships, with the fin-like lateen sails which at some uncertain date replaced the square ones of the ancient Mediterranean world. If it is Venice, we tether a boat, as we might a horse, at every door.

And the people? How shall we clothe the manikins which dot the piazza? Trousers have conquered the land of the toga, or, to be accurate, long narrow leggings destined to evolve into medieval hose. Bishop Liutprand does not mince matters in his acidulous *Report of the Constantinople Mission*:

The ruler of Greece has long hair, trailing garments, wide sleeves and feminine headgear. He is a swindling liar. By contrast the King of the Franks has fine short-trimmed hair, a cap, and unmistakably masculine clothes.

Charlemagne had intensely disliked the effeminate finery of the Byzantines and had worn it only under protest for ceremonial occasions. After his time, Western Europeans relegated Byzantine fashions to royal robes and ritual vestments. So our imagined townsmen have long belted tunics, cloth leggings, shoes, and cloaks pinned at the right shoulder. If trouble looms, they have knee-length tunics of mail, slit fore and aft to facilitate leg-movement. It is these slits which, in the Bayeux Tapestry, give the misleading impression of metallic combinations. In general the tapestry serves as a reliable fashion-plate for the Italians of a generation or two earlier.

The women have longer tunics, like dresses, cover their heads with a kerchief, and fasten their cloaks centrally over the bosom. Liutprand is never in any doubt as to which sex is which. He himself has his head shaven in the tonsure of St. Peter. For that reason he probably (like most clergy) favours a cloak with a hood, as worn by travellers, shepherds, and others particularly exposed to the weather. Only later does the hood become general with the laity.

.   .   .   .

Rome herself had little share in this lively commercial development. Her only distinctive trade was in sacred relics, and she certainly did her best to satisfy the demand. It was popularly assumed that every skeleton found in the catacombs was that of a martyr, and it seemed contrary to the best interests of the Church to query transactions so edifying to the purchaser and so productive of revenue. The hair and bones of some very surprising people must have found their way to the shrines of Christendom. The most that can be said for these unexpectedly venerated individuals is that they had probably been more virtuous in life than the average pilgrim entering Rome. He was often a convicted criminal, whom a merciful bishop had rescued from the civil courts and ordered to make the pilgrimage in lieu of a more painful punishment. Sometimes, no doubt, it had the reformative effect intended.

The Pope had long been the political as well as the spiritual leader of the Romans, filling the vacuum left by the disappearance of effective imperial authority. In anarchic times most cities had turned instinctively to their bishops and later (as we have seen) the Frankish rulers rather favoured them as local representatives. In Rome the position had been consolidated by successive pontiffs. Their lands were known as 'the Patrimony of Peter'. Just as spiritually they claimed to be the heirs to a special authority granted to that Apostle, so they based their territorial rights on another inheritance. This was known as 'the Donation of Constantine', by which the emperor, when establishing his capital in the East, was supposed to have made arrangements for the future government of the West.

Wherefore, that the pontifical crown may not become too cheap, but may be adorned with glory and influence even beyond the dignity of the earthly empire, we hereby hand over and relinquish our palace, the city of Rome, and all the provinces, places and cities of Italy and the western regions, to the most blessed Pontiff and universal Pope Sylvester; and we ordain that they shall be governed by him and his successors, and we grant that they shall remain under the authority of the holy Roman Church.

Unfortunately the first mention of this not unimportant document was in 777, four and a half centuries after the event, and it is now generally supposed that it was faked by a well-meaning and imaginative scribe soon after 750. It gained

wider currency by inclusion in what are now known as the
False (or Forged) Decretals of Isidore, a collection of papal
letters and decrees dating from the earliest period, so skilful
a pastiche of the genuine and the fictitious that it was not
questioned until the fifteenth century. Though fathered on a
Spanish archbishop, the Decretals were probably concocted
by a Rhineland monk about 850. The Popes of those days
were careful not to rely too much upon them, but, whatever
their private doubts, they did not attack the authenticity of
documents so helpful to their claims. Only long afterwards
did the Donation and the Decretals in general become the
subject of controversy.

How in those days did a man become Pope? We must
forget all we know of modern elections. There was no Sacred
College, no mustering of august voters from distant lands.
It was a local matter. 'Cardinal' was a term applied only to
the senior clergy of the city, who came increasingly to speak
for the others, just as the laity was represented by the nobles
descended from old senatorial families or Byzantine officers.
Thus the practice of the early Church, whereby the bishop
was chosen by clergy and people, was to some extent preserved,
though the role of the majority was reduced to 'acclaiming'
the Pope selected by their betters. How far that selection was
also subject to the emperor's approval was another question
pregnant with controversy.

With elections on this local basis, and largely at the mercy
of powerful laymen, it is understandable that not all the
Popes were equally worthy of their office. Whether or not
they were at all times infallible in their pronouncements on
doctrine and morals (a view not dogmatically affirmed until
1870), even the most devout Catholic is not asked to believe
that they were anything but fallible in their own conduct.
If he forgets this reassurance, he may find many indisputable
episodes in Italian history unnecessarily painful.

A particularly regrettable period began with Pope Formosus, elected in 891 after previously being excommunicated
and then absolved. The last Frankish ruler having been
deposed, there were several candidates for the nebulous title
of emperor. Formosus favoured the German Arnulf, who,
though illegitimate, was at least a nephew of the discarded
Charles the Fat. When Arnulf marched through Italy and

stormed into Rome, Formosus willingly crowned him in St. Peter's, untroubled by the recollection that he had performed the same ceremony for Lambert, Duke of Spoleto, a few months before. Unluckily for the Pope, Arnulf was taken seriously ill as he advanced to fight Lambert, and was compelled to retreat from Italy. Formosus himself died shortly afterwards, which, in view of what followed, was probably as well for him.

The next Pope lasted just fifteen days. The cause of death is now uncertain. The next, Stephen VII, was a virulent enemy of Formosus, whose embalmed body he now exhumed and subjected to a solemn trial in the council chamber of the Lateran Palace. The defunct Formosus, robed and enthroned, was searchingly questioned. As, not surprisingly, no answers were forthcoming, silence was taken to imply guilt. Sentence was pronounced. The assembled clergy broke ranks and rushed at the corpse, stripping it of the papal vestments and hacking off the three fingers of the right hand which had so often given them benediction. The body was then thrown into the Tiber, from which it was retrieved by a monk and given secret burial. Political reaction came within a year. The rehabilitated Formosus was restored to his tomb in St. Peter's, while Stephen was imprisoned and then strangled. At this time there were eight Popes in as many years. The occupational hazards rivalled those of the Roman emperors in the worst period.

Real power had slipped into the hands of a layman, Theophylactus, consul and leader of the Senate, and his wife, Theodora, who assumed the title of 'Senatrix' and whose will was as firm as her morals were flexible. Their son became Pope John IX at the remarkably early age of eighteen, but died at twenty. John X, fourteen years later, had the double advantage of Theophylactus as patron and Theodora as mistress. In an era of papal puppets he was a strong man. He organized the decisive victory over the Saracens at the Garigliano, and survived from 914 to 928, when he was strangled on instructions from Theodora's beautiful daughter, Marozia.

Like her mother, Marozia was conspicuous for vitality rather than virtue. She married Alberic, a soldier of fortune who had made himself Duke of Spoleto, and bore him a son, also christened Alberic, but she had a lover who became

Pope Sergius III, having had the two opposing candidates strangled. Her son by Sergius was himself to achieve the papacy as John XI. Meanwhile her husband, Alberic senior, had died or possibly (as seems very understandable) just disappeared, and Marozia married Guido, Margrave of Tuscany, erroneously calculating that he would soon be recognized under the grander if vaguer title of King of Italy. This went instead to his half-brother, Hugo of Provence. She was considering how best to correct her mistake when, by the happiest coincidence, Guido died and Hugo lost his wife. To a woman of Marozia's serpentine fascination the next move was obvious. A quiet wedding was arranged in the massive Castel Sant' Angelo, which she had prudently made her home, and to preserve the family character of the ceremony it was performed by the Pope, her bastard son by Sergius. Her legitimate son, Alberic, now eighteen, was reluctantly present as a page.

A queen at last, Marozia set her heart on becoming empress. What simpler? Her new husband would proclaim himself emperor and her papal son would crown him. She was frustrated by a trivial accident. Hugo was washing his hands in a basin sullenly held by young Alberic. A few drops of water splashed the king, who gave his stepson a resounding clout. Alberic, true to his fighting stock, rushed out and stirred the citizens to revolt. They were already tired of Marozia, who, with her mother before her, had run the affairs of Rome for thirty or forty years. Nor had they any enthusiasm for her foreign bridegroom. She herself had not trusted him to the extent of letting him bring his soldiers inside the fortress, so, since her own supporters abandoned her, there was no one to stop Alberic when he came raging back with his followers. Hugo slid down a rope in the dark and fled to Lombardy, Marozia was consigned to a dungeon, and Pope John was imprisoned in his own Lateran Palace on the far side of the city. Alberic took few chances. Neither his mother nor his half-brother was ever released.

For twenty-two years he gave Rome efficient government, ruling like the dukes of other cities but with the style of 'Prince and Senator of All the Romans'. To safeguard himself against Hugo and other external enemies he reorganized the militia in twelve companies, based on the wards into which Rome was divided. The Popes all this time were politically innocuous figures who fully understood that spiritual matters were their proper concern. Alberic himself shared that concern. He was keenly aware of how the Benedictine monasteries had degenerated in Italy, as in France and England, and he knew of the reforms begun at Cluny. On his invitation Abbot Odo came to Rome to supervise the overhaul of the Italian houses. Alberic gave him his own palace on the Aventine for the use of the Order.

As happens in history with almost monotonous frequency, this prince possessed a quite dissimilar son, was blind to his faults, and bequeathed power to him under an arrangement foredoomed to failure. Octavian was sixteen when Alberic's last illness came upon him. Not satisfied with leaving the youth his secular authority, Alberic—who himself had managed perfectly with Popes of his own selection—planned to merge spiritual authority in the same individual. He made his assembled nobles swear that, when next the papacy fell vacant, they would secure Octavian's succession. He was dead within the year, and the Pope too. The seventeen-year-old duly succeeded to both dignities. In his papal capacity he took the name of John XII, to differentiate between his two functions, thus starting the tradition that each new pontiff should change his name.

Such concentrated power would have imposed a strain on any youth, no matter how virtuous or precociously sage. John, though the son of Alberic, was also the grandson of Marozia. His nine-year reign was a period of irresponsibility and self-indulgence. No respectable woman dared set foot in the Lateran, which resembled a seraglio. John did not trouble even to pay outward observance to the decencies. He would drink toasts to the Devil and the old pagan deities. Once he consecrated a ten-year-old boy as bishop, perhaps reasoning that, if he himself had been thought old enough to become Christ's Vicar at seventeen, ten was not too young for the controlling of a single diocese.

The man who ended this scandal came to Rome, ironically enough, as John's guest. He was Otto I, the great Saxon leader who had just built up a powerful German kingdom and destroyed the Magyar horde at Lechfeld. From this time onwards, let us note in passing, the Empire becomes a predominantly German institution. There is a separate kingdom of France, divided from Northern Italy by the kingdom of Burgundy. Italy's other Alpine neighbours are, from west to east, Swabia, Bavaria and Carinthia, all part of the Empire, and it is over their mountain passes that the emperors will ride into Lombardy, time without number, in the centuries to come.

John was having trouble with Berengar, one of those nominal 'Kings of Italy' whose authority extended as far as their swords. An effective King of Germany seemed the perfect ally to put Berengar in his place. Otto was willing. The Nordic hero swept splendidly down, awful in anger but magnanimous in victory. He deposed Berengar and put the Iron Crown on his own head; then, memories of Charlemagne stirring, rode on to Rome. John anointed him emperor. Thus was the Holy Roman Empire born, or, as some maintain, reborn.

The Roman citizens were unenthusiastic. John himself was quite ready to change sides. When Otto turned his back, there was a popular rising against the Germans. Otto reappeared and suppressed it, deposed John and called a meeting in St. Peter's, at which the Romans sullenly swore 'neither to elect nor to consecrate a Pope without the consent of the Lord Emperor Otto and his son, King Otto'. From this historic meeting all subsequent emperors dated their claims over the Papacy. John took to the hills and, as soon as it was safe, re-entered Rome in force and expelled his successor. Again the tall German came thundering back, but John escaped his vengeance by suddenly dying, beaten to death (it has been said) by an indignant husband.

Otto the Great continued to have difficulty with the unruly Romans. One insurrection he put down with Teutonic severity, hanging the twelve company-commanders of the militia and suspending the city prefect by his hair from the mounted statue of Marcus Aurelius, which then stood in front of the Lateran. His unpopularity sprang from his treatment of Italy as a German fief and the Church as an instrument of government; for, not content with dictating the choice of Popes, he built up the regional powers of the bishops and imported Germans for Italian sees. On the other hand he was no narrow nationalist. Unlike Charlemagne, he spent nearly all his remaining years in Italy and chose a Byzantine princess, Theophano, as bride for his son.

Otto the Red became emperor at eighteen. Small in stature, he had his father's courageous and impulsive nature, the same knightly prowess with considerably more culture. His ten-year reign was a breathless serial of military adventures, usually successful. In Southern Italy, however, he was crushingly defeated by a combined force of Saracens and Byzantines, and himself escaped only by swimming to a Byzantine vessel whose crew did not recognize the young man they helped aboard. Otto did not correct them. He waited until the ship drew near to Rossano, his base-camp in Calabria, and then dived overboard again. It seems sad that so picturesque a monarch did not live longer to brighten history. The next year he died of fever in Rome, while planning to bring the pro-Byzantine Venetians to heel. He left three daughters and a son, who succeeded him as Otto III with his mother, Theophano, as regent.

Thirteen years elapsed before the new emperor (still only sixteen) came to Rome to claim his crown. During the interval the regency had been in general respected, but Rome had reasserted her independence. Successive, and sometimes concurrent, Popes had been deposed, imprisoned, expelled, strangled, poisoned or lynched. The popular anti-German party had dominated the stage. Its leader, Crescentius, had revived the ancient title, 'Patrician of the Romans', and had ruled with something like Alberic's absolute power.

Otto III was a remarkable boy, blending the Germanic and Greek qualities of his parents, influenced equally by his Byzantine tutor and the French Benedictine scholar, Gerbert. His taste for worldly pomp degenerated into megalomania, yet he sometimes yearned for monastic austerities. He dreamed dreams but he could also enact nightmares, as in his diabolical mutilation of the old tutor who accepted the papacy against his own nominee.

Otto's choice was his own cousin, Bruno, who at twenty-four became the first German Pope, Gregory V. The emperor's other main act on arrival in Rome was to deprive Crescentius of his position. When he went away again, there was the usual uprising of citizens; when he came back, the usual punishments. He decided to make Rome his permanent capital, building himself a new palace on the Aventine and introducing a court ceremonial which recalled Diocletian's. Wearing robes of imperial crimson and purple, he dined alone at a crescent-shaped high table. Gerbert encouraged him to plan a wonderful new order in which the glories of pagan Rome should be revived and transmuted by Christian piety. He assumed magniloquent titles, 'Consul of the Roman Senate and People', 'Servant of Jesus Christ', 'Servant of the Apostle'.

When Gregory died in 999, Gerbert, already Archbishop of Ravenna, became the first French Pope, Sylvester II. Otto had now the partnership he really wanted, emperor and Pope, pupil and teacher, working harmoniously to remodel the Western Empire as a federation of Italians, Germans and Slavs. Italy was to be the centre. It was said of him, 'He would not visit delightful Germany, his native land, so great a love of Italian life possessed him.'

Italy did not altogether reciprocate his love or share his enthusiasm for an imperial dream which few understood. It was less real to the citizens than the commercial competition of the next city or the class-conflict within their own gates. In the latter the prospering bourgeoisie were aligned with the lesser barons and knights against the bishops, abbots, and greater noblemen. As the bishops in particular had become increasingly identified with the emperor's authority, he shared their local unpopularity.

Nowhere was Otto more disliked than in Rome. In February, 1001, the citizens came out on the streets once more and besieged him for three days in his palace. Otto talked himself out of an ugly situation, withdrew to Ravenna, and went into the monastery at Classe for some quiet reflection. He considered retiring from the world, but finally decided to persevere with his imperial schemes. Gathering an army, he rode south for yet another punitive reoccupation of Rome. A Byzantine bride was already on the high seas. There would be just time to clean up the rebellious city in all senses and then to change the hangings for something more decorative and bridal.

He never reached Rome. Like his father he caught fever. He died in the castle at Paterno, near the Tiber, aged twenty-one. He had asked to be buried beside Charlemagne at

Aachen. To fulfil that wish, his men had to fight their way out of a hostile Italy, an empire crumbling about their ears. Another Crescentius proclaimed himself Patrician of Rome, the Marquis of Ivrea grabbed the crown of Italy, Pope Sylvester followed his young pupil quickly to the grave, and once more the country reverted to confusion.

9. Pope or Emperor?

WHILE THE northern half of Italy was in turmoil following the death of the third Otto, the southern saw the irruption of a new force, the Normans.

They first appeared there about fifty years before their conquest of England. The original 'Northmen' settled in France had by now softened their name to 'Normans' and, with their flair for assimilating themselves to their neighbours, had rapidly turned from pagan Scandinavian rovers into French-speaking feudal Christians. Their adventurous, ruthless qualities remained. Normandy was too small to hold such an explosive people.

It happened that some Norman pilgrims were passing through Salerno when the city was attacked by Saracens. They naturally helped in the defence, and, though only forty in number, played a decisive part. Their fighting qualities made such an impression that offers were made for their services. In the next few years a number of landless Normans emigrated to Southern Italy, where there was a ready market for their swords. In 1022 came three of the redoubtable de Hauteville brothers. That there were nine other brothers indicates the kind of pressure behind the Norman expansion. In 1025 the trio helped the Byzantine expedition against Sicily, which, though unsuccessful, had long-range results by revealing that island's possibilities to the shrewd blue eyes of the de Hautevilles. About 1029 the Duke of Naples gave another Norman leader, Rainulf, the first grant of land, making him Count of Aversa, a nearby Campanian town where he would be a buffer against the Duke's alarming neighbour, a prince of Capua nicknamed 'the Wolf of the Abruzzi'. The de Hautevilles soon acquired similar territories. The eldest, William Iron-arm, made himself Count of Apulia, and in 1047 another brother, Robert, came out to join the family enterprise. Robert gained the nickname 'Guiscard', or 'Weasel', a reference to his craftiness rather than his massive physique. Even more than his brothers he typified that remorseless ambition which we associate with the Conqueror himself. He played the dominant role in the Norman expansion over Southern Italy.

The landmark date is 1053, when the Normans quarrelled with the Pope. For the past half-century the papacy had been passing through another period of degradation, controlled by a single dominant family, first the Crescentians, then the Counts of Tusculum. Rome had seen a twelve-year-old pontiff, Benedict IX, and three simultaneous rival Popes, defying one another from their respective strongholds in the Lateran, St. Peter's and St. Maria Maggiore. This scandalous situation had been ended by the Emperor Henry III, and it was now his cousin who was restoring the lost credit of the office as Pope Leo IX.

The clash with the Normans arose over Benevento, which Leo had just acquired with imperial assistance. Its disgruntled former ruler enlisted the Normans to raid the duchy from which he had been ejected. Leo, an active not to say aggressive man, took the field with thirty thousand men, including a company of outsize Swabians lent him by Henry. Against them moved a negligible Norman force of three thousand mail-clad cavalry and a few hundred foot-soldiers. Seldom, however, was Norman superiority more terrifyingly displayed. The surprised Swabians were hewn down like forest trees. Leo's other troops demonstrated that, if nothing else, they had mobility. He himself was captured.

The 'Weasel' now showed his craft. The victorious Normans knelt before the pontiff and apologized for what they had done to his army. They then conducted him with exaggerated deference to Benevento, where they entertained him as a guest, brushing aside all suggestions of departure, for the next six months. In that period they grew to know each other, and an understanding began to emerge which Leo's successors developed into a firm settlement. Under this the Pope gave the Normans his blessing and ratified not only all their conquests up to date but others (notably Sicily) which existed only as ideas. The Normans, in turn, appreciating that this papal approval was meaningless unless it derived from the Donation of Constantine, endorsed that dubious document, agreed to hold their lands feudally as vassals of the Church, and swore to support the Pope as their overlord. The Pope thus secured valuable backing against the emperor and also checked any Norman temptation to expand Rome-wards. The Normans got a free hand against the Greeks and Saracens.

Their conquest of Sicily was roughly contemporary with their compatriots' invasion of England, but theirs was a more modest effort and therefore slower. Messina fell in 1061, Palermo in 1072, Syracuse in 1085. By 1091 Roger de Haute-ville was undisputed lord of the whole island. His forces were small, resembling rather the *conquistadores* of Cortez than the Conqueror's host at Hastings. How then did they succeed? Partly because the Saracens were disunited under three squabbling emirs, partly because they underrated the Normans, and partly because the masses, being Christian, did not actively oppose the invasion.

Roger called himself Count of Sicily, but his son, Roger II, managed to amalgamate his territory with the mainland con-quests of his late uncles, the 'Weasel' and the others, and on Christmas Day, 1130, was crowned king in Palermo Cathedral. Thus was born the strangely styled 'Kingdom of the Two Sicilies', which did not finally disappear from the map until the nineteenth century. The mainland part soon embraced everything south of the papal states. Thus was added yet another cultural factor perpetuating that division (of which the tourist is so quickly conscious) between the North, with its Etruscan-Celtic-Lombard-Germanic influences, and the South, where the comparable influences have been Hellenic and Byzantine, Saracen and Norman.

Of these the Norman — the distinctively Norman — was perhaps least, for the Normans were not by nature the inno-vators we might suppose them to be from their achievements in England. In Italy, and especially Sicily, they found a finer civilization than they could create themselves, and they were content to be assimilated. But the fusion they achieved in the Norman-Saracen-Byzantine culture of twelfth-century Sicily was something unique and memorable.

The reigns of Roger II, his son and grandson, were a golden age for Sicily, which they governed directly as a royal domain, whereas the mainland was delegated to feudal lords. In the island the tolerant policies of the Saracens were continued, the multi-racial society flourished as before. Muslim and Jew went unmolested, the Byzantine Christian was not bullied by the adherents of Rome. Saracen craftsmen adorned Catholic churches: the clock which Roger installed in his superb new Capella Palatina was inscribed in florid phrases more applicable to a caliph, and the date given not as 1142 A.D. but as the 536th Year of the Hegira. Latin, Greek, Arabic and Hebrew were all used in official documents. Though the king spoke Norman French with his knights and ladies he did not disdain to learn Arabic. Indeed, he may have needed the language with some of his ladies, for the harem was one of the Saracen institutions which the Norman rulers took over with most enthusiasm.

The glories of Palermo under the emirs were enhanced by the Norman conquest. Ibn Jubair, the Arab poet who visited Sicily in 1185, wrote that '*the King's palaces encircle the city like a necklace adorning the graceful throat of a girl.*' One such palace, La Zisa, bore the deserved inscription: '*Here the earthly Paradise opens before your eyes.*' A hint of its splendours may still be gained from the banqueting hall, with its mural mosaics depicting huntsmen and peacocks and strange trees, products of the royal studio in which local craftsmen were trained by artists from Constantinople. The air is cooled by a runnel of clear water whispering timelessly across the paved floor from a fountain in an alcove, under a fretted ceiling with a stalactite motif. In Norman times this hall opened upon one of those exotic courtyard gardens at which the Saracens excelled.

All this was not achieved without a struggle, and it would be a great mistake to picture a little band of northern adventurers softened and seduced by languorous Oriental comforts. Roger's assumption of the crown landed him in a ten-year struggle with assorted adversaries. The Pope, the emperors (both Byzantine and Holy Roman), the republics of Pisa and Genoa, rebellious mainland Normans — he fought them all and, despite more than one disastrous defeat, emerged finally victorious, largely owing to the loyalty and ferocity of his Saracen troops.

Roger cared nothing for race, only for ability. He made a

Greek his senior admiral, an Englishman Bishop of Syracuse, a Hungarian Bishop of Agrigento. He developed a silk-weaving industry by having skilled Greek workers shanghaied from Thebes. They wove the robes which, like all forms of court ceremonial, followed the Byzantine fashion; but it was Saracen seamstresses who then embroidered Christian texts in Arabic script, before they were laid upon the broad shoulders of the fair-haired Norman. If we visualize Roger thus — bearded, with leonine features as harsh as his voice, standing in one of those palace apartments in which the architecture and decor of several traditions blend in a strange new harmony — we have this whole phase of Sicilian history vividly personified.

.   .   .   .

Meantime, what had been happening elsewhere?

We have seen how the papal dignity had been rehabilitated by Henry III's clean sweep of three rival claimants and the subsequent election of his cousin as Leo IX. We have seen how Leo, after his initial fiasco against the Normans, reached an understanding with them which his successors turned into a definite agreement. There were four other Popes in that brief period. That Rome pursued a consistent policy was due to a Tuscan named Hildebrand, who by various stages, now as legate in France or Germany, now as a Pope's confidential chaplain, now as Archdeacon of Rome, had become the real power behind the papal throne. Hildebrand conceived of the Church as the supreme earthly authority. He wished to tighten its discipline by enforcing the rule of celibacy on the clergy, but even more he wanted to assert the Pope's supremacy over the mere laymen ruling other parts of Christendom. It is interesting that during this period even the preoccupied Macbeth made the long pilgrimage from Scotland, and Duke William felt it important to win papal support for his claim against Harold.

Henry III was succeeded by the six-year-old Henry IV, whose political views were necessarily unpredictable. Hildebrand saw that the present harmonious partnership of Pope and emperor might not continue. He also saw the opportunity offered by the youth of the new monarch. In 1059, a council at the Lateran passed a momentous decree, which, while making a formal bow in the direction of the Empire, laid down the principle that the only people entitled to elect a Pope were '*the cardinal-bishops and cardinal-priests of the Roman territory*'. By something more than coincidence the Pope visited Guiscard only four months later at Melfi, the capital of his Apulian duchy, and the bargain with the Normans was finally sealed. It was a timely act of reinsurance against possible trouble with the Germans. The years passed. Henry came of age at fifteen. He showed the wilful tendencies not seldom developed in youthful sovereigns frustrated by long regencies. Hildebrand too may have felt a little frustration, for the next Pope proved less frail than his recent predecessors and reigned for eleven years. Only in 1073 was Hildebrand able to step from behind the throne and take his seat at last upon it, as Gregory VII.

The stage was now set for the drama, the protagonist an imperious German of twenty-three, the antagonist a shrewd Italian in his fifties. The immediate cause for conflict was the archbishopric of Milan, to which the late Pope had appointed one man while the emperor had invested another. This was, of course, no isolated problem. The whole business of 'investiture' was one of the great controversial issues of the period, notably between Henry I of England and his Archbishop of Canterbury. It was rooted in the dual nature of a bishop as a dignitary of the Church and as a feudal lord, owning vast estates and controlling armed forces, in which capacity he became a vassal of the sovereign. As a man, however, he was indivisible and in the last resort only one of his two masters could invest him with his authority. *Which* of the two could be a question of enormous political importance.

One of Gregory's first pronouncements declared that such investitures by laymen were unacceptable. Henry reacted by installing two more bishops in Italian sees and, somewhat illogically, investing a second of his supporters as Archbishop of Milan though the first was still available. Gregory sent him a sharp letter, bidding him appear and explain himself at the Lenten Synod in Rome. This was no way to talk to an emperor. Henry called the German bishops to a conference at Worms and secured a unanimous vote for Gregory's deposition. He forwarded their resolution with a covering letter of his own.

'How dare you,' he wrote, *'you who have won your power
by cunning, flattery, corruption and violence, stretch out your
hand against the Lord's anointed? Vacate the Apostolic Chair
and let another take it, who will preach the sound doctrine
of St. Peter. We, Henry, by the Grace of God King, with all
our bishops, say to you: " Get down, get down."'*

This in turn was no way to write to a Pope. If Henry could
mobilize German bishops against the authority of the papacy,
Gregory could just as easily muster allies among the rebellious vassals of the Empire. He had a trump for Henry's ace
—excommunication—a card never played against a ruling
sovereign since Theodosius. In playing it now, Gregory knew
very well what he was doing. He was giving the German
dukes the respectable excuse they wanted for turning against
the young master to whom they had sworn allegiance. To
remove all doubt, he expressly released them from that oath
and declared Henry deposed. The immediate effect was all
that could have been desired. The German nobility assembled
at Tribur in October to discuss the situation. It was decided
to suspend Henry from his imperial functions. Deposition
would follow automatically, and the election of a new
emperor, if he could not obtain papal absolution within a
year and a day.

The sting lay in the last clause. The time-limit was calculated not from that moment, but from the actual pronounce-
ment of excommunication. Henry had only until 22nd
February to get out of his predicament, and his enemies were
determined to make this impossible. Another conference was
convened for 2nd February at Augsburg, ready to exploit
Henry's failure without further delay. Gregory was invited
to preside and was promised a safe-conduct through the Alps,
no empty courtesy since Lombardy was hostile to him.

Thus began the comedy of Canossa. It was vital for Henry
to see the Pope in private, before he reached Augsburg, and
strike a bargain. His dukes, well aware of this, barred the
Alpine passes against him. Only the Mont Cenis lay in friendly
territory. Henry slipped through and reached the plains of
Lombardy, themselves white with an unusually severe winter.
Gregory had already started for the conference. He halted
at Canossa, the stronghold of his staunch supporter, Matilda,
Countess of Tuscany. There he waited, perhaps for better

weather, but chiefly for the German escort without which he could not trust himself among the Lombards.

Time was running out. Clearly the chairman was going to be late for the conference — but what did Gregory's lateness matter compared with Henry's? It was 25th January when the anxious young emperor arrived at the castle gates, only to be refused admission. Sober historians have queried some picturesque details of the scene. It may be that we must reluctantly abandon the touching spectacle of the royal penitent, clad only in a woollen shirt, standing barefoot in the snow for three days and nights until the Pope judged that he had learnt his lesson. Whatever Henry wore, and however many times he retired from the threshold for greater comfort, there is no doubt that he was publicly humiliated and that the humiliation lasted until the 28th. And the legend, if not historically accurate in every detail, is the account which must have been passed gleefully from mouth to mouth through Christendom. In propagandist effect it mattered more than the strict truth.

Gregory would only grant absolution. Whether Henry was to be deposed or not was a question he referred to the conference. He himself abandoned his journey to Augsburg. Henry went back in a glow of blended embarrassment and virtue restored. The Canossa incident, though dramatic, proved indecisive, for the dukes, determined to get rid of him, managed to convince themselves that he had broken his oaths again and that his absolution was thereby nullified. They deposed him and tried to establish a rival emperor. The internal strife continued in Germany, and the struggle between Henry and Gregory was resumed. Again the Pope excommunicated the emperor and pronounced his deposition, again the emperor countered by deposing the Pope.

Gregory held on in Rome. He was disappointed in his hopes of Norman aid, for Guiscard chose this moment for a distant adventure against the other emperor in Constantinople, but he would not yield. Twice Henry besieged Rome. The second time, Gregory was penned in Castel Sant' Angelo, for the Romans, tired of the struggle, had allowed Henry into the city. A proposal to settle matters by a congress of bishops came to nothing, because Gregory barred all Henry's bishops on the grounds that they had been excommunicated and

Henry effectively obstructed the arrival of Gregory's supporters. Eleventh-century diplomacy had little to learn from
the twentieth. Henry broke the deadlock by appointing
another Pope, who obediently crowned him in St. Peter's with
traditional solemnity. Gregory glowered from the battlements
of his circular stronghold, and wrote again to Guiscard.

At last Guiscard came, with thirty-six thousand men, many
of them Saracens, hastening somewhat incongruously to the
rescue of Christ's Vicar and the Eternal City. Outnumbered,
Henry hastily withdrew from Italy. Some of his sympathizers,
however, staged a rising against the newcomers, who were
looting as though they were conquerors rather than rescuers.
Guiscard repressed this with characteristic brutality. The
whole district between the Lateran and the Colosseum was
deliberately fired. Gregory either could or would not restrain
his Norman protector. Perhaps he was resentful against the
citizens; certainly they were now more than ever resentful
against him. The flames which the Normans had kindled left
Rome too hot for Gregory. When Guiscard retired to his
duchy, the ageing Pope had to go too. A year later he died
in Salerno, his last words a wry adaptation from the Psalms:
'I have loved righteousness and hated iniquity: therefore I
die in exile.'

.   .   .   .

The investiture dispute did not end with his death. It
could not. The issue was fundamental. Urban II also had to
spend most of his time as an exile in the Norman South,
while a rival, subservient to Henry, occupied the Lateran.
Henry had rivals too, and was finally betrayed by his own son,
so that his last twenty years were wretchedly unhappy, and
he was even forbidden Christian burial. Henry V carried on
the vendetta for sixteen more years, matching Pope with
Anti-Pope of his own selection. At one time the true Pope, an
Italian, had to seek refuge in France while a Portuguese
Anti-Pope held Rome for his German master. Only in 1122
was a compromise accepted under the Concordat of Worms
(similar to an agreement reached some years earlier in
England) whereby the religious and the political aspects of
investiture were distinguished in the manner of appointment. But it was only a compromise, made because

everyone was weary of the struggle. The hatchet was buried, but no one forgot where it was.

Meanwhile, Popes and emperors being absorbed in their own quarrels, the cities nominally subject to them developed more and more independence. Venice, Pisa and Genoa took an active part in the First Crusade, and, though the outstanding general was Guiscard's son, Bohemond of Taranto, it was mainly their fleets which captured Tyre, Sidon, Haifa, and other ports, during these years. It may be debated whether these cities were chosen primarily because they offered bases for disembarking the soldiers of the Cross or because they formed the seaward termini of prosperous caravan routes. The commercial interests of the Italian republics never suffered by their participation in the Crusades.

Whereas the South was becoming unified under the Normans, even Naples and Amalfi being absorbed into the Kingdom of the Two Sicilies, in Lombardy even the smaller cities were becoming more and more independent communes. Under their chosen leaders there was a three-tiered structure of civic government. There was the Consiglio di Credenza, or privy council, answerable to the Gran Consiglio of several hundred leading citizens, chosen to represent the various wards. Only on special occasions were the masses consulted by assembling them in the piazza for a Parlamento.

These city-states were as quarrelsome as those of ancient Greece. Their fitting symbol, evolved about this time, was the *carroccio* or sacred war-chariot, a large rectangular dray painted red and surmounted by the civic banner, with an altar at which the militia could hear Mass before starting to batter and disembowel their neighbours from the next town. The protection of the *carroccio* was entrusted to picked warriors, and its capture by the enemy was the ultimate embarrassment.

Among the smaller cities which revolted against the domination of their bishops in this period was Brescia, and among the ringleaders was a young monk named Arnold, an idealist and an ascetic, who deplored the Church's intervention in worldly matters and dreamed of a return to the purer religion of days gone by. He studied at the University of Paris when Abelard was delighting the students and scandalizing their seniors. Back in Italy, he suffered in the general persecution of Abelard's supporters and was banished to Zurich by the Lateran Council. After a few years there he heard interesting news from Rome.

The Romans had revolted and expelled their own bishop. Tired of being a perpetual battleground for Popes and emperors, Popes and Anti-Popes, sickened by the corruption of the papal court, they had claimed the autonomy already won by lesser cities. They had set up a Senate again of fifty-six prominent citizens, under a Patrician. The Pope had fled. The nobles had fought neither for nor against him. Some had followed him, others were helping themselves to outlying papal possessions as opportunity offered.

It was two or three years before Arnold made his way to Rome. Once there, though little interested in practical politics, he became the popular spokesman of the reforming movement. The citizens hung on his words when he compared the hated Curia, the papal court, with a thieves' kitchen. They cheered when he declared: 'There can be no salvation for priests who possess estates, for bishops who hold fiefs, for monks who own property! '

Pope Eugenius, fulminating against the rebels from his refuge at Viterbo, hurled at Arnold the ultimate thunderbolt of excommunication. The monk and his followers remained unmoved. There was, indeed, only one way to move Arnold, and it was found by an Englishman, Nicholas Breakspear, who became Pope a year or two later as Adrian IV, and managed to resume occupation of the Leonine half of Rome. He clapped an interdict on the rest of the city until such time as the Senate should agree to banish Arnold. This meant that all churches were closed, no sacraments were administered except baptism, Christian marriage and burial were suspended, and, in a hundred and one ways, regular life was made impossible. By imposing the ban in Holy Week, when Rome was about to profit from the seasonal influx of pilgrims, he ensured that it would have the maximum persuasive effect upon the citizens. So, after being for nine years the idol of the republican party, Arnold found himself banished. He took shelter in a castle not far away, reasoning no doubt that the seesaw of revolution would soon raise his fortunes again.

As well it might have done, but for the entry of a new and formidable character in the last act of the drama. This was

the new emperor, the red-bearded Frederick I of Hohenstaufen, who had just appeared in Italy and who was later
to win the nickname 'Barbarossa'.

Barbarossa (let us call him, for history has too many
Fredericks) was a stalwart Bavarian of complex make-up, cruel
and chivalrous by turns, a Wagnerian hero-king yet a shrewd
statesman, even something of an intellectual, knowing Latin
and having as keen a taste for history as for the hunt. This
love of history spurred him to copy Charlemagne and dream
of a Holy Roman Empire in direct line with Augustus.

He became emperor in 1152, when he was about thirty
and had already proved himself a vigorous soldier in the
disastrous Second Crusade. He was elected partly because he
had links with both the rival factions in Germany, the parties
of Waiblingen and Welf. These names, Italianized into
Ghibelline and Guelph, became completely divorced from
their original meanings and were applied, south of the Alps, to
the ideological divisions which bedevilled Italian history for
generations. The Ghibellines supported the emperor, the
Guelphs the Pope. The schoolboy trick of remembering which
was which by the number of syllables is not altogether to be
despised. The distracted Italians themselves were reduced to
even more elaborate mnemonics — papal cities built their
battlements square, as at Florence, while imperialist cities
favoured the swallow-tail shape, as at Verona. Partisans
declared their allegiance by a dozen trivial mannerisms and
conventions.

After two years spent in restoring order in Germany, Barbarossa came to Italy to do the same. The vigorous communes of Lombardy made no appeal to a man who looked
backwards through history. Could one imagine Charlemagne
or Constantine allowing little republics to grow like mushrooms all over his realm? But on this first visit Barbarossa
had only small forces. When Milan defied him he could only
vent his displeasure on the lesser towns. Similarly, he could
not afford to quarrel with the Pope until after his coronation
in St. Peter's. Adrian took advantage of this. Among his
demands to Barbarossa was the person of Arnold of Brescia.
Though the emperor might have found the monk's propaganda helpful, notably in its insistence on the purely spiritual
role of the Church, he was himself too much of an authoritar-

ian to sympathize with a rebel. He had Arnold seized and handed over to the papal prefect. Arnold was tried and executed, and his ashes thrown into the Tiber.

Adrian came out to meet Barbarossa at Sutri, some distance north of Rome. Pope and emperor eyed each other warily, eager for advantage. The Pope, riding a mule, wished the emperor to lead it, a symbolic gesture of subordination which Barbarossa was reluctant to make. He did so at last under protest, and the impermanent allies went forward to Rome with a conscientious show of cordiality.

Now came a hitch. Though Arnold was dead, a convenient scapegoat for the unrepentant Romans, the republican Senate still held the main city and Adrian could speak only for the Leonine quarter. When the Senate asked Barbarossa for assurances that he would respect the liberties of the people, he refused to commit himself. The Senate thereupon barred its gates.

It was all distinctly embarrassing, especially for the Pope. However, there was no reason why the coronation should not be performed, though, in the present state of public opinion, it seemed imprudent to follow it with the customary 'acclamation' of the multitude. A quiet ceremony was indicated, with minimum publicity. So, on 18th June, 1155, Barbarossa slipped unobtrusively into St. Peter's, and was crowned Holy Roman Emperor.

It was now possible to relax and follow a hasty coronation with a leisurely banquet. Hardly had this got under way when the irate Romans, feeling that they had been outwitted, mobilized their militia and poured across the bridges to attack the unbelted Germans. A bloody struggle took place. Finally the citizens were driven back. Barbarossa would gladly have taught them a lesson, but he had not the forces for a siege. Soon the midsummer heat of Rome was enervating his northern warriors and malaria assailed them from the marshes. His main purpose had been achieved: he was crowned. He rode back to Germany.

For a time now emperor and Pope maintained contact by correspondence, not always with the happiest results. On one occasion the Pope wrote of conferring *beneficia,* which nearly provoked a physical assault upon his representatives at the imperial court, since the word was taken to mean 'benefices' in a specific sense with highly controversial implications, though the Pope (as he hastily explained, apologizing for the classical flavour of his Latin) had meant only ' benefits ' in a general way.

In 1158, Barbarossa returned to Italy, marching over the Brenner with a hundred thousand men, to assert his authority over the Lombard cities. Again Milan resisted him. There was a brief but savagely contested siege, then a moderate settlement, since the Milanese were not provisioned for a long resistance and his army, though large, was none too large for the extensive fortifications confronting it. The Milanese gave hostages and promised to stop bullying their weaker neighbours at Como and Lodi. Barbarossa said that they could go on electing their own consuls, subject to his approval.

Not content with this sensible arrangement — for it went against the instincts of a hero-king to make bargains with municipal councillors — Barbarossa called a conference at Roncaglia and invited four learned lawyers from Bologna University to give an impartial opinion on his imperial rights. They assured him that, as heir to the Roman emperors, he had absolute power, and there was no constitutional basis for locally elected consuls. Thus encouraged, he decided to govern each city, as Charlemagne had tried to do, through a personal representative, or *podestà*. Barbarossa was too intelligent to appoint a German, yet he saw the impossibility of finding a local man who would put loyalty to the emperor before civic patriotism. He therefore decided that the *podestà* should be an Italian chosen from another city. This compromise worked so well in practice, such a man standing outside the cliques and feuds of the community, that it was continued by independent cities long after Barbarossa was forgotten.

For the moment, though, the proud Lombards were not prepared to see its possible advantages. They saw only a threat to their liberty, and they reacted explosively. When the emperor's officers arrived in Milan to appoint the new *podestà* in place of the consuls, the citizens rose in arms. Even the little town of Crema, with no more than twenty thousand inhabitants, defied Barbarossa — and it was the ensuing seven-months siege which first earned him his nickname, an allusion as much to the blood on his beard as to its natural colour. On one occasion he had fifty captives, including children, lashed

Swallow-tail battlements proclaimed Ghibelline sympathies at Castello Scaligiero, Sirmione, the lakeside stronghold of Verona's ruling family.

Square Guelf battlements on the Palazzo dei Priori indicated Perugia's loyalty to the Pope.

'Venice, by the close of the 14th century unrivalled among the maritime republics.' A manuscript of this period, now in the Bodleian Library, shows Marco Polo departing in 1271, against a 14th-century background.

'The urbanity of Florentine society . . . ' A fashionable wedding, recorded by an unknown artist on a marriage chest now in the Academy, Florence.
'Lorenzo loved to ride out with his falcons.' A contemporary hunting party, on a marriage chest in the National Museum, Florence.

to the front of his siege-towers as a living shield. In the end it was famine more than terrorism which forced the city to surrender on terms. The survivors were allowed to evacuate Crema with such possessions as they could carry. The city was then plundered and burnt, principally (it must be said in fairness) by the people of Cremona near by. Had the various cities stood together Barbarossa would have been impotent. He throve on their enmities.

Meanwhile, Pope Adrian died. The succession was bitterly contested and the result disputed. Once again there was a Pope backed by the emperor and another, canonically elected, who, despite the support of France, England, Sicily and a large opposition movement in Germany, had to take refuge abroad. It was this Pope, Alexander III, who excommunicated Barbarossa. As was inevitable, he became the ally of the northern cities in their struggle for freedom.

In the summer of the next year Barbarossa decided to deal with Milan. Strong reinforcements came from Germany, the city was blockaded, and a belt of territory twelve miles deep was devastated all around it. As far as the eye could see not a fruit-tree, not a vine, was left standing. Countryfolk caught smuggling produce into Milan had their hands struck off. Then, as the hungry winter went on, Barbarossa had an undeserved stroke of luck — unless indeed it was sabotage: fire destroyed the city's granaries.

Milan could hold out no longer. The citizens had to surrender unconditionally. The *carroccio* was brought out, its standard lowered in homage. The townsmen knelt for mercy. But it was not a commodity that Barbarossa dealt in. He was determined to destroy Milan, yet cunning enough to shift the infamy to other shoulders. He gravely consulted the neighbouring cities, Milan's rivals and for the moment his own supporters: Cremona, Pavia, Como and the rest. The Milanese were ordered to evacuate their town and distribute themselves among the villages. Their enemies then moved in like birds of prey. The empty houses were looted, many were burnt, only churches and monasteries were spared. Each contingent was allotted a section of fortifications to demolish, and the walls were pulled down amid scenes of exultation like those at Athens after her humiliation in the Peloponnesian War.

But there were other cities which took no pleasure in this spectacle. The *podestè* were behaving tyrannically, but with the awful example of Milan before their eyes the citizens saw that isolated action would be suicidal. Secret emissaries passed to and fro. Finally a meeting was called in a monastery at Pontida, with delegates not only from Verona, Brescia, Mantua, Ferrara and the Milanese villages, but even from repentant Cremona. A solemn oath was sworn that they would all stand together and fight for their former liberties. The first act of this Lombard League was to rebuild the walls of Milan, so that, after five bitter years, the refugees could return. Then, as Barbarossa was occupied elsewhere, the League built a new city in Piedmont, calculated to vex him not only by its strategic value but also by its name, Alessandria, given in honour of the Pope he was trying to displace.

The final trial of strength was delayed, for Barbarossa's forays into Italy were only spasmodic. For six years he did not set foot there and the League was able to consolidate its position. Nearly all the cities which had previously supported the emperor found it advisable to join. Then he came down over the Mont Cenis and laid siege to Alessandria. Although the newly founded city was still defended only by earthworks, it managed to hold out until the following spring, when a relief-party, composed of militias from the different League cities, forced him to suspend hostilities. The war flared up a year later, in 1176, and the rival armies met for a decisive battle at Legnano, fifteen miles from Milan.

Barbarossa attacked with his German knights. They charged for the standard of Milan, which they recognized, raised up on the *carroccio*, above the sea of helmets. For some minutes the Italian ranks reeled under the impact of the armoured horsemen. But the *carroccio* had been entrusted to two body-guards of young men, the Company of the Carroccio and the Company of Death, who vied with each other in heroism. The knights were forced to a standstll. Then, encouraged, the whole Italian array began to push them back. The emperor's own standard-bearer went down, Barbarossa himself was hurled from the saddle and vanished. The Italian horsemen counter-attacked, the Germans wavered and broke, many were driven into the Ticino. Victory seemed complete. A search of the battlefield produced Barbarossa's standard and shield but not his body, which was thought to have been swept down-river like so many others. But days later came the disquieting news that he was alive and safe, though wounded, at Pavia, almost the only place which had remained consistently loyal to him.

Was all to do again? Would the terrible red-beard prove doubly terrible in his thirst for revenge? Italy was soon reassured. Though Barbarossa had usually displayed the more monstrous side of his nature in his actions south of the Alps, he was no fool, and he knew when to swallow unpalatable necessity.

The next year a settlement was agreed in Venice, under the chairmanship of the doge. The cities were to govern themselves but acknowledge the emperor as overlord. Barbarossa was to recognize Alexander as the true Pope and be given absolution. So that the situation of rival pontiffs should not recur, the present election rule, requiring a two-thirds majority, was introduced shortly afterwards.

So, on a summer's day in 1177, before the doors of San Marco on a spot still marked by a slab of red Verona stone with a white marble lozenge, the emperor humbly knelt and set his red-bearded lips to kiss the Pope's foot. And for a time there was peace.

10. Crusaders and Friars

In 1 1 8 9 the indefatigable Barbarossa, then in his late sixties, went off on the Third Crusade. A year later his flamboyant career ended with a drowning accident in a Cilician river.

The real hero of this Crusade (apart from Saladin) was Richard I. At Marseilles he 'hired two large busses and twenty well-armed galleys', the 'busses' being transports, and sailed down the west coast of Italy, with leisurely shore-excursions at Ostia and Naples, to meet the French king at Messina. Local relations were not easy and there was trouble over supplies. *'But for God and the navy'*, runs the slightly ambiguous record, *'many would have had a poor time.'* Coeur-de-Lion was not without his more personal embarrassments. The French king demanded a definite answer: did Richard still wish to marry his sister Aloysia? In December Richard had to do penance for homosexual practices. A few months later his formidable old mother, Queen Eleanor, came out with Berengaria, the 'Damsel of Navarre', met Richard at Reggio, and in a brisk four-day visit arranged that Berengaria, not Aloysia, should be the next Queen of England. As if this was not all sufficiently distracting for a keen Crusader, Richard had to settle the future of his sister Joan, the recently widowed Queen of Sicily and at that moment the prisoner of the new king.

Joan's husband, William II, had died childless a year or two before. It had been arranged that the kingdom should pass to the only legitimate survivor of his grandfather's brief dynasty, Constance, Roger's posthumous daughter by another marriage. When the time came, this solution recommended itself less and less to the people of the two Sicilies. Besides her sex, Constance had two other disadvantages: she had married, at thirty-one, the twenty-year-old son of Barbarossa, who now became emperor as Henry VI and would obviously be the effective ruler of his wife's domains; and secondly, as

134

several years of marriage had produced no issue, it seemed likely that in due course Sicily would fall into the hands of Hohenstaufen rulers without a drop of Norman blood in their veins. This would create an enlarged Holy Roman Empire and leave the Papal States uncomfortably sandwiched between a North and South equally imperial.

There was an alternative. Roger II's eldest son, though never married, had left a son, Tancred, who made up for what he lacked in inches (he was nicknamed 'Tancredulus') by his talent for war and intrigue. Illegitimate he might be, but he was a truer de Hauteville than Sicily was likely to find elsewhere. At that moment Barbarossa was still alive, crusading, and his son, Constance's husband, was fully occupied as regent in Germany. So when Coeur-de-Lion arrived at Messina, he found that Tancred had brought off a successful coup, made himself King of Sicily, and clapped the widowed queen into prison as a sympathizer with the outmanoeuvred Hohenstaufen faction.

It was to discuss this matter of his sister that Richard met Tancred in Catania. The encounter between the towering Plantagenet and the bantam-weight de Hauteville must have had its amusing side, especially when Richard presented Tancred with a large sword purporting to be the original Excalibur. The two kings took to each other and formed an alliance, which was to win Richard the bitter enmity of Henry VI and prolong his imprisonment when he later fell into the emperor's hands. Meantime, however, Richard secured Joan's release and when the Crusaders sailed she went with them as chaperone to Berengaria until her marriage to Richard, who now passes out of Italian history.

Tancred remained, but not for long. Henry entered Italy that year, was crowned Emperor in Rome, and marched south to Salerno. There Tancred drove him back and indeed captured Constance, but the Pope persuaded him to set her free. Early in 1194 Tancred died, leaving his wife regent for his infant son. Henry swept down again with an irresistible army. Constance followed at leisure, being now, at forty, after nine years of marriage, pregnant for the first time. On Christmas Day her husband received the crown of Sicily in Palermo Cathedral. The next day, in a little town near Ancona, with nineteen cardinals and bishops mustered as witnesses that there was no deception, Constance was delivered of a son, Frederick, destined to be known later (but for quite another reason) as *Stupor Mundi,* 'the wonder of the world'.

For a few years Henry ruled with a cold Teutonic severity hateful to his southern subjects. All sighed for the golden days of William II, 'the Good', or even William I, 'the Bad', so termed because he had been rather too sympathetic to the morals of Islam. Hopes rose when Henry died of dysentery at Messina and Constance, acting as regent for her son, *qua* King of Sicily, cleared out the German troops and put the government back in the hands of the local nobility. But within the year she had followed her husband to the grave, leaving little Frederick as the ward of the strong, newly-elected Pope, Innocent III. And there for the moment we too must leave the three-year-old orphan to grow up in the garden-girt palace at Palermo where alone (he used to say in later times) he felt truly at home.

.   .   .   .

That year Innocent preached the Fourth Crusade, to redeem the failure of the Third. Saladin was dead. Richard lived, and had long ago expressed his 'hope and resolve, with God's will, to return' to the Holy Land. But he died while the Venetians were still haggling over charter-rates for the expedition, and the Crusade, when at last it got under way, was hardly one of which he would have approved. Its members indeed might appropriately have taken as their emblem a double cross.

Venice dominated the affair from the start. Doge Enrico Dandolo, an octogenarian of incredible vitality, proposed to crusade in person. Venice was to contribute fifty galleys, together with transports sufficient for 4,500 cavalry and 29,000 infantry, and provisions for twelve months—an impressive indication of her resources at this date. In return, she was to receive a cash payment from the other Crusaders of 85,000 marks and a half-share of any territorial acquisitions. The second condition was easy to promise, the first impossible to fulfil. Dandolo then suggested that it could be postponed if the Crusaders would, as they sailed down the Adriatic, re-capture for Venice the Dalmatian port of Zara, then in Hungarian hands. There was some demur over this, since the King of Hungary had himself taken the Cross, but there seemed no other way of getting the long-frustrated expedition started. So at last, in 1202, an armada of three hundred vessels left Venice with Dandolo in command, plundered Zara, and settled down there to wait for spring.

The Fourth Crusade, as one might expect after such an unholy beginning, never went near the Holy Land. Instead, it made for Constantinople, Dandolo having made a cynically opportunist deal with the exiled Alexius Comnenus, son of the Emperor Isaac II recently deposed and blinded by his brother Alexius III. The assault on the city, heroically led by the old doge, was repulsed, but it touched off a revolution inside which threw out the usurper and restored Isaac. He, however, found difficulty in honouring the promises his son had made to the Crusaders. There was a counter-revolution. Isaac died of shock, Alexius Comnenus was murdered, and the Crusaders within the city had to get out quickly. Regrouping, they made a furious assault on the great sea-walls, which was successful at the second attempt. This was the notorious sack of Constantinople still commemorated by the ancient bronze horses in front of San Marco. But Venice gained more than these statues, more than a share of the stupendous loot which fell to the conquerors. She kept part of the city itself as a Venetian quarter, most of the Morea or Peloponnese, Crete and numerous smaller islands, in short the command of the Aegean. The other Crusaders (the 'Franks', as the natives called them) staked out feudal claims for themselves over the rest of the dismembered Byzantine Empire. Dandolo died, presumably well content, in the following year.

·   ·   ·   ·   ·   ·   ·   ·

The hypocrisy of the Fourth Crusade was not an isolated aberration — the whole Church, from cardinals and curia downwards, had strayed from the track blazed by its founder, and even Innocent III, most forceful of pontiffs, was only indifferently successful in pulling it back. Many bishops were corrupt, and the parish priests only less so because their opportunities were smaller. Frequently the disgusted congregations rose up and expelled them: Piacenza was without a priest for over three years. Where the clergy did officiate, they merely followed the ritual and could not, even if they wished, expound Christianity in sermons, for preaching was still a privilege reserved for bishops, and by some of them seldom exercised. The monasteries were spiritually sick. Even if the Pope discounted as slanderous gossip what was generally reported by the man in the street, he could not ignore the documents which poured in, appealing against assaults, murders, rapes, adulteries and incests committed by professed monks. Small wonder that Innocent, distracted by the miscarriage of his Crusade, by disputes with King John of England and other foreign princes, and by half a dozen such problems, declared that he had no leisure to meditate on other-worldly things. 'Scarcely can I breathe! So much must I live for others that I am almost a stranger to myself.'

There was nothing novel in this situation. There had been corruption in the Church before, and it had provoked reaction from idealistic reformers. Usually they had been defeated by a mixture of their own human weakness and the strength of the ecclesiastical establishment. Many, like Arnold of Brescia, had been condemned as heretics. Now, though, something of more lasting consequence was about to happen. While the Crusaders in Constantinople were washing the Greek Christian blood from their hands, a young man in Assisi was undergoing spiritual birth-pangs which were to produce not only a transformation in himself but a far-reaching religious revival.

Francis was the high-spirited son of a well-to-do textile merchant. Whether in fact his mother was a Provençale, or it was merely that his father had business links with France, the boy learnt French as he grew up and his mind was tinctured with the ideals and symbolism of chivalry. At this period the Provençal troubadours were touring Italy and even the local poets versified in Provençal because there was as yet no vernacular Italian developed for literary use. Later, Francis was to see himself and his brotherhood as the troubadours and jongleurs of the Lord and to speak in their fashion of the 'Lady Poverty' as the 'mistress' of his heart.

In 1199, when he was seventeen, the middle class of Assisi rose against their overlord, the Duke of Spoleto. They tore down the castle dominating their town and used the masonry for ramparts of their own. The local aristocracy opposed the movement. Some fled to their country mansions, others barricaded themselves in their town houses, which rose cliff-like from the steep alleys. Appeals were sent to the sympathetic nobles of neighbouring Perugia. This was typical of a new tendency in civic politics. Whereas cities had hitherto been more or less unitedly Ghibelline or Guelph, they were now split internally on class lines. Soon the tocsin was sounding in both cities to mobilize the respective militias. Francis, the cloth-dealer's son — but as deeply imbued with the *Chanson de Roland* and the Arthurian cycle as any knight — took his place eagerly in the ranks.

Nothing so vividly brings home to the modern traveller the scale of these medieval wars as the sight of the two little cities, each on its hilltop, a dozen miles of green Umbrian plain between them. In that plain the miniature armies clashed and hacked until the men of Assisi were defeated, and across that plain, for a long year, the captive Francis gazed yearningly towards the home he could see on the lower slopes of Mount Subasio. The sobering effect of this period was intensified by a serious illness after his liberation.

The next few years turned the playboy into the missionary and the mystic — yet, wonderfully, without apparently diminishing the charm and gaiety for which he was well known. He preached penitence but not doom, joy of life not fear of death, embracing austerity as though it were a luxury. His extravagant generosity was regarded as the behaviour of a lunatic. In 1206 his perplexed parent disinherited him, feeling that, while he could have tolerated a sinner in his cloth-business, he could not cope with a saint. Francis took the disinheritance quite literally, retired briefly from the public assembly convened by the bishop to deal with the matter, and reappeared stark naked, carrying his clothes in a bundle which he deposited, with a handful of small change, at the bishop's feet. 'Henceforth,' he announced, 'I have but one Father, Him that is in Heaven.' The cloth-merchant, with a shrug, picked up the clothes and money and went out, while the embarrassed bishop threw his own cloak round Francis. This dramatic episode reversed the volatile sympathies of the townspeople. From that date there was more respect than ridicule for the tall, dark-eyed young man, once so elegant, who now went about in a rough woollen garment girt with rope.

Soon others began to share his vision of a life based directly on the New Testament. In 1210 the whole group, twelve in all, went to seek papal approval for some simple form of organization.

Innocent and his advisers eyed the plan warily. Such movements often developed into heresies. Francis was a layman. He seemed set against anything institutional and clerical. And, though his sincerity was impressive, was his Rule practicable? 'Poverty, chastity, obedience.' The last was admirable, for it meant proper subordination to papal authority. The second was perhaps more difficult than as yet this young man realized, but it was not for Rome to suggest that it was beyond human achievement. But the first? The experienced churchmen considered it with pursed lips. However, the draft wording of the Rule was hard to fault, for Francis, whether with innocence or cunning, had composed it largely by stringing together quotations from the Gospels.

So the 'Penitents of Assisi' went home with provisional permission to found what became the Franciscan Order. Like the first disciples they went out preaching, living roughly and simply with the people, often sharing in their work. Once a year they gathered together in the cluster of wattle huts they had built round the ancient little shrine of Portiuncula, at the foot of the mountain to which Assisi clings, where Francis had once had the decisive mystical experience from which he dated his conversion. Soon the preaching tours developed into missionary journeys as far afield as Spain, France and Africa, Francis himself visiting Egypt and the Holy Land. In 1212 a wealthy young heiress, Clare, founded a parallel sisterhood.

Before long, the movement became too much of an institution to please Francis. Sadly he resigned his leadership to Brother Elias, who headed the group pressing for more rigid organization. He himself, and others who regretted but would not fight the change, sought consolation in withdrawal. His own favourite refuge from the world was a hermitage in the forest, two or three miles up the mountain. But these retirements were only temporary. Francis remained to the last a soldier in the field.

He died in 1226, in his middle forties, prematurely worn out by illness and voluntary austerities, yet in spirit the debonair youth who had once scandalized the bourgeoisie of Assisi. He had sung then, he sang now as long as breath

remained. On his death-bed at Portiuncula, he improvised
an additional verse for his Canticle of the Sun:

*Praise be, O Lord, for our Sister Death: whom no man
     may escape. . . .*

He had asked to lie outside the city in the ground where
criminals were buried and rubbish was thrown. Brother Elias,
however, started almost immediately to build the immense
Italian Gothic church which now enshrines his body. It was
only two years before Rome canonized him, merely endorsing
what the instinct of the common people had long ago
recognized.

   If St. Francis had not transformed the religious life of Italy,
he had at least given it a much-needed injection of pure
Christianity. The Franciscans went on to do important work,
though it was often remote from his design. Their preaching,
like that of the brotherhood founded almost simultaneously
by the Spaniard, Dominic, took religion out of the realm of
ritual and into the sphere of daily conduct. Their missions
went far into Asia, John de Plano Carpini appearing in 1245
at the court of the Great Khan in Mongolia, thirty years before
Marco Polo. Though St. Francis had himself distrusted
intellectualism, his successors penetrated the universities, a
sphere originally left to the Dominicans, and soon the Grey
Friars were making as great a contribution as the Black,
tending to rather more freedom of speculation than their
Dominican colleagues. They were not so liberal, however,
as to prove unsuitable officers of the Holy Inquisition, and
soon after this was set up (in 1233) Central Italy was one of
the regions for which they were made responsible, while
Lombardy was assigned to the Dominicans. So, within a
decade or two, the troubadours of God turned to torture and
executions.

   Meanwhile, artists like Cimabue vied with each other in
adorning the great two-storeyed basilica which juts precipit-
ously from the flank of Assisi, and here, just before 1300,
Giotto depicted the saint's life in those twenty-eight murals
which are probably his earliest extant work. The mosaic was
giving place to the fresco. Cimabue had already begun the
departure from its stiff, stylized Byzantine tradition. Giotto,

his pupil, now ventured to portray characters almost within living memory and settings unchanged, adjacent and familiar to every eye.

So, in achieving what his contemporaries accepted as the supremely lifelike, Giotto began a revolution in art as far-reaching as that inaugurated in religion by St. Francis. In that upper church at Assisi, perhaps more than in any other one spot, modern painting was born.

.   .   .   .

It is time to return to the exotic palaces of Palermo. Here, while the Crusaders were storming Constantinople and St. Francis was first scandalizing Assisi, Barbarossa's orphaned grandson, Frederick of Hohenstaufen, was growing up under the remote control of his guardian, Innocent III. The Pope in fact never saw his ward. There was little systematic provision for his welfare and education. It may be unduly cynical to relate this fact to his adult career, when he showed himself probably the greatest European ruler between Charlemagne and Napoleon, and in intellectual versatility the precursor of the Renaissance. In a Sicily which was an anarchic battle-ground of faction and intrigue young Frederick somehow survived, neglected, at times in physical danger. One thing helped: this Palermo was the girlhood home of the mother he had scarcely known, and for her sake there was kindness from officials and servants, who remembered that this boy, though a Hohenstaufen, was also half a Norman, Roger's grandson too. So, despite everything, his childhood memories were strangely happy. He always loved Sicily, and declared irreverently that, if God had known of it, He would never have chosen Palestine.

Frederick's inquiring mind sought satisfaction in many directions. His tutors ranged from the papal legate (afterwards Pope Honorius III) to the learned Saracens of Palermo. He learnt Arabic and eventually had a working knowledge of six languages, being also one of the first men to write passable verses in Italian. He was interested in mathematics, medicine, pharmacy and other sciences: later he formed a menagerie of rare animals — lions and lynxes, cheetahs, an elephant, the first giraffe to be seen in Europe — and wrote a treatise on falconry displaying accurate observation and a courageous readiness to disagree, where necessary, with the revered Aristotle. He loved architecture and the arts; he probably designed some of his own castles, which he adorned with antique sculptures. His greatness as a legislator, his shrewdness as a diplomat, and his very fair skill as a general must have owed something to the haphazard, eclectic self-education of his precocious boyhood. That education had glaring gaps. Though he learnt all the knightly tricks of horsemanship, archery and swordplay, there were no feminine influences to impose the refinements of chivalry, and he grew up crude of speech and manner.

Always he knew himself a king. Practically his first memory must have been the coronation in Palermo Cathedral. '*He thinks it shameful to be subject to a guardian and considered a boy,*' ran a report to the Pope. '*He talks with all and argues.*' It irked him that his kingdom was being governed for him, and indeed misgoverned, by the Pope, who was allowing himself generous expenses for the purpose. It irked him that he was king only of Sicily: the imperial crown which his father and grandfather had worn belonged now to Otto IV of Brunswick. But at last came his fourteenth birthday, when he assumed his full responsibilities, which included a staggering bill from Innocent for extra expenditure as trustee, and made him almost bankrupt at the outset.

He soon showed that he had indeed come of age. Before he was fifteen he married Constance of Aragon, the twenty-four-year-old widowed Queen of Hungary. Her initial attraction was that she brought with her five hundred Spanish knights, led by her own brother, who (Frederick calculated) would enable him to tame his unruly barons. But an epidemic attacked the bridal party; within a couple of months the prince and most of his knights were dead, and Frederick and Constance had to flee to Catania to escape the infection. Despite this tragic beginning, and the disparity in their ages, the marriage did not turn out too badly. Constance was good for the boy. She improved his manners and he was not criticized for uncouthness again. She must have been in some sense a mother to Frederick himself before, after a year or so, she became the mother of his child.

Though he had lost the Spanish knights, Frederick soon managed to put his house in order. There was a purge of disloyal councillors and insolent vassals. In a circular letter addressed to all bishops and barons, the amazing adolescent showed himself master of the propaganda weapon which he was often to wield so effectively on later occasions. There was no doubt that Sicily had a king once more.

Meanwhile, the Emperor Otto was proving increasingly obnoxious to the Pope and threatening to extend his power southwards. The papal nightmare of an isolated Rome returned, a Rome sandwiched between a Northern and Southern Italy united under one emperor. Innocent, confident of his ability to control his late ward, decided that Frederick would be a much safer emperor, especially if an agreement were made that North and South should not come under a single ruler. If Frederick were helped to gain the imperial crown, that of Sicily must first be handed over to his infant son, Henry. There was also an understanding that Frederick should lead a Crusade to the Holy Land. On these terms Innocent excommunicated Otto and secured Frederick's election in his place. So, at eighteen, the youth became Holy Roman Emperor, though it was another six years before Otto's death left him unchallenged master of Germany, by which time Innocent too had died, spared from seeing the full consequences of his unwonted naïvety.

For Frederick had no intention of dividing his new-won power. Little Henry was carried to Germany and crowned there too, which was the recognized way of marking him heir-apparent to both realms. In fact, as he grew up, it was Germany rather than Sicily which was delegated to him, for Frederick's own heart remained ever in the South. As for going on a Crusade, this, with the best will in the world, he had to postpone indefinitely. He must consolidate his power in Germany, an ancestral but unfamiliar country. And in Sicily he must deal with a serious ten-year revolt of the Saracens, touched off by a terrible famine in 1212, and ended only by a wholesale deportation of the Muslim population to the mainland. Harshness of this sort made him unpopular in the island he loved. Though he gave the Sicilians peace and order, they never forgave him for his outside preoccupations. They looked back nostalgically to the Norman kings whose lives had been centred in Palermo. Yet it is fair to remember that Frederick's Saracens remained his most faith-

ful soldiers. He treated them well. At his great Apulian stronghold of Lucera he built them a miniature Baghdad complete
with mosques.

In 1225 he assured the reigning Pope (his old tutor, now
Honorius III) that he would positively sail for the Holy Land
within two years. Constance had died. Political motives made
him marry the twelve-year-old Yolande, daughter of John, the
nominal King of Jerusalem. Though John was still very much
alive and at seventy-five indefatigably touring Christendom to
enlist support for his claims, Frederick insisted on anticipating nature and adding 'King of Jerusalem' to his own collection of titles. In 1227 a new Pope, Gregory IX, reminded him
sharply that the two years were up, whereupon Frederick
mustered an army at Brindisi and sailed.

Within a few days he was back, having been taken gravely
ill at sea. His second-in-command and hundreds of other
Crusaders died in an epidemic which had been raging through
their ranks before they started. But Gregory disbelieved the
explanation and excommunicated Frederick. Frederick
retorted without mincing his words. Denunciations flew back
and forth. The old contest was on again, Pope versus emperor,
with Frederick's propagandist circulars providing a new
element.

The next year he left for the East. Gregory felt that an
excommunicated Crusader was a contradiction in terms. To
remove any grounds for misunderstanding, he excommunicated Frederick all over again, and, lest he be thought to
fight only with words, sent his own troops to ravage Apulia.
Frederick continued serenely to the Holy Land where he
enjoyed, on the whole, a highly successful Crusade. He
regained possession of Jerusalem, Bethlehem and Nazareth
by peaceful negotiation and, though he had lost his sixteen-
year-old wife a few months earlier, crowned himself King
of Jerusalem in that city, no priest daring to perform the
office for him. Returning to Italy, the deliverer of the Holy
Sepulchre was welcomed with a third excommunication.
Imperturbably he chased the papal troops out of Apulia and
compelled Gregory to grant him absolution as the price of
peace.

Now for some years he concentrated on administering his
southern kingdom. From Melfi, the old Norman capital of

Apulia, he promulgated the new legislation which made his reputation as a law-giver. He liked the lofty fortress, fifteen hundred feet up amid the breezy woodlands clothing the once-volcanic slopes of Monte Vulture, but to escape from business he was increasingly compelled to use remoter castles as hunting-boxes. For the rest of his life he was a great castle-builder. Lagopesole, Castel del Monte, Oria, Gioia del Colle, and the other Apulian fortresses, 'our places of solace', combined military value with sporting attractions. The strongholds with which he dotted Sicily were more purely strategic in purpose.

Frederick did much for his mainland territories. Fairs were established, seafaring guilds encouraged, special privileges granted to the ports of Bari, Barletta, Brindisi and Taranto. He took a keen interest in the medical school at Salerno, added to it a department of anatomy, and made its diploma the essential qualification for anyone practising medicine. He had already, in 1224, established a university at Naples which, following the Italian rather than the French or English pattern, was a secular institution and taught no divinity until 1360. One of its earliest students, Thomas Aquinas, whose critical approach to Aristotle must have appealed to the sceptical Frederick, had to move on to Paris for his theological degree.

The imperial court had something of the atmosphere of the senior common room. Learned men, Christian, Jew and Muslim, disputed at his table with a freedom which sometimes appalled the orthodox. Here gathered the scientists, Giordano Ruffo, Master Theodore, Adam Charter of Cremona, Jacob Anatoli, Jehuda ben Salomon Cohen, and many more, writers on veterinary medicine, diet, ophthalmology, and hygiene for crusading armies. Here came the ingenious Michael Scott, astrologer, mathematician and translator of Aristotle, and Leonardo of Pisa, who introduced algebra and Arabic numerals to the West. With them mingled the poets of the Sicilian school, busily creating a vernacular poetry from Provençal models: Giacomo da Lentini, perhaps the first sonneteer, Pietro della Vigna, Rinaldo d'Aquino, and Frederick's eldest illegitimate son, Enzio.

The atmosphere of an (old-style) senior common room was no doubt enhanced by the comparative absence of feminine

Lodovico il Moro: 'strong will, subtle intelligence, infinite ambition.'

Strong Men of the Quattrocento.

Pope Julius II: 'aggressive campaigner, blunt statesman, bold townplanner.'

Cosimo de' Medici: 'banker with higher enthusiasms.'

Doge Foscari: 'astute party-manager.'

'In his country villas Cosimo was the centre of a coruscating intellectual c
Villa Cafaggiolo, built for him by Michelozzo in 1451.

Alfonso's 'triumphal arch so incongruously squeezed between the plain cylin
towers of the Castel Nuovo' at Naples.

influence. After Yolande's death Frederick remained for some years a widower and in any case his attitude to women was rather Oriental. During this period he began what was probably the one satisfactory relationship in his life, with Bianca Lancia, member of a noble but impoverished Piedmontese family which had emigrated to the South. She bore him a son, his favourite, Manfred, and it seems likely that, long afterwards, she and Frederick entered into a secret morganatic marriage.

Meantime, in 1235, he married Isabella, who was beautiful, twenty-one, and the sister of Henry III of England. She had been engaged to Frederick's son, but he was now disgraced and in prison, so Frederick married her instead. She received the Oriental treatment from the start. Nearly all her English servants were packed off home and she found herself practically in purdah, attended by negro eunuchs 'hideous as old masks'.

. . . .

Having consolidated his power in the South, Frederick now embarked on a long struggle to bring Northern Italy similarly under control. 'Italy is my heritage,' he told the Pope bluntly, 'and all the world knows it.' At first things went well. He defeated the Milanese at Cortenuova, captured their *carroccio* and sent it as a trophy to Rome, a symbol that he had wiped out the shame of his grandfather's defeat at Legnano. But soon the Pope assumed his traditional role as champion of the communes. He excommunicated Frederick. Against that skilful propagandist he threw into action a new form of spiritual shock-troops, the wandering friars. Frederick then overran most of the papal territories and threatened Rome. The beleaguered Pope summoned a Lateran Council to mobilize Christian opinion against him. As Frederick held the roads, the delegates were to come secretly by sea from Genoa, but Frederick countered this move brilliantly, arranging for his obedient Pisans to attack the Genoese convoy. This they did, capturing the whole reverend cargo of some hundred bishops and abbots, who were sent to meditate in the various castles of Apulia.

The next Pope, a Genoese, had to abandon Rome and seek refuge in France, where he once more went through the routine of excommunicating Frederick, proclaimed his deposition, and preached a Crusade against him. Frederick was over fifty now, red-faced, bald, short-sighted, yet dynamic as ever, still capable of twenty-four hours in the saddle. He was ready to storm through the Alps and beard the Pope in his French refuge, but trouble broke out behind him in Lombardy, where Parma, one of his most dependable supporters, revolted against him. An eight-month siege, stained by atrocity and reprisal, could not subdue the citizens. One winter's morning, when the emperor had ridden off for a few hours' sport with his falcons, the famished defenders saw their chance, made a surprise sortie, and overran the imperial camp. Too late he galloped back. The camp was in flames. His treasure, his throne, regalia and great seal — even his books and his Saracen harem — were in enemy hands. The humiliation of Legnano was repeated. Frederick had to ride for his life to Cremona, nearly forty miles away.

These years were dark and bitter. Frederick, essentially lonely from childhood, felt himself increasingly isolated. Manfred was a charming companion, but still only a boy. His heir, the rebellious Henry, after seven years in prison had committed suicide. His beloved Enzio had been captured by the citizens of Bologna, who vowed never to release him. He felt, often without cause, that he could no longer trust his entourage. When his personal physician was caught trying to poison him, Pietro della Vigna, for years his closest adviser ('the half of my life!') was accused of complicity and committed suicide to escape the appalling tortures which lay ahead. For Frederick, who had not been a cruel man by the deplorably low standards of the thirteenth century, was now descending to the most inhuman punishments conceivable by the medieval mind.

In 1250 his fortunes seemed to be rising again. He passed that summer in Apulia, where for eight years he had been gradually building an immense castle at his favourite Lagopesole. In the autumn he was taken ill with dysentery while on a hunting expedition. For a fortnight he lay dying in the castle of Fiorentino, where he had time to summon his state officers, make his will, and put all his business in order, down to the smallest detail. Then he rallied, talked of getting up, and had a sharp relapse. His life-long friend, Archbishop

Berard of Palermo, braved papal displeasure by giving him the last sacrament as he lay, conventionally but somewhat incongruously swathed in the white robe of a Cistercian monk. That day, the 13th December, he died.

'Let the heavens rejoice,' commented the Pope when the news reached him in France. To him and to his supporters the death of Frederick was the death of Antichrist. But more men remembered the emperor as ' *Stupor Mundi* ', the wonder of the world.

11. *Anjou, Aragon and Avignon*

FREDERICK'S OFFSPRING ('the brood of vipers', as the Pope termed them) had been numerous, for his vigour and versatility had been as conspicuous in this field as in others. But when he died, just short of his fifty-sixth birthday, he left only two sons in a position to carry on his work.

The legitimate heir was Conrad, whose birth had cost poor Yolande her life at sixteen. Conrad was now twenty-two, King of Jerusalem and King of the Romans, but in fact absorbed in the administration of Germany which he, a more typical Hohenstaufen than his father, regarded as the essential Empire. The other son, Frederick's favourite and faithful companion to the end, was Manfred, now a dashing, charming youth of eighteen, 'fair, handsome and of noble countenance', as Dante assures us. Frederick did as much as he dared for him. In his will he made him Prince of Taranto and regent of all Italy until Conrad could travel south.

The new emperor and the old exiled Pope converged upon Italy with alacrity. Unable at once to regain Rome, then held by an independent commune, Innocent established himself in Perugia. Manfred meanwhile handed over control to Conrad with as good a grace as possible. Conrad rewarded him by reducing his inheritance and cancelling some grants he had made to his maternal uncles.

It was not long before the Pope resumed his vendetta with the Hohenstaufens, the basic motive being, as always, to block any effective union of Germany-and-Lombardy with Sicily-and-the-South. He soon found an excuse for the routine step of excommunicating Conrad and for preaching a Crusade against him, of which nobody took much notice. Things would probably have gone badly for the Pope, had not one of those sudden attacks of fever, which play so frequent and important a role in Italian history, carried off the young emperor at the age of twenty-six.

Conrad's heir was Conradin, his two-year-old child far away in Bavaria. The dying man realized that the German princes would not elect an infant emperor. Sicily, however, might be held as it had been before. He appointed a trusted follower, Berthold of Hohenburg, as regent, and somewhat optimistically appealed to his papal adversary to protect the interests of the helpless child. He pointedly omitted Manfred from these arrangements.

It was soon apparent that Manfred was indispensable. The Pope, indifferent to Conrad's death-bed plea, saw a chance to control Sicily himself. The whole military balance had been reversed — so catastrophic in those days was the death of a personal leader — and the imperial forces, though irresistible under Conrad, could now offer no adequate opposition to the Pope. Even Berthold saw that the only man to deal with the situation was Manfred, who had not only been fathered by the mighty Frederick but trained by him too. He asked him to take over the regency.

Manfred began cautiously, with an astuteness which would have pleased his father. Having no choice, he accepted the Pope's terms and welcomed him to the South with a show of deference. But he was well aware that his liquidation was planned. Hostile troops were infiltrating into his lands, his jurisdiction over Calabria was already promised to another. After narrowly escaping death in an ambush, he threw off the mask of obedience and rode hard for Lucera, where Frederick's faithful Saracens were guarding the imperial treasury. Papal troops, under a cardinal, were making for the same objective, cheered by prospects of long-deferred pay. Manfred got there first, harangued the Saracens, and won them over, together with some of Berthold's Germans, though others defied him. These he defeated in a short, sharp engagement, and they fled to meet the advancing cardinal. The latter's unpaid warriors deserted as soon as they heard the facts, and Manfred was saved the trouble of further fighting.

At this point the Pope died. His successor, Alexander IV, though less virulent personally against the Hohenstaufen family, could not alter the basic policy dictated by the political needs of the papacy. He was a native of Rome, and local sentiment helped him to return there, but he was in fact very much in the hands of the Florentines, who for generations had been loyal Guelphs and were now leading the struggle against Frederick's successors. Alexander had the backing of their bankers, fast becoming the foremost financial power in Europe, having just coined their own gold 'florin', usurping the imperial prerogative, and made it the favourite international currency. It was a Florentine cardinal, too, Octavian, who was the real force in the Lateran.

This cardinal acted promptly against Manfred. Some of the Sicilian and Southern towns wished to set up Northern-style communes. He promised them papal support for a confederate republic, though secretly he was looking for an alternative King of Sicily to pit against Manfred. Meanwhile, with Berthold, he took the field against the young Hohenstaufen. In the course of the campaign Berthold decided to change sides again and, by supplying Manfred with information and denying provisions to Octavian, he landed the cardinal in an untenable position. Octavian signed a treaty, immediately repudiated by the Pope, which recognized Manfred as regent for the young Conradin and left him unchallenged master of the mainland South.

In a year or two, having scotched the republican movement, he was equally master of Sicily. Then came false news, possibly inspired by him or at least by his supporters, that the child in Bavaria was dead. In that century one could not afford to wait indefinitely for confirmation. Manfred was quickly crowned in Palermo. When news came that Conradin was alive and well, it seemed a pity to confuse simple folk by nullifying the coronation, especially since the boy (unlike his grandfather at the same age) had never been seen in the island and meant nothing to its people.

Regional patriotism, then as later, was the obsession of the Sicilians. Manfred himself lost much popularity by not keeping his court in Palermo: he had an understandable fondness for Lucera, the depot of his faithful Saracen troops. This might have been forgiven. Lucera was after all in Apulia, a mainland region of the Regno, as the Southern kingdom was called. But Manfred, a Lombard on his mother's side, surrounded by Lombard uncles, wanted Lombardy as well. He vexed the Sicilians by taking their men and money for campaigns against the North.

At first he was remarkably successful. The cities of the

Lombard League had no hostile emperor to unite them in mutual defence: the German princes for the moment preferred to be under a figurehead, some outsider and absentee, but they could not decide between Richard Earl of Cornwall and Alfonso King of Castile. This left the Italian cities free to pursue their local rivalries under the increasingly irrelevant labels of Ghibelline and Guelph. More and more, individual strong men were establishing local dictatorships; the Guelph, Martino della Torre, in Milan, and the Ghibelline party-bosses, Ezzelino da Romano and Mastino della Scala, who successively ruled Verona. By skilful diplomacy, and the loan of a few hundred German troopers where they would be most effective, Manfred was able to exploit the situation.

Florence was the hardest nut to crack. She had driven out her Ghibelline minority, who had taken refuge with her rivals, the Sienese. Manfred lent some Germans. After a murderous battle at Montaperti, the Guelphs were routed and the exiles swept triumphantly home. Florence had to join Siena, Pisa and other cities in a Ghibelline league, and accept Manfred's representative as *podestà*. Within the year Manfred was master of nearly all Italy save Rome, where the Pope with difficulty kept his foothold.

The papacy rather, for the holder of that office was changing frequently and in a summary 'the Pope' may mean different men in consecutive sentences. It was a new French Pope, Urban IV, who, in 1262, two years after Montaperti, offered the crown of Sicily to the French king's brother, Charles of Anjou; but by the time Charles had mustered an army and reached Rome it was yet another pontiff, Clement IV, who welcomed and crowned him King of Sicily. As Manfred was in the field with his army it was easier to perform the ceremony in St. Peter's than, as was more usual, in Palermo.

But Manfred had missed his chance. Charles had received large reinforcements and mustered thirty thousand men, their spirits high at the prospect of winning a kingdom under the pretext of waging a Crusade. Manfred's feudal levy, their morale lowered by eight months of indecisive manoeuvres, had no desire to die in his defence. Now, when Charles moved out of Rome, Manfred fell back, intent on barring the road south across the Apennines. Charles pressed forward, his ranks

swollen with Florentine Guelphs and even Apulian rene-
gades. Battle was joined on the plain north of Benevento. The
Saracens fought with their usual ferocity. So did the Germans.
But when Manfred gave the signal to throw in his Apulian
reserves, he was appalled to see the southerners wheel and
gallop off the field. He knew this was the end. He charged
into the mêlée and was overwhelmed. When his body was
found three days later, the chivalrous knights of Anjou urged
Charles to give it honourable burial, but Manfred had been
excommunicated and Charles dared not offend the Pope.
All he could do was to mark the unhallowed grave with a
cairn, on which every Angevin soldier threw a stone as he
marched by. Manfred's wife and daughter, with his three
illegitimate sons, were thrown into prison, from which only
the girl ever emerged alive.

One viper of the brood remained at large, most dangerous
of all, Conradin, the legitimate heir. Ghibelline sentiment
swung back to him. Emigrés streamed northwards with tales
of Angevin extortions and atrocities. Conradin, a handsome,
romantic boy of fifteen, saw himself as a predestined liberator.
Last of the Hohenstaufen, grandson of the stupendous
Frederick, great-great-grandson of Barbarossa, he would ride
forth under the eagle banner of his house and claim his
imperial heritage. His mother, his uncles, and most of the
German princes tried to dissuade him but it was useless.
With a mere four thousand men Conradin rode over the
Brenner.

The adventure, though risky, was not hopeless. Charles
was already hated. There was unrest in Sicily, the Saracens
at Lucera were in armed revolt, Tuscany was unreliable. All
over Italy, a great number of people were sitting on a great
number of fences. Though Conradin gathered strength as he
went, his southward progress would have been impossible if
all Charles' supporters had done their duty. Conradin reached
Rome and the city went wild with delight, greeting him with
flower-strewn streets, music, banners, and torchlight processions, as though the victory were already won. The Pope,
barricaded in Viterbo forty miles away, was no less wild with
chagrin.

Charles broke off his siege of the mutinous Saracens at
Lucera and rode north. The armies came face to face across

the River Salto, high in the Apennines. Charles' slightly smaller forces were veterans like himself. It was usual to divide one's array into two parts and to stay with the reserve division, ready to charge at the decisive moment. Charles, however, made up a third division which he kept out of sight under his own command, while Henry of Cousances, donning Charles' surcoat and taking the royal standard, posted himself conspicuously at the head of the second. Naturally the Angevins, still further outnumbered by the subtraction of the hidden reserve, soon gave ground. Henry of Cousances was cut down, the standard captured. Conradin's men had broken ranks to pursue the fugitives when Charles and his thousand fresh horsemen appeared from nowhere and devastatingly reversed the situation. Conradin fled to the coast but was captured before he could get a ship to Genoa. Two months later, after a formal trial, he was publicly beheaded in Naples with many of his followers. All Christendom was indignant, not so much because he had been handsome, high-spirited and only sixteen, but because the spilt blood was royal.

Charles, a penniless adventurer three years before, was now supreme in the peninsula. He had, by pitiless elimination, destroyed the 'brood of vipers'. There was still no sign of the German princes agreeing on a new emperor, no fear of competition from that quarter, and now the Pope, to whom Charles owed so much in more senses than one, died within a month of the boy for whose execution he had pressed so emphatically. Charles had lost his chief creditor, and could postpone awkward settlements. Three years passed before another Pope was chosen. The numerous French cardinals appointed by their compatriot Urban would not vote for an Italian and the native cardinals did not want another Frenchman who might be the pawn of the Angevins. When at last this party got their way, and the conciliatory Tedaldo Visconti became Gregory X, one of his first decrees established the Conclave, literally the 'lock-up', providing that, in future, when a Pope died, his cardinals should be locked up together until they agreed on a successor. To accelerate their decision, the meals taken in were to be progressively reduced in bulk and interest as the days went by.

So, from 1268 to 1271, there was neither Pope nor emperor, though the strife of Guelph and Ghibelline continued unaffected by their absence. Charles was already by papal appointment the 'Senator' or civic head of Rome for ten years. He dominated Tuscany and Central Italy, and got many of the Lombard cities to confer their *signoria,* or over-lordship, upon him. In the South he was at last in full control: even the Saracen mutineers of Lucera had laid down their arms, had been demobilized, and were now dispersed in family groups throughout the country. The capital of the Sicilian kingdom was in due course transferred to Naples, where the waterfront fortress of Castel Nuovo, built for Charles by Pierre de Chaulnes, remains a massive reminder of his heavy-handed rule.

Heavy it was. Charles brought a dour, northern efficiency to the government of his unwelcoming subjects. Much that he did was doubtless admirable. He had roads improved and harbours enlarged, himself designing a new lighthouse for Brindisi. He built ships with timber from his own forests. He encouraged mining and agriculture — it was he who introduced Barbary sheep from Africa. To all these schemes he gave tireless supervision, and, apart from one Crusade, spent all his time touring his domains.

All this was more admirable than admired. It involved heavy taxation and a complicated system of licences, controls and inspections worthy of our own century. To operate it he was forced to import French officials. Already he had dis-possessed many landowners by refusing to recognize any grants made since the Pope's 'deposition' of Frederick twenty-five years before. Seven hundred Frenchmen received fiefs in their places. When to these newcomers were added all the Florentine bankers, northern merchants, and other outsiders who flocked in, it was no wonder that the South felt the resentment of an occupied country. One of Charles' most trusted lieutenants was Guy de Montfort, an exiled survivor from Evesham, until he blotted his copybook, not so much by murdering his Plantagenet cousin, Henry of Almain, as by doing so in church at Viterbo. For this lapse of taste Guy was dismissed by Charles and assigned by Dante to the seventh circle of Hell.

Not content with Italy, Anjou and Provence, Charles began to dream of empire. He had no hopes of the Western: that vacuum was now filled by Rudolf of Habsburg, a papal nominee. But the Eastern Empire was back in the uncertain hands of the Byzantines, who, having managed after more than half a century to overthrow the regime imposed by the Fourth Crusade, were defending themselves with difficulty against Bulgarians, Tartars and Turks. It seemed to Charles a good season to launch another Crusade which should regain Constantinople for the West and win him an imperial crown, a grand conception which was by no means impracticable and would have had immeasurable historical consequences. By the spring of 1282 his preparations were complete, his main armada ready in the harbour at Messina, and a supporting convoy of ornate, castellated vessels in every Southern port, eager for the King's messenger from Naples with word to hoist their graceful lateen sails.

Simultaneously an armada was being fitted out in Aragon, ostensibly against the infidel in Africa, really against the Angevin in Sicily. The viperous brood of the Hohenstaufen was not in actual fact extinct. As Charles well knew, though he had long ceased to worry about it, Manfred had had a daughter, Constance, by his first marriage. She, twenty long years ago, had married Peter, the King of Aragon's son. After the death first of Manfred and then of Conradin, their surviving supporters had made a bee-line for Spain, where Frederick's grand-daughter became the last hope of the Hohenstaufen party. Charles had lost little sleep over their conspiracies. Constance's husband Peter could do nothing while his father lived, and the King of Aragon seemed immortal. He reigned in fact for sixty-three years and his excommunication at the end was for adultery with the wife of a vassal. When at last he died, his son succeeded to more pressing problems than the belated claim to Constance's inheritance.

Charles was wrong, though, to ignore the threat from Spain. A few years sufficed for Peter to put his own kingdom in order. Meanwhile, he sent out his agents, some to move secretly through Italy and Sicily, others to negotiate with the nervous Byzantines. It was agreed with the latter that, when Charles moved east, Peter should stab him in the back, the thrust being delivered in the softest place, Sicily, where the Angevin government was most detested.

The schemes of both sides were anticipated by unforeseen

events. The Sicilian conflagration, when it came, was touched off by spontaneous combustion.

It began on Easter Monday evening, 1282, at the hour of Vespers. The people of Palermo were taking the air, the rigours of Lent over. The free-and-easy atmosphere encouraged a besotted French sergeant to press his attentions upon a young married woman, whose husband, with the normal reflex action of his nation, promptly knifed him. A fight started, grew to a riot, and ended as a wholesale massacre of the French, whose very friars were dragged from their convents and butchered. About two thousand men, women and children died that night.

What next? The promptitude with which the revolution threw up its leaders, the decision with which they acted, show that though the incident was unpremeditated much thought had already been given to means of national liberation. Before the night was out, messengers were galloping all over the island. A commune was quickly proclaimed, and an appeal for protection drafted, not to Queen Constance or her husband, but to the Pope. Within the next few days there were risings everywhere except in Messina, where Charles' main armada lay. Everywhere else rose the cry, 'Death to the French! ' and there were savage massacres, costing perhaps another two thousand lives in all, except in two towns where the garrisons were allowed to move out unharmed. Finally, after a month Messina too rose in revolt, penned the French in the citadel, and burnt their ships.

The Sicilian idea was a federation of communes under papal protection, but the reigning Pope was again a friend of Charles and refused recognition. In July Charles crossed from the mainland, tried to storm Messina, but was beaten back. By now the Sicilians had the help of a small contingent of Aragonese 'volunteers' from North Africa where King Peter was campaigning against the Arabs. The Spaniard was biding his time. The Sicilians had committed themselves. Their hoped-for protector, the Pope, had disowned them and they now faced the vengeance of the French. Throughout August Charles stepped up the military threat to Messina, while diplomatic emissaries galloped or sailed in all directions. Then the ripe fruit dropped into Peter's patient lap: the Sicilian communes offered him the crown and he sailed across to Trapani on the western tip of the island while the siege of Messina was still at its height. It was some time before Charles heard the news and he launched a general assault in the hopes of overwhelming the citizens before they too learnt that Peter was advancing to their aid. The attack failed. Unwilling to risk a battle with Peter, Charles withdrew across the straits. He never set foot on the island again. What was more important to the general history of Europe was that this 'war of the Sicilian Vespers' caused him to abandon his Eastern designs.

The struggle dragged on for another twenty years. Queen Constance arrived at Messina with her children in April 1283, and a parliament met to settle the future. Peter's eldest son would naturally succeed to the throne of Aragon, but the second, James, would inherit Sicily, with Constance if necessary acting as regent. Meanwhile, there had been a picturesque proposal that Charles and Peter, each assisted by a team of one hundred knights, should settle the issue between them by personal combat. This chivalric encounter was fixed for 1st June at Bordeaux (then an English possession) but no hour was agreed, and this diplomatic loophole allowed each champion to appear in the lists separately, hurl defiance at his absent adversary in the prescribed terms, and claim victory by default. Four days later, far away in the Bay of Naples, there was a more serious conflict when Charles' son was lured into a naval battle by Peter's brilliant admiral, Roger of Lauria, and ignominiously taken prisoner. This disaster for the Angevins sparked off anti-French risings and massacres ashore. There was a good deal of fighting, but the Angevins managed to hold the mainland while the Sicilians, with their Aragonese protectors, kept their own island inviolate. Two years later the rival kings both died.

James gave Sicily some valuable political institutions, including a parliament on the Aragonese model. Unfortunately his elder brother died and his interest shifted to his Spanish inheritance. In 1295, as part of a larger deal, he agreed to restore the island to Anjou. This was unacceptable alike to the Sicilians themselves and to his younger brother, Frederick, whom he had left as viceroy. Frederick was popular, having grown up far more a Sicilian than a Spaniard. He proclaimed himself King and war ensued between the brothers.

Roger of Lauria won two naval battles for James, but on land Frederick was a match both for his brother and for the Angevins. The latter were routed at Falconaria, in Western Sicily, and peace was made at last in 1302, leaving Frederick king of an independent Sicily, which remained so until 1435. The Angevins kept Naples and the mainland, and somewhat confusingly continued to style themselves 'Kings of Sicily' though they did not control an acre of the island.

Rome's long vendetta against the House of Hohenstaufen — extending, as we have seen, throughout the thirteenth century — had unforeseen consequences for the Popes. They had eliminated the old imperial threat in the North, by sponsoring emperors too preoccupied in Germany to interfere in Italy. Further south, by backing the hated Angevins at all costs — even to the extent of ignoring the cry of the Sicilian patriots in 1282 — they had forfeited more and more popular sympathy. No longer did the papacy stand out as the obvious champion of the free Italian cities against foreign domination. Rather did it seem itself the agent of foreigners, not German now but French.

Even at home the Popes had forfeited the loyalty of many through the intrigues and feuds of the Curia. Not only were the French cardinals in natural opposition to the Italians, but the Italians were disunited among themselves. Two factions, the Orsini and the Colonna families, were continually at strife. This culminated in the excommunication of two Colonna cardinals and a miniature war, in which the Roman *palazzi* of their relatives were burnt, their country castles stormed, and the little town of Palestrina, of which they were lords, razed pitilessly to the ground.

When to such unstable conditions we add the uncertainties of human life and remember that the average papal reign was only a few years, we can appreciate the anxieties of other rulers whose plans and policies were inextricably involved with the papacy. One such was King Philip of France, Philip le Bel, who came into conflict with Boniface VIII when he wished to tax the clergy. It occurred to Philip that a Pope resident in France might be more amenable to reason, and he sponsored an enterprising scheme whereby Sciarra Colonna, with five hundred horsemen, should kidnap the old pontiff from his summer palace at Anagni. The coup failed through the fumblings of the conspirators, and before they could get away with their captive he was rescued by Cardinal Orsini and a posse from Rome, aided by the townspeople of Anagni. The excitement, however, had not been healthy for Boniface, and it was not long before another papal election was needed, shortly followed by yet another, which enabled Philip to attain his objective in a less melodramatic fashion.

The next Pope was a Gascon. As he was not a cardinal, the news of his election reached him at Bordeaux, where he was archbishop. Instead of starting for Italy he announced that he would be crowned at Lyons, and the cardinals, together with the Curia and all their bureaucratic apparatus, were summoned to join him in France. It was seventy years before they went back to Rome.

This was the beginning of what Petrarch called, with some exaggeration, 'the Babylonian captivity'. Of the seven Popes, all French during this period, only one made a short-lived attempt to return to Rome, and he was soon thankful to go back to Avignon, which, from 1309, was the seat of the papacy. Avignon was not strictly in Philip's kingdom. It lay within the Provençal possessions of the Angevin Kings of Naples and was further encircled on three sides by a direct papal possession, the Comtat Venaissin. But this technical independence of the French king was illusory. On the fourth side the Palace of the Popes looked straight across the Rhône to Villeneuve, where Philip's massive new castle of Saint André was an ever-present reminder of political realities.

12. A Patchwork of Cities

WHILE ANGEVINS and Aragonese fought over the South, cutting one kingdom into two, the North remained a political patchwork. Patchwork perhaps suggests too static a conception. Boundaries changed continually, weaker units were absorbed by stronger, only to regain their independence with the fortune of war or the division of a despot's power between several sons. From year to year the map resembled not so much a patchwork as some animated biological diagram, depicting cells in a feverish alternation of union and fission.

Nowhere can we isolate a clear, simple pattern. Some territories are communes, some feudal domains; for feudalism survives, though not so strong as in the old Norman South. Some states have a republican constitution which is respected, with power held firmly by the leading citizens. Others, though they retain old forms and names, are dominated by an autocrat, who may be a blue-blooded feudal lord, self-made banker, or a soldier of fortune. Each city's story is distinct, and would fill, indeed has filled, a book. Here we can only note a few general characteristics and glance at half a dozen cities to illustrate the complexity of the situation.

Every city was predominantly either Guelph or Ghibelline with the minority party usually in exile plotting revenge. The authority of Pope or emperor was taken just as seriously as the circumstances demanded. Their representatives might be welcomed with bells and strewn roses or with barred gates and showers of arrows. When it came to legal quibbles over recognition and non-recognition, the medieval Italian had nothing to learn from modern diplomacy. Essentially, each major city and its surrounding countryside, or *contado*, was independent. Even when beaten by a neighbour, it preserved its own government, merely accepting the *signoria* or 'overlordship' of the conqueror. When, as frequently happened, that conqueror was an individual despot, it was he or his nominee (not his city) who received the *signoria* as a personal acquisition. There was no administrative merger. It needed only a military defeat or an assassin's dagger and the association of the two cities was at an end.

The class-structure at least was consistent. Each community was a triangle of forces. First, there were the feudal nobility, fighting the usual rearguard action against the advance of capitalism. Their town houses were miniature fortresses with tall slender towers commanding the adjacent alleyways and rooftops. Florence, by 1200, had seventy-five such towers. Later on, even the much smaller town of San Gimignano boasted seventy-six, of which thirteen survive today. The families living in such houses were called the *società delle torre*, 'tower-folk', rather like the 'carriage-folk' of Victorian England.

Opposed to this declining aristocracy was the ascendant bourgeoisie of bankers and merchants. The massive *palazzo communale,* still with its square or swallow-tailed battlements a dominant feature of Florence, Siena, Perugia and other cities, was the middle-class answer to the petty strongholds of the nobility. The *palazzo communale* was at once a guild hall and a party headquarters. In towns where Guelphs and Ghibellines achieved co-existence, each party might possess such a building.

No such impressive architectural memorial exists to the third class, the small traders and workmen. Theirs was a hole-and-corner existence, without political rights or economic security. Housing was squalid, wages low, conditions repressive, unemployment frequent. Sometimes the men were goaded to strike, but more often they migrated with incurable optimism to another town. It was not only Giotto and the artists whose labour was mobile. The nameless also were on the road in their thousands. Local patriotism was the luxury of the prosperous, and against the fierce civic individualism of these states we must set that feeling of a common culture which enabled not only scholars, artists and political exiles to change their addresses freely and frequently, but journeymen and labourers too.

These, then, were the three classes. Most commonly, the middle class held political control, and the nobility from time to time sought the incongruous partnership of the workers against them. The mutual distrust of the three sections was shown in the substitution of mercenaries for the old militia. The time had long gone by when the able-bodied men of the city turned out with unanimous enthusiasm to beat off a common enemy. Wars were fought over remote and complex issues. As a rule the bankers and big business-men favoured wars, as likely to win new foreign markets and damage their competitors. The shipping interests did well out of any sea-borne crusades, and conflicts irrelevant to Italy offered a profitable opening for loans, whether of money or of mercenaries who would otherwise have been eating their heads off at public expense. Edward III of England borrowed 1,365,000 gold florins from the Florentine bankers to finance his adventures in France, and his royal opponent hired from Genoa those crossbowmen who were so impressively outshot by the English archers at Crécy.

The rising middle class of Italy were not inclined to do any fighting themselves; nor were the lower orders, who had a shrewd instinct that none of the profit would trickle down to them. Only the nobles were eager for military service, being fit for little else, but the business-men could not trust their traditional enemies. They preferred a characteristically commercial solution, putting out the city's defence to contract. A professional *condottiere* or soldier of fortune, with a few hundred mercenaries, disciplined, skilful, toughened by innumerable campaigns, could make mincemeat of conscripted amateurs. Many mercenaries were German, like the notorious Company of Baumgarten, but there was the Company of the Star from Provence and the White Company of Sir John Hawkwood, the Essex-born veteran of Crécy and Poitiers, who, after fighting impartially for several Italian states against each other, completed sixty years of campaigning as the servant of Florence. A foreigner like Hawkwood had no political preference beyond a vested interest in strife and suspicion between the cities, but the native *condottiere* introduced a fresh variation.

When oligarchy gave place to a single despot, he might be a pedigreed nobleman (Este of Ferrara) or an archbishop (Visconti of Milan) or a parvenu (della Scala of Verona), but he might also be an adventurer like Castruccio Castracane of

Pisa. Elsewhere, as in Venice, the oligarchy might never lose power at all.

The political forms varied locally, but two officials were usually found at the head of affairs. There was the *podestà*, by tradition an unbiased outsider. At Verona he served for a year and received 4,000 lire, with free board and lodging for his staff, but was forbidden to bring wife or family with him, to dine out, or to accept presents. His year of office must have been somewhat austere, but it was the only way to prevent corruption. The very success of this institution was its own undoing. The ruling clique found that a supreme magistrate who was above party might sound admirable but was in fact highly inconvenient. They therefore created the second post, that of *Capitano del Popolo*, a professed partisan, whose prime duty was to promote 'the will of the people'. Out of this office, which gradually gained in real importance at the expense of the theoretically senior post, the permanent despotisms developed.

We might turn now from the generalized picture to a few particular cities.

· · · · · · · ·

Florence already possessed many of the landmarks which, however altered, are known to the modern traveller. The Bargello was begun in 1254 as a palace for the *podestà*. The Palazzo Vecchio and the cathedral were under construction when Dante left Florence for ever in 1301. Between these years the various religious orders had vied with one another in church building, the Franciscans with the restoration of Santa Croce, the Dominicans with Santa Maria Novella, the Cistercians with Santa Trinità. The octagonal Romanesque Baptistery had already stood for centuries in the heart of the city, but it was not until about 1336 that Andrea Pisano executed the earliest of the famous bronze doors, which originally hung on the side facing the new cathedral. There, just across the road, his master Giotto was simultaneously at work on the bell-tower which he was destined to continue. And down by the river the city fathers were, no doubt, shaking their heads over the bridge, which had to be rebuilt in 1345 as the present Ponte Vecchio.

This was the Florence Boccaccio knew. Born in Paris in

1313, he was brought home to his father's native city and educated. As a young man he spent some time at Naples, but in 1348, the year of the Black Death, he finally returned to Florence on the death of his father. The plague hit Florence as hard as the rest of Europe, killing perhaps a third of her hundred thousand people. The personal effect upon Boccaccio was not entirely unhappy. He at once began to write, or rewrite, the hundred short stories of the *Decameron,* linking them with a narrative thread suggested by the recent pestilence. From his father, a rich merchant, he received an inheritance which not only freed him for his own writing but enabled him to indulge his passion for collecting Greek and Latin manuscripts, and in due course to establish a professorship of Greek literature in Florence. The Revival of Learning was already in the air. Only three years after Boccaccio's death, the Loggia dei Lancei, that graceful forerunner of Renaissance architecture, was begun.

The original prosperity of Florence was based on textiles. She imported wool from Flanders, Spain, Portugal, and eventually England. Two hundred workshops turned it into cloth and soon the merchants had their subsidiary workshops, staffed with skilled Florentines, in England, France and Holland. The minor guild of *ciompi,* or wool-carders, formed the organized part of the city's proletariat. Their short-lived revolt in 1378, under an outstanding leader, Michael Lando, who soon became disgusted with their violence and went into exile, was one of the rare mass movements of the age, preceding by just three years the Londoners' rising at the time of Wat Tyler.

Soon banking was added to textiles. Fleece and florin made Florence ever greater. Her merchants evolved the new capitalism, worked out the ABC of stocks and shares, currency manipulation and foreign credits. They abolished serfdom in 1289 and decreed that no one could vote or be eligible for office unless he belonged to a guild, thus neatly disfranchising the nobility unless they were prepared to pocket their pride and join the Skinners, Furriers, Bankers, Clothiers, or one of the other organizations. Active participation in the business was no more obligatory than it is today in the Livery Companies of the City of London, which preserve several fossilized characteristics of Florence seven centuries ago.

Dante participated in the civic government as Prior of the Apothecaries' Guild, but there is no record of his ever dispensing a prescription. By vesting power in the major guilds, a few thousand Florentines created a closed shop for themselves in the political sphere.

Except for a brief interlude after the Ghibelline victory at Montaperti in 1260, they were staunchly Guelph and as papal bankers could not afford to be otherwise. But, with a characteristic Italian impatience of monotony, the Guelph party soon divided into two antagonistic wings, the Blacks and the Whites, whose sanguinary feuds amply made up for the absence of Ghibelline opposition. In 1301 Pope Boniface, who had a scheme of his own to bring Florence under his domination, persuaded the citizens to receive an arbitrator in the person of Charles of Valois, brother to King Philip le Bel and an Angevin leader in the last episode of the Sicilian conflict. Charles used his position in Florence to bring off an armed coup. The government of the Whites was overthrown, six hundred of their supporters exiled, and their leaders, including Dante, sentenced in absence to death by burning. Charles went on his way, leaving the Blacks firmly in control. As a consequence the outlawed White Guelphs were forced into sympathy with the Ghibellines, and when a few years later the Emperor Henry VII came over the Alps in a final, fruitless attempt to reassert the old imperial authority, Dante hailed him as 'Bridegroom of Italy and Solace of the World', even when he tried to besiege Florence. Henry's effort to turn back the clock ended in a fatal bout of fever near Siena, and the poet's chance of a triumphant homecoming faded for ever.

.   .   .   .

Verona, one of Dante's refuges in exile, presents a contrast to Florence in several respects.

Nearness to the Brenner made her traditionally Ghibelline: had she been Guelph, she would have had the unenviable honour of the first blow from each invading emperor. This position also gave her commercial importance. Traders converged from all quarters on Verona. Their operations were severely controlled. Each foreigner had to lodge at the inn assigned to his nationality. The landlord was held responsible for his behaviour and strict regulations debarred him from activities which competed with those of the local merchants. These merchants, through their guild, provided each inn with interpreters. The Germans alone had four.

Verona, again unlike Florence, had accepted the benevolent despotism of a single family, the della Scalas, whose ladder emblem was both a pun upon their name and a symbol of their social ascension. The founder of the dynasty was Mastino, who came of a family of lawyers and business-men. He was serving as *podestà* of a small town thirty miles away when, in 1259, he was offered, unusually, the same honour in his native city. Three years later he was proclaimed 'Perpetual Captain of the Veronese People', and in 1277 he was succeeded by his brother, Alberto, who ruled Verona until 1301. Altogether, eight successive della Scalas governed the city from 1259 to 1375. Then the line petered out ingloriously under two illegitimate sons of Can Signorio, one of whom murdered the other and died in exile in 1388, when Verona lost her independence, first to the Visconti of Milan and soon afterwards to Venice.

The most noteworthy of these despots, Can Grande I, Dante's patron, ruled from 1311 to 1329. His quaint name ('Big Dog') echoed that of his uncle Mastino ('Mastiff') and was commemorated in the canine crest which he and his successors bore on their helmets. Can Grande would have adorned any boys' adventure story. He despised soft living and adored pugnacious action. He took Vicenza in his first three months and spent the rest of his reign campaigning to conquer Padua and Treviso. His life was full of disguises, stratagems, headlong gallops and fearless exploits. He was always first in the charge, first into the moat or river, first up the scaling ladder. Perhaps the most remarkable thing about him was that he lasted for eighteen years and died in his bed.

This fire-eater was, by the undemanding standards of his time, comparatively humane and moral. He had no love of unnecessary bloodshed and, victory won, would check the pursuit. Generous and loyal to friends, he was fair — if formidable — to his opponents. His gay smile won forgiveness for his quick temper, while his free-and-easy manner gained him the devotion of all classes.

Can Grande's interests went far beyond war and sport—though he did keep three hundred falcons and innumerable hounds and hunters. He loved literature and intellectual conversation. The Veronese themselves preferred tournaments and had to import troubadours. At least Can Grande's encouragement made his court a rendezvous for writers from elsewhere. Dante spent little time there himself but wrote regularly from Ravenna, sending Can Grande his *Paradiso* a few cantos at a time as written.

Not least of Can Grande's achievements was his protection of the trader. He agreed with the Venetians to guarantee the safe transit of merchandise between their city and Bergamo. Every other week, if the freight justified it, an escorted convoy started from either terminal, the Venetians supplying guards as far as Verona, and Can Grande for the rest of the journey. A minimum convoy was twenty-five wagon-loads of Italian cloth or eighty of miscellaneous goods. Can Grande charged toll according to the contents of the wagon, four florins for spice or cloth, a florin and a half for salt, and so on.

Other revenue came from central taxation, special imposts, private rents, mineral rights, monopolies and legal fees. The army was at first maintained by militia levies from Verona and the lesser towns which came under della Scala rule. Each place had to contribute not only so many infantrymen, crossbowmen, and sappers, but a full complement of military 'tradesmen', including a surgeon, and a meticulously detailed list of supplies, ranging from a hundred wagon-loads of corn or wine to twelve pounds of crossbow cord, four demolition tools, and two pounds of glue. Cavalry were seldom asked for: most governments preferred professionals, usually Germans. As time went on the citizens found it more convenient to supply money instead of men; the army lost all resemblance to a feudal levy and was recruited entirely from mercenaries.

· · · · · · ·

The biggest inland city was Milan which, with 200,000 population, equalled Florence and Verona combined. Here there was rivalry between the Guelph family of della Torre and the Ghibelline Visconti, who gained the upper hand in 1277 under Archbishop Ottone Visconti. His great-nephew, Matteo, was ejected in 1307 by Guido della Torre, who, supported by a personal bodyguard of a thousand mercenaries, got himself elected Captain of the People for life, with a free hand to rewrite the city statutes. But after four years Matteo turned the tables, and the Visconti family was back to stay.

They were aggressive, like Can Grande, but on a larger scale. Azzo Visconti, ruling from 1328 to 1339, conquered ten cities, murdered one of his uncles, and was, with poetic justice, succeeded by two others. The second of these, Giovanni, who combined the archbishopric with the secular power, dominated most of Northern Italy by the time of his death in 1354. His lands were divided between three nephews, of whom the most remarkable, the handsome Galeazzo II, kept a brilliant court in Pavia, founded a university there, and continued his uncle's friendship with Petrarch. Edward III of England did not disdain Galeazzo's daughter as bride for his son, the Duke of Clarence, or the useful dowry of 200,000 gold florins promised with her. Milan was treated to a spectacular June wedding. Unhappily the groom died in the following October, almost before the festivities were completed.

The recurrent problem of the Visconti was the division of territory when a ruler left more than one son. This produced a tendency to murder uncles. Following Galeazzo's death, Pavia was ruled by his son Gian Galeazzo, while his uncle Bernabò, who had five sons, continued to hold sway in Milan. Bernabò sought to bring Pavia into his orbit by marrying his daughter Caterina to his nephew, but Gian Galeazzo outwitted him, put him and his sons to death, and entered Milan as a popular liberator, a reputation he consolidated by a judicious distribution from Bernabò's treasury and by favouring the bourgeoisie against the nobility.

Gian Galeazzo was a single-minded statesman of great intellectual power. The aggrandisement of his state was his compelling interest. He relaxed only in books and scholarly conversation, having no taste for sport, women or frivolities. Like a new Philip of Macedon he relied on treachery to open city gates to his soldiers. He drove the last della Scala bastard from Verona and went on to take Padua. After a pause for digestion he swallowed Pisa, Siena, Perugia, Lucca, Bologna. He was attacking Florence in 1402 when he died, having hammered out for his son, Filippo Maria, a dominion as durable as the armour for which Milan was renowned.

.   .   .   .

The maritime cities, Pisa, Genoa, and Venice, seemed less prone to despotism. All were immensely wealthy and avidly competitive, reaching throughout the known world in quest of markets. Their ship-builders were quick to learn from those of Northern Europe. Early in the fourteenth century they began to imitate the square-sailed, stern-ruddered cogs introduced to the Mediterranean by the pirates of Bayonne.

Their merchantmen — two- and three-masted vessels up to eighty-five feet long — transported not only goods but armies; their lean war-galleys could be hired like mercenaries, and constantly were. The Emperor Henry IV used Pisan galleys to attack Naples, and Genoese to capture the ports of Sicily; Charles of Anjou called in Pisa, Genoa and Venice too, to replace the fleet he lost at Messina after the Vespers.

In 1135 the Pisans (this time commissioned by the Pope to fight the Normans) took the opportunity to smash their nearest business rival, Amalfi. Thereafter Pisa enjoyed an unparalleled prosperity, which reached its apex early in the thirteenth century. Then, with an opulent gesture, her merchants brought fifty-three shiploads of earth from Jerusalem to make the Campo Santo graveyard, wherein the humblest citizen might sleep with an enhanced prospect of Paradise, though the best positions, under the surrounding arcades added later, were reserved for people of means. Work was in progress on the three adjacent buildings which are today so impressive a memorial to Pisan greatness — the circular baptistery, the cathedral, and the eight-tiered campanile, already leaning at the familiar angle, though the architect had not yet given up hope of correcting it.

This was the age of Niccolo Pisano, who, whether actually a native of the city or not, was specially identified with it. He and his son Giovanni revived the art of sculpture and launched the movement which was carried on by Giovanni's pupil Andrea and the latter's sons. The 'Pisani' worked all over Italy, turning their versatile hands to a fountain at Perugia, a pulpit at Siena, or a castle at Naples for Frederick II or Charles of Anjou. In Pisa itself Niccolo carved the baptistery pulpit which Sir Kenneth Clark has called 'that false dawn of the Renaissance'. Giovanni carved the pulpit in the cathedral, and both father and son worked on the building itself.

Pisa's glory endured two centuries. Always a bitter rival of Genoa, she earned in time the hatred of her inland neighbour, Florence; for it irked the Florentines to have a Ghibelline seaport straddling the Arno and blocking their outlet to the sea. Threatened from both sides, the outnumbered Pisans engaged the Genoese in a tremendous naval battle near Meloria, a craggy islet off the Tuscan coast. Their fleet was annihilated, only a dozen ships escaping out of more than a hundred. Eleven thousand prisoners were carried off to Genoa and it was said bitterly, 'Who would see Pisa, let him go to Genoa.' One of the commanders who survived was a nobleman of Guelph sympathies, Ugolino della Gherardesca, and in the moment of disaster it seemed best to put the government in his hands, as the man most likely to secure merciful treatment from the Guelphs of Florence. Ugolino unscrupulously used this opportunity to establish a personal dictatorship, deliberately obstructing the release of the prisoners at Genoa because he knew that his power would not survive their repatriation. He was overthrown in a Ghibelline counter-revolution led by his enemy, Archbishop Ruggieri, who, having imprisoned him in the Gualandi Tower with his sons and grandsons, threw the dungeon key into the Arno and left them all to slow death by starvation.

The Genoese were now supreme on the west coast but in ever acuter rivalry with Venice. Their widely scattered outposts included former Saracen strongholds in Spain and North Africa, fortresses in the Levant, the Peloponnese and the Crimea, on the Euphrates and the Don. In Constantinople they enjoyed extra-territorial rights over the walled suburb of Galata, their Venetian competitors being no less firmly entrenched in another quarter of the city. Their enterprising navigators discovered the Canary Islands and the Azores; one, Vivaldo, anticipated the explorers of two centuries later by seeking an Atlantic route to India, but never returned.

Civic affairs were turbulent with family feud and class struggle. There were two predominant Ghibelline families, Doria and Spinola, and two Guelph, Grimaldi and Fieschi, but, with that contrariness which repeatedly frustrates any effort to simplify the chronicles of Italy, the main battle for power was between the two Ghibelline houses, each seconded by one of the Guelph. In 1339 the people sought stability by electing a doge, Simon Boccanegra, then popular for his victories over the Moors, Turks and Tartars, but now better remembered as the inspiration of Verdi's opera. Boccanegra was elected for life, but compelled to resign after five years, only to be recalled from his retirement in Pisa when the political pendulum swung back in 1355.

The conflict with Venice continued through the thirteenth and fourteenth centuries, open war alternating with hypocritical peace. Neither city could assail the other by land: Genoa's mountain-wall, the *corniche*, was a defence no less effective than the Venetian lagoons; only the hapless Pisans had had an open plain at their back door. So, instead, the Genoese and the Venetians fought in every sea where their interests clashed. If dissension split the Byzantine Empire they were to be found inevitably supporting rival factions. Had the chance offered, they might have fought as cheerfully for York and Lancaster.

The fortune of war swung fairly evenly. In 1298 the Genoese were victorious at Curzola in the Adriatic, but there was only one permanent consequence: the eight thousand Venetian prisoners included Marco Polo, who had been given command of a warship after his recent return from China, and his enforced leisure now led him to dictate his travel experiences to Rusticiano of Pisa. In 1353 it was the turn of Venice to win a sea-fight off Sardinia with the help of Aragon, but in the following year the Genoese got their revenge at Sapienza, off the Peloponnesian coast. These three battles sufficiently illustrate the geographical range of the conflict. The decisive round came in 1379 and 1380.

Nominally, the war broke out over the Greek island of Tenedos and a massacre of Genoese in Cyprus, but very soon it was raging at the sea-gates of Venice herself. The Venetian admiral, Vettor Pisani, overruled by the Senate, reluctantly accepted battle. His fleet was annihilated, he reached port with only six vessels, and his government, determined to save their own faces, clapped him into prison. The triumphant

Genoese admiral, Pietro Doria, aware that the rest of the Venetian navy was in the Levant, sailed through the southern gaps in the Lido into the great lagoon itself and captured the islands of Pellestrina and Chioggia, not twenty miles from the city.

For once, if only briefly, the Venetians despaired of their city. Envoys were sent to Doria, asking for terms, which he refused. He had come, he told the envoys, to bridle those horses in front of San Marco. He settled down to wait until his blockade should enforce complete surrender.

That was late summer. The Venetians made good use of the next few months. A message was sent to Carlo Zeno, the other admiral, recalling him and his fleet from the Levant. An unsuccessful attempt was made to secure the professional services of Sir John Hawkwood. Finally Vettor Pisani was released and restored to his command, where his popularity did much to raise morale. A palisade was built across the channel from San Spirito to the Lido, a new fleet of thirty-four galleys was somehow fitted out and manned, and even small boats were mobilized to harass the besiegers. As Christmas approached it was touch and go whether Zeno would arrive before the Genoese attacked again. On the evening of December 23rd Pisani took a chance, slipped out with his scratch fleet into the Adriatic, and, by scuttling two stone-filled hulks in the channel from Chioggia, blockaded the blockaders.

It was an impudent gamble, doomed unless Zeno arrived. Doge Andrea Contarini, who was over seventy, showed his faith in Pisani by coming with him, and vowing not to return unless victorious. But the flotilla's position was exposed both to the weather and to the primitive cannon of the enemy, provisions were scanty, and there was soon a murmur of mutiny. Sadly the doge warned the admiral that if Zeno did not arrive by New Year's Day not only the adventure but the city of Venice itself must be abandoned, and the capital of the republic moved to Crete. The miracle happened. Zeno's galleys were sighted on the morning of January 1st. The tables were now completely turned. The Genoese were attacked at Chioggia, Doria killed. In June, the Genoese surrendered, and this was virtually the end of their naval greatness. Thereafter, though their nominal independence survived until Napoleon, they were usually subservient to a stronger neighbour, France or Milan.

Thus, by the close of the fourteenth century, Venice was unrivalled amongst the maritime republics. She had regained with interest the supremacy won in the Fourth Crusade and largely lost when the Greeks had recovered Constantinople from the Latins in 1261. Soon enough she would face other competition, when the Turks blocked her trade-routes to the East, when the Portuguese found an alternative route via the Cape, and when the Spaniards (ironically, under a Genoese) sought another such route but found America. In Italy, though, she no longer had a competitor. From 1338 onwards, too, she had been enlarging her mainland territories, primarily at the expense of Verona, until by 1405 that city, together with Padua and Vicenza, came under her sway.

The independence of Venice was always her salient characteristic. Guelph-Ghibelline squabbles meant nothing to her. This impartiality caused her citizens to be in great demand by Bologna, and other cities requiring a really neutral *podestà*. Similarly, the cities of the Lombard League favoured Venetian banks for the deposit of their funds. The Venetian gold ducat, first struck in 1282, was the one currency which could hold its own with the earlier florin, and was minted with that object. She was independent even of the Pope. No priest or bishop served in the city unless Venetian-born, and it was abundantly demonstrated that his first loyalty was to the republic.

This independence was less evident in the life of the individual. Venice anticipated the totalitarian state. The marble lion's mouth, letter-box for anonymous denunciations, was the vivid symbol of her elaborate police system, embodying spies at home and abroad, informers, and assassins ready to liquidate disloyal elements at any distance and any risk. A Murano glassworker who quitted Venice with his trade secrets was self-convicted as a public enemy and was liable to come to a violent end in whatever distant city he tried to start a new life. Yet we should not allow the lion's mouth and the later 'Bridge of Sighs' to give us too ugly an impression of the republic. Her severities were at least dictated by public policy, not by the caprice of some perverted individual. The object in many cases was the maintenance of honest standards and the good reputation of Venice. If punishments were often terrible, it was because no one in that age ever questioned the efficacy of deterrence. Usually there was full investigation and patient trial, with a conscientious observance of the rules. The treatment of prisoners was relatively humane. The doge's coronation-oath made him individually responsible for persons in custody and for bringing them to trial within a month.

No republican constitution could have been less democratic. All power rested with the top families. They formed the Great Council, which rose in time to over a thousand members. A *serrata,* or 'closed shop', was established in 1297, after which recruitment was entirely hereditary. Every member had to report his marriage and children for inclusion in the *Libro d'Oro,* which was at once the electoral register and the stud-book of Venetian society.

Even the 'Most Serene Republic' could not entirely escape the occasional bread-riot or political conspiracy and the normally stable government was shaken by a brief but bloody insurrection in 1310. Thereafter executive power was concentrated in the Council of Ten, elected from the Great Council with elaborate and typically Venetian safeguards. No two members of one family could serve at the same time, membership was for one year only without re-election, there was no pay, and it was a capital offence to accept any sort of gift. The Council elected three of its members as joint leaders, serving a month at a time, during which they were forbidden to visit shops or public places where they might be accessible to corruption. If any relative of a member was accused before the Council, that member was bound to withdraw during the case. The doge and six of his privy council attended *ex officio* and a watching brief was held by a law officer, without vote, to see that all the regulations were observed.

The efficacy of this system was demonstrated in 1355, when the new doge, Marin Faliero, planned a coup which would have made him a despot. A large-scale revolutionary organization was created. Ingenious tricks were used to discredit the oligarchy and win mass sympathy: hired agents impersonated well-known noblemen and roistered through the streets at night, addressing each other loudly by their assumed names and molesting harmless people. But the Ten proved equal to the situation. The plot was detected, prompt measures taken. By dawn the doge was under arrest. He was tried by the Council, who wisely co-opted twenty more of the most respected citizens. Twenty-four hours later he was beheaded on his palace staircase, where so lately he had sworn to defend the constitution. So powerful was the Venetian respect for that constitution, so traumatic the realization that a doge could betray it, that the sentence was not recorded in the Council minutes, but only the words, *Let it not be written.*

Trade was subject to a good deal of governmental organization. Ships were state property, though chartered to private merchants of proved standing. At her zenith the republic sent out half a dozen annual convoys, each comprising several hundred vessels. One went to the Black Sea, another braved the Atlantic to visit the ports of Flanders and England. There was strict standardization, inspection and control, punctilious regard not only for the reputation of Venice but for the welfare of her seamen. Everything was taken care of. At Southampton, for instance, the Venetians reserved a burial vault for their nationals in North Stoneham Church.

The wealth which these thousands of vessels carried back to the long quays of Venice was unimaginable. The city burgeoned into magnificence as the first Rialto Bridge replaced the old pontoon and new Gothic *palazzi* sprang up along the shimmering canals.

·   ·   ·   ·   ·   ·   ·   ·

In sad contrast to all this thrustful prosperity was the stagnation of Rome. Her staple industry was, put bluntly, the papacy with all its many material by-products, and after 1309 these were transferred to Avignon. The papal states had disintegrated until only two castles acknowledged the Pope's remote authority. In the forsaken city this was still accepted in theory. There was a senator whom he nominated, King Robert of Naples picking up this additional title in 1313, but in practice there was anarchy. The old nobility did as they liked, making themselves private strongholds from the massive ruins of antiquity. The Colonna family adapted the mausoleum of Augustus, the Orsini fortified Pompey's theatre, others converted temples, baths, and even triumphal arches.

Lesser folk lived timorously where they could in holes and corners. At one stage the population of this ghost-town sank to a mere twenty thousand.

What could be done? Was the eternal city to perish after all? Men recalled the golden days before the departure of the Popes. The year 1300 had been especially golden, for it had been declared a jubilee, with plenary indulgence for all pilgrims visiting St. Peter's. There had been two million of them, their gifts clinking and scintillating in heaps before the altars, the attendants wielding long rakes as though for autumn leaves. Even the humble coppers had been equal to fifty thousand gold florins. The total benefit, to Church and tourism, had baffled estimate.

Why, someone asked in 1343, wait till 1400 for another Holy Year? Surely the interval was unnecessarily long? Millions of the faithful were automatically denied the chance of earning plenary indulgence for their sins. A jubilee in 1400 was of no more use to them than to the present inn-keepers and tradesmen of Rome. Let a spokesman be sent to Avignon with a respectful suggestion: would His Holiness declare 1350 a Holy Year and return for the celebrations?

The man chosen was a persuasive young lawyer, Cola di Rienzi, who was later to inspire Bulwer Lytton and Wagner as much as he inspired Petrarch and the mass of his contemporaries. Son of a tavern-keeper and a washerwoman, Rienzi was well qualified to represent the interests of tourism. His brother had died in a street-fight, victim of some aristocratic vendetta. Rienzi had been quite unable to secure justice, and this fact, added to the marked contempt with which the nobility treated him, gave him a sharpened class-consciousness.

At Avignon he made a deep impression upon Clement VI, who saw that a jubilee might revive both the morale and the finances of the Church. The papacy had recently been under heavy criticism. Marsiglio of Padua in *Defensor Pacis* had submitted the relations of Church and state to an all too acute examination. The unruly Franciscans were once more in revolt. Their doctrine of Poverty had been declared heretical by a Dominican Inquisitor, and the then Pope, John XXII, having in his eighteen-year reign amassed twenty-five million gold florins, had found it hard to disagree with the Dominican. Clement had inherited the ill-feeling but not the florins. He announced that a 1350 jubilee would be an admirable idea, though he did not see his way to being present.

Rienzi's reception at Avignon and on his return to Rome encouraged him to go further. He was well read in the Latin classics which his generation (he was born in the same year as Boccaccio) was eagerly rediscovering. His study of Livy and Cicero made him ache to revive the ancient glories. The impending jubilee furnished a text on which to preach. How could Rome, in her present condition, welcome millions of pilgrims? Even a chamber of commerce would have seen that the case for reform was unanswerable.

Rienzi was handsome, brilliant, eloquent, idealistic. He hypnotized the masses, he had charmed the Pope himself. With these two assets he assumed power in 1347, styling himself 'by the grace of Jesus Christ, Severe and Merciful, the Tribune of Freedom, Peace and Justice, and the Liberator of the Holy Roman Republic'. He expounded his policy to a mass meeting on the Capitol. The power of the nobility was to be broken. Bridges, gates and strong places were to be taken over by the people's militia, the safety of the roads ensured, banditry put down, murderers executed. Rome was to be made once more the capital of a unified 'Sacred Italy'.

The nobles sneered but dared not refuse the oath of allegiance. Many of their private towers were at once pulled down and an energetic start made in cleaning up the city's affairs.

Rienzi's meteoric rise made him giddy. Soon he was a prey to delusions of grandeur and religious megalomania. To his earlier titles he added 'Candidate of the Holy Spirit, Friend of the World, Tribune Augustus', claiming that he was filled with the Holy Ghost and that his true father had been the Emperor Henry VII, which, though highly unlikely, was not geographically impossible. He flaunted his power by arresting the principal nobles and sending them to the scaffold — and then paraded his magnanimity by pardoning them at the last moment and giving them high positions in the government. The Colonnas and Orsinis were not to be won over by such cheap tricks. There was a counter-revolution and a bloody battle at the San Lorenzo Gate, in which the citizens slaughtered so many nobles that the old Roman aristocracy never fully recovered. But Rienzi himself was no hero, and his conduct disgusted his followers. When news came that the Pope had disowned him and was threatening excommunication, Rienzi abdicated, slipped out of the city, and spent the next few years in the wilderness of the Abruzzi.

The Holy Year was duly celebrated, despite the disruption of the Black Death in 1348 and 1349. The pilgrims flowed in: the two-million mark was reached at Whitsuntide. But all remarked upon the roofless churches and general decay. Law and order hardly existed, and many must have regretted Rienzi's fall. The Pope had sent two cardinals to dispense indulgences on his behalf. One was driven from the city by a howling mob and the other, having had his hat transfixed by an arrow, never appeared again without wearing a helmet under it and a mail shirt beneath his robe. At one stage the Pope had to place the irreverent city under an interdict for a week, Holy Year or no Holy Year, and when he died during the summer, with several of his relatives, poison was credibly suspected. Otherwise, the jubilee was a success and achieved its main material objectives.

Restoring papal authority in the countryside was a longer task. The next Pope gave it to a Spanish cardinal, Albornoz, who besides being a fine administrator had fought successfully against the Moors. Albornoz took with him Rienzi, who had reached Avignon after various adventures and regained favour through the change in Popes. While the cardinal was energetically suppressing the rebellious country barons, he sent Rienzi to Rome as senator. Perhaps he hoped that Rienzi's demagogic appeal would be of temporary value in winning over the city. Perhaps he thought it was the best way to get rid of an embarrassment. For the idealist had gone to seed. He was drinking hard, he looked bloated and debauched. Despite a tumultuous welcome home, he lasted just two months. Then an even more tumultuous assembly stormed the Capitol, crying 'Death to the tyrant!' Rienzi put on his armour, came out on his balcony, and attempted the old magnetism, but attracted only a volley of stones and arrows. He tried to escape in disguise, cutting off his beard and dirtying his face, but his gold bracelets were noticed, and he was stabbed to death at the foot of the palace steps.

Albornoz continued with the restoration of order. In Rome

he set up a popular government from which the uncontrollable aristocrats were specifically excluded. In the papal states
he patiently reduced castle after castle, town after town, until
after fourteen years, when the Pope at last revisited Rome
in 1367, the cardinal was able to welcome him with a wagon-
load of surrendered keys. Having made this impressive report
of his stewardship, Albornoz died a few months later.

The next decade saw much of his work undone. The Pope
went back to die in Avignon and his successor was content to
send legates to his Italian territories. These men were corrupt, immoral and cruel. Also they were French. Their
maladministration stirred the people to revolt. The last straw
was their cynical employment of the godless mercenary Free
Companies to restore their authority. When the Legate of
Bologna sent Hawkwood trespassing into Florentine territory,
the normally Guelph Florentines forgot their devotion to the
papacy. They summoned all Central Italy to arms, sending
out a great red banner inscribed with the word *Liberty* in
silver letters. Eighty cities, including Bologna herself, threw
out their papal garrisons. Hawkwood replied with a massacre
of four thousand people at Faenza, but his English cut-
throats could not terrorize a whole population.

What was the Pope to do? Men like Albornoz did not grow
on every tree. Other legates had shown the danger of sending
the wrong men to Italy. Surely the Pope should go in person?
Petrarch, for all his own attachment to Provence, had urged it
until his dying day. Now a new voice was heard, that of a
working-class Dominican nun, Catherine of Siena, today the
patron saint of Italy. She travelled to Avignon, and begged
Gregory to return to Rome and bring peace to the agonized
peninsula. Gregory was impressed. He did in fact return,
early in 1377, though he took the precaution of sending a
horde of Breton mercenaries to supplement the carnage
wrought by the English Company.

It was almost an accident that the papal exile ended that
year. The Curia, comfortably entrenched in Avignon, had
always resisted the idea of change, and after a couple of
months the Pope, with peace discussions already under way,
was planning a return to his palace beside the Rhône. Suddenly he was taken ill and died. As a result, the election had
to be held in Rome, with a mob outside clamouring that the

new Pope should be a Roman or at least an Italian. Thus was the French sequence broken at last.

The choice fell on the Archbishop of Bari, who became Urban VI. But thirteen opposition cardinals held their own conclave at Fondi, in the Pontine marshes, declared the election invalid, and chose one of themselves, Cardinal Robert of Geneva, as Pope Clement VII. Urban had, in his first few months, proved so unfortunate a choice that even the Italian cardinals now swung round and endorsed the change, but he deftly overcame this difficulty by creating a complete new college of twenty-eight cardinals.

Each Pope promptly excommunicated his rival and engaged the services of the most savage Free Company available. Urban's Italian mercenaries having trounced Clement's Bretons, Clement withdrew to Avignon, where he was recognized by France, Savoy, Naples, Spain and Scotland, while the emperor, England, Hungary and Scandinavia followed the remainder of Italy in supporting Urban. This was the start of the Great Schism which lasted for the next forty years.

13. Quattrocento

THE FIFTEENTH century or *Quattrocento* ('the four hundreds') as the Italians term it, somewhat confusingly to our ears, is a period of special brilliance. Between 1400 and 1500 the Renaissance flowered and fruited. The seeds, carried northwards over Europe, produced later crops there, but by the time those first seedlings were springing up in, say, early Tudor England, the Renaissance was over in Italy.

Politically, the *Quattrocento* saw a progressive tendency for the smaller states to become absorbed in the larger. The patchwork gradually simplifies. The first half of the century, up to the Peace of Lodi in 1454, is one of incessant, bewildering warfare, which makes sense to us only because we know the solution to which it was all tending. That solution is the division of Italy into five main blocs, which find it good business, at least for the time being, to respect each other's sphere of influence. The five blocs are the Kingdom of Naples, the Duchy of Milan, the Republics of Florence and Venice, and the Papal States of Romagna, in which many cities are ruled by local despots whom the Popes recognize as 'Vicars' because they are powerless to displace them. Besides the big five a limited number of independent states survive, varying from the secondary but not inconsiderable cities of Genoa and Lucca and the Este domains round Ferrara to the microcosmic San Marino. This simplified pattern is achieved only by half a century of fighting, in which not only the *condottieri* continually change sides like transferred footballers but so do the belligerent states themselves. It is an intricate dance, full of twists and turns, of purely formal hand-clasps and exchange of partners. To follow the details would make us dizzy. Fortunately we need only remember the net result, together with a few salient persons and episodes so picturesque in any case as to be almost unforgettable.

This fighting varies in intensity. Some battles are

15TH CENTURY ITALY

minor territories

DUCHY of SAVOY

DUCHY of MILAN

REPUBLIC of VENICE

MANTUA

FERRARA

MODENA

R. of GENOA

LUCCA

R. of FLORENCE

R. of SIENA

PAPAL STATES

DALMATIA (Venetian)

CORSICA (Genoese)

SARDINIA (Aragon)

KINGDOM of NAPLES

KINGDOM of SICILY (Aragon)

W.B.

Miles 0   100   200

remorselessly bloody, some sieges desperate. Others are
quaintly professional: the rival *condottieri* were colleagues
last year and may be again next year, if they take care not to
hurt each other. They are as free from personal animus as
opposing barristers. They want neither crushing victories nor
peace, only security of employment. Elaborate plate-armour
minimizes casualties, so long as no one is unsporting enough to
introduce gunpowder or anything really dangerous. Machiavelli alleges that a four-hour battle between the Florentines
and the Milanese resulted in only one death, when a steel-
encased warrior fell off his horse. Not all battles achieve this
Tweedledum standard, but not all are markedly homicidal.
Much of the blood flows between engagements, and is that
of the hapless civilians.

.   .   .   .

We have seen how even the rival Popes used *condottieri*
against each other during the Great Schism. The Schism continued into the fifteenth century and, though one pontiff had
been driven back to Avignon, life in Rome remained chaotic.
Albornoz' democratic reforms were forgotten: the government, such as it was, reverted to a senator appointed by the
Pope. So little harmonious was this arrangement that when
the Pope and the citizens disputed the ownership of the
Ponte Molle, the only acceptable solution was to demolish
the middle of the bridge, making it useless to both. There was
a monotonous cycle of public disorder, papal flight, papal
return in triumph and public hangings. The cardinals maintained their own virulent vendettas.

Naples now comes into our picture again. We must glance
quickly at what had been happening there in the century
since the Sicilian Vespers.

Frustrated in his wider ambitions, Charles of Anjou had
concentrated on making Naples a worthy capital for his
shrunken kingdom. New fortifications and churches had been
built. Thousands of flagstones had been brought from the
Appian Way to pave the streets. The nobility had been
encouraged to move into the town, the university had been
extended. Charles II had continued this policy with a somewhat lighter touch. Artists were summoned from Tuscany, a
cloth industry established, the city exempted from taxes. His

son, Robert the Wise, developed the patronage of art and learning. He corresponded with Petrarch and commissioned frescoes from Giotto. Young Boccaccio, coming to Naples on business for his father, found lasting inspiration in the gay and amorous atmosphere there. His beloved 'Fiametta' was the king's illegitimate daughter, Maria.

Three generations of progressive government were followed by more than half a century of turmoil. Robert was succeeded by his temperamental grand-daughter, Joanna I. She was married to a singularly dull young man, Andrew of Hungary, who seemed in all ways unsatisfactory. She now took a lover, Louis of Taranto. Whether or not (as picturesque scandal suggested) she actually wove the cord with which Andrew was strangled and then suspended from a balcony — whether indeed she was even aware of the project — she certainly lost no time in marrying Louis. In all she had four marriages, equally childless, so it may be that in some respects Andrew had been misjudged. Civil commotion filled her long reign. In 1381 Charles of Durazzo, great-grandson of Charles II, won papal backing and captured Naples, his cavalry wading through the sea to surprise the defenders. He had his cousin murdered the next year, smothered not inappropriately with her own bolster.

The succession, however, was disputed by another of Joanna's distant cousins, Louis of Anjou, and the matter was still unresolved when Charles died in 1386, bequeathing his claim to his little son, Ladislaus. The struggle went on intermittently. Ladislaus had the support of Pope Boniface in Rome, himself a Neapolitan, but Louis was backed by the Avignon Pope and the French king. Not till he was over twenty did Ladislaus manage to eject his rival and drive him back to Provence. The dawn of the *Quattrocento* found Ladislaus firmly established in Naples, a cunning, ambitious, dissolute young soldier. The royal patronage of culture was a dim memory. His taste was for the tourney, and for the seraglio collected in the Castel dell' Ovo, but above all he thirsted for power. Soon, as the papacy changed hands and the confusion in Rome intensified, he decided to intervene.

The Great Schism had now lasted thirty years. Many influential men, the practical-minded no less than the spiritual, felt that Christendom could no longer tolerate the scandal. Others had an interest in its continuance, no one more than Ladislaus, whose position in Naples rested on the support of a Pope independent of France. In 1408 the rival pontiffs, under pressure from the supporters of reunion, reluctantly set out to meet each other near Genoa. Ladislaus promptly occupied Rome and advanced northwards, determined that if there was any kind of summit conference he would be present and predominant. The two Popes, approaching each other with the enthusiasm of small boys being egged on to box against their will, now gave way to panic. The Avignon Pope retreated hastily to Perpignan: his Roman rival took sanctuary with Malatesta, Lord of Rimini. Their cardinals showed more determination. Ignoring the displeasure of Ladislaus, they called a General Council for the following May at Pisa, a city newly absorbed by the Florentines. This Council, holding that there was an even higher authority in the Church than the Pope's, deposed both claimants and elected a cardinal as Alexander V. As the Council's decisions were not universally accepted, the result was that, instead of reducing the Popes from two to one, it had raised the number to three.

Alexander died in ambiguous circumstances after only ten months, and the reunion party replaced him with Cardinal Baldassare Cossa, who had prefaced his ecclesiastical career with some useful experience as a corsair. Although (or perhaps because) he was born a Neapolitan aristocrat, John XXIII felt no affection for the King of Naples. He transferred papal support to the Angevin pretender, and by enlisting the two best *condottieri* available, Sforza Attendolo and Braccio da Montone, succeeded in driving Ladislaus out of Rome. Ladislaus soon returned to the offensive and sent John scuttling to Lombardy, where he met the newly elected Emperor Sigismund, an active and experienced statesman, keen to end the Schism. Catching the fugitive Pope at a disadvantage, Sigismund made him agree sulkily to summon a General Council of the Church at Constance. An imposingly learned and cosmopolitan assembly gathered in the cathedral there, including the alleged heretic John Huss who attended under promise of safe-conduct. Having disposed of various preliminary matters (including the unfortunate Huss whom it was quickly agreed to burn at the stake), the Council proceeded with admirable impartiality to depose all three existing Popes and to make a fresh start. One of the Colonna family was elected as Martin V, and thus, in 1417, the Great Schism ended.

During these tortuous manoeuvres Ladislaus was taken ill and returned to die in Naples. The crown passed to his elder sister, Joanna II, a childless widow of forty-five with morals no better than those of Joanna I. She at once took a twenty-six-year-old lover and made him seneschal of the kingdom. Her reign promised endless trouble, for the South was still a region of mettlesome feudal barons, very different from the northern bourgeoisie. A king's childlessness, however tiresome, seldom leaves his people with no ray of hope, but in Joanna's case the certainty of a disputed succession hung cloud-like over the country for more than twenty years, and her scandalous behaviour made the present as dark as the future. While she ruled, Naples slipped back into medieval anarchy, untouched by the Renaissance which was transforming other parts of Italy.

.   .   .   .

When, in 1420, Martin V made his somewhat delayed entry into his native Rome, it was a city as derelict as the one which had distressed Petrarch seventy years before. The interim had been filled with incessant violence, giving no encouragement to constructive effort, public or private. Churches stood roofless, rubble blocked the streets, the ruins were dens for bandits, beggars, and the dregs of humanity. An English chronicler recorded that he had seen wolves fighting stray dogs in the shadow of St. Peter's. Hardly had the Pope taken possession of this depressing heritage than the Tiber flooded all the low-lying districts, its muddy waters rising to the high altar of the Pantheon, but this disaster may have helped rather than hindered him in cleaning up the city.

What he could do, he did. Life and property were made more secure, and repairs put in hand, but the programme was halted by his sudden death from apoplexy in 1431. Eugenius IV tried to carry on the work, and revived the university which Boniface had founded in 1303. Otherwise Eugenius, a Venetian of mercantile origins and monastic tastes, had little sympathy with his aristocratic Roman predecessor. Martin had relied on his Colonna relatives, without whom no doubt he could have done little against the daunting problems which faced him. But the Colonna family had demanded their price in papal favours, and now Eugenius assailed them, enlisting their perennial rivals the Orsini. Once more the exhausted city became an arena. Eugenius hanged two hundred Colonna supporters and demolished their palace. The people, who had genuinely mourned Martin, stormed the Capitol and demanded a return to republican government. Eugenius fled, pursued with shots and stones, scrambled into a boat and escaped down-river. It was nearly ten years before he dared to re-enter Rome.

Most of that period he spent in Florence, where Martin (who banked with the Medici) had also passed much of the first part of his reign. No two places could have presented a more startling contrast than decadent, moribund Rome and the ascendant city on the Arno.

Florence was now more than ever pre-eminent in Central Italy. Turret and tower and campanile rose in a forest of pink and fawn and white masonry on both banks of the swirling river. Life pulsated across each bridge, through every narrow street and broad piazza. The city had had some narrow escapes: in 1402 only the sudden death of Galeazzo Visconti had saved her from disaster at the hands of her northern rival, Milan, and a decade later the providential illness of Ladislaus had removed the threat from Naples. In general, though, she had gone from strength to strength. Hegemony rather than conquest was her theory, but on occasion she could be ruthless. Thus, Pisa, taken over by the Visconti in 1399, was transferred to her six years later for cash, during the weak period of Milanese government after Galeazzo's death, but when the affronted Pisans objected to the transaction the Florentines did not hesitate to take possession by force.

During all this period the small controlling group was headed by the Albizzi family. But in 1417, the year which ended the Great Schism, the death of Maso degli Albizzi removed the dominant member of the clique and allowed the gradual emergence of another family, the Medici.

   .   .   .   .

An early Medici, Silvestro, had been behind the

short-lived *ciompi* revolution of 1378. He died in 1388, and it was then a long time before the reinstated oligarchy could be effectively challenged. Giovanni de' Medici, who died in 1429, concentrated on building up the business which was to provide so massive a base for the political power of his descendants.

Our very word 'bank', derived from the *banco* or money-changer's table, is a reminder that Italy gave us not only cultural standards but also the financial techniques of international trading. The Medici bank was only one of scores operating in Florence and other cities, but Giovanni and his son Cosimo made it the greatest.

It was essentially a family business under close personal supervision, though the directors found time to engage in the silk and woollen trades. The branches were really subsidiary companies, the manager being a director of the parent house in Florence and very often a relative by marriage. The Medici themselves always kept the controlling interest. In London, for example, the manager took twenty per cent of the profits, while the rest went to the senior partners at home. The Venetian branch financed Florentine trade with the East, the Pisan branch, with offshoots in Barcelona and Valencia, handled business with Spain. There were branches in Avignon, Geneva, Bruges and other cities. When, later, Cosimo de' Medici helped his friend Sforza to the dukedom of Milan, Sforza took the Milanese branch manager as his minister of finance.

The services provided were as varied, and sometimes as exotic, as could be demanded by the most eccentric customer today. Banks were commissioned to search for Greek manuscripts, to buy French tapestries, to recruit boys for the papal choir. Mercenaries used them for the safe transmission home of their pay. Papal due-collectors in far-off countries used them to remit funds to Rome. When a foreign bishopric was for sale, the Bull approving the appointment might be sent to the nearest Medici branch, whose manager would hand it over only in exchange for cash. Along with the safe routine business, like the purchase of the Cotswold wool-clip, there were speculative ventures in the political field. Later Medici lost considerable sums which they had been unwise to advance to Edward IV and Warwick the King-maker. But that was all

in the game. More often their financial power was used
shrewdly and successfully, to the benefit of Florence no less
than the family.

This power was fully deployed by Cosimo, as deft a banker
as his father but with higher ambitions and enthusiasms. As a
young man he accompanied Pope John to the Council of
Constance, an educative experience even for one already far
from naïve. When John was deposed, Pope Martin became
one of the bank's most valued customers, with the obvious
corollary that the Medici became one of the most valued
papal allies.

The same financial lever could be applied to other operations, large or small, and not least to acquire control of the
Florentine government. That government did not lend itself
to the open predominance of any one leader. The head of the
state, the Gonfalonier of Justice, served for only two months
at a time, and the council, or Signoria, were elected by lot
from the upper social stratum with a complicated set of safeguards. The Medici came to dominate Florence by indirect
methods: by revision of the rules, by securing the disqualifi-
cation of their opponents, by increasing whenever possible
the number of their well-wishers. Methods varied from reforming the taxation-system to juggling with individual assess-
ments and precipitating or preventing bankruptcy. By
furnishing a dowry for the superfluous daughter of some
financially embarrassed Florentine, they would make one
more citizen politically reliable, and by confining their own
family marriages within the narrow circle of the local bourgeoisie they were for ever extending their influence. Crude
bribery was unnecessary. So was the formality of public office.
Cosimo was to control Florence for thirty years and in all
that period to have only three two-monthly terms as Gonfalonier of Justice.

'Keep in the background as much as possible,' his father
once advised him. 'Never express an opinion that runs
counter to popular sentiment, even if what the people want
is something perfectly useless. Don't lay down the law. Give
an impression of gentle, well-intentioned discussion.'

The net result of these devious policies was not to destroy
a democracy but to widen appreciably the narrow class-basis
on which the government rested. Nor was the power so

gained used to aggrandize the family at the expense of the republic. On the contrary, it was the lavish expenditure of the Medici and the patriotic use of their bank which made Florence great and glorious in the fifteenth century.

First, though, they had to come to power.

While the Albizzi policy of war against Lucca was popular, Cosimo gave judicious support. When reverses came, he found good grounds to criticize. The Albizzi decided to silence him. He was summoned to the Palazzo della Signoria, arrested by the captain of the guard and locked up in a small dark cell, high in that tower which is still the city's most distinctive landmark. Never, before or after, was Cosimo in such mortal danger. He had been warned and could have escaped, but only to become a discredited fugitive. He gambled on his popularity and his money power. The captain of the guard was well-disposed and, though he could not let his prisoner escape, took his meals with him and thereby scotched any attempt at poison. He also allowed visitors, one of whom received Cosimo's authority to draw one thousand ducats and bribe the gonfalonier, whom the Albizzi supposed they had already bought over. In the end, all they achieved was a ten-year banishment. Cosimo made a stately exit. Padua received him with deference. Thence he moved to Venice where his bank had an important branch. Here he lodged quietly in a monastery, biding his time.

He had not long to wait. At home his friends and his money were active. The Albizzi grew ever more unpopular. Soon there was a mounting demand to recall him. The Albizzi attempted an armed coup, abortive because their main allies, the Strozzi, drew the line at violence. The snarling factions then agreed to arbitration by Pope Eugenius, arrived that moment as a fugitive from Rome. He ruled that Cosimo's banishment should be annulled. Cosimo returned in triumph, a year almost to the day after his departure, and it was the turn of the Albizzi and the Strozzi to make a hasty exit. 'Never mind,' said Cosimo, 'new nobles can be made with two lengths of crimson cloth.' The Medici were firmly in the saddle at last. It was sixty years before they were knocked out of it.

The first thirty of those years were Cosimo's. He dominated Florence without needing to hold office. He had his bank and his party, manipulating both with dexterity and tact. The bank was the essential instrument of foreign policy, while at home his control of the party enabled him to fill every post with a dependable supporter — or, in time of crisis, to fill the streets with the loyal rank and file, bellowing their war-cry, ' *Palle! Palle!* ' an allusion to the *palle* or balls which were the Medici arms. This discreet dictatorship, though firm and unsentimental, was benevolent. Cosimo loved peace, external as well as internal. He did not foment wars for profit. Although, for the safety of Florence, he had to accept his share of the marchings and counter-marchings, he was the most pacific statesman of his age, consistently working towards that general settlement which, after twenty years, he achieved at Lodi.

Though Cosimo bequeathed a comfortable fortune to his family, it was only half what he spent in his lifetime on charity and the encouragement of culture.

The Renaissance was now in full blossom. Boccaccio's collection of classical manuscripts had helped to make Florence a focal point in the revival of learning. Cosimo bought more books, opened public libraries, and sponsored a complete translation of Plato, but into Latin, not Italian, which was still struggling for recognition as a literary medium. Greek studies, soundly organized by Manuel Chrysolaras in 1396, received a special fillip from the Council of Florence in 1439, when the Eastern Emperor, John Palaeologus, together with the Patriarch of Constantinople and a multitude of theologians, came to discuss with the Pope a possible union of the Greek and Latin Churches against the Turkish threat. Later, when that threat materialized in all its horror, the fugitive academics found a warm friend in Cosimo.

In the century since Giotto, Florence had become a hive of artists. When Ghiberti won the open competition for designing the baptistery doors, his six rivals included his friends Brunelleschi and Donatello. Masaccio, so revolutionary in his technique of suggesting mass, lived out his brief life under the Albizzi, while Uccello, master of fascinating perspectives, painted his *Rout of San Romano* a year before Cosimo's expulsion. So, when the great age of the Medici arrived, there was infinite scope for the patron. Cosimo made good use of it. Michelozzo built his modest palace, Fra Lippo Lippi decorated it, Donatello made *Judith and Holofernes* for its courtyard. Fra Angelico was brought down from Fiesole to paint frescoes in every cell of the San Marco monastery, restored by Michelozzo, Brunelleschi worked in Cosimo's parish church of San Lorenzo, and Luca della Robbia made the massive sculptured doors for the cathedral sacristy which were one day to save Lorenzo the Magnificent from assassination.

To these artists and scholars Cosimo offered not only patronage but personal friendship. In his palace, in his country villas, in the streets and shops of Florence, he was the centre of a coruscating intellectual circle. His table was the high table of an invisible college. Among its fellows was the future Pope Nicholas V, the first humanist to wear the tiara, a lively little bibliophile who developed in Florence the passion for culture which he was soon to lavish on Rome.

.   .   .   .

Meantime in both Venice and Milan no less remarkable men had taken the stage.

In Venice it was Francesco Foscari. Like Cosimo, he was ambitious, rich, of comparatively newly risen family, a challenger to the establishment. Like Cosimo, he was an astute party-manager and used similar means of building up his popularity, not forgetting discreet help with dowries. Unlike Cosimo, however, he was forthright in his own views, which were in direct conflict with traditional policy. That policy was to look eastwards to the sources of Venetian greatness — the sea, Constantinople, the Levant, the caravan-terminals from Central Asia; to thank God for the lagoons and avoid dangerous involvements in Italy.

Foscari led the new 'mainlander' school of thought. It had been safe to disregard Italy while she was divided into innumerable city-states, but those days were over. Milan was extending in all directions. Venice had already committed herself to the mainland by taking Verona under her wing. She must consolidate her position or Milan would absorb all Northern Italy and monopolize the land-routes into Europe.

So raged the debate. 'Can we afford to go into Italy?' 'Can we afford *not* to?' 'Should we waste resources which ought to be used against the Turks?' 'Suppose the Turks

Palazzo Chiericati (1551-1557), in 'Palladio's own little town of Vicenza'.

Ingenious perspectives are offered by the permanent scenery of Palladio's Teatro Olimpico, 'the first permanent playhouse erected since classical days'. A drawing from the collection of Inigo Jones.

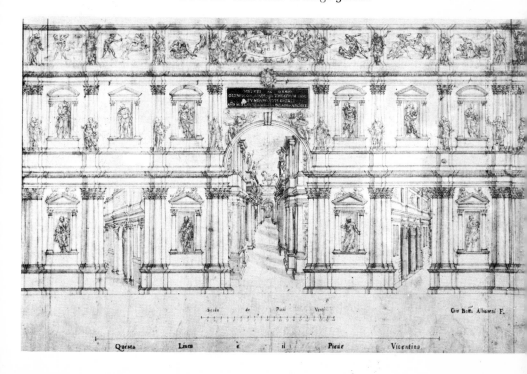

'That uneven, unhappy genius Borromini' added this typically baroque facade to the church of Sant'Agnese in Rome, about 1653.

cannot be stopped anyhow? Suppose they take Constantinople? Suppose we have to write off many of our Eastern
markets — is not that the strongest argument for a policy of
re-insurance in Italy? '

In 1423 Doge Tomaso Mocenigo, knowing his end was near,
called his councillors around his bed and reviewed the list of
possible successors. There was no shortage of suitable men.
Loredan, Bembo and half a dozen others were each capable
of guiding the republic along sound lines. Only Foscari
would be an unmitigated disaster. Foscari must not be elected
at any price.

When the election came, Foscari managed it with a dexterity which Cosimo de' Medici would have appreciated. The
electoral college consisted of forty-one men, chosen by a
fantastic procedure, a mixture of lottery and ballot, which
ensured that, although no one could become an elector without the right social qualifications, no one could be absolutely
certain of inclusion. The procedure started (after the invoca-
tion of divine assistance) with the youngest councillor going
out into the Piazza San Marco, seizing the first boy he met
and bringing him back into the palace to draw the ballots
out of a hat. The subsequent stages whereby the thirty chosen
reduced their number to nine, the nine increased themselves
to forty, and the assembly successively expanded and con-
tracted itself, from twelve to twenty-five to nine to forty-five
to eleven to forty-one, were more suggestive of a test in mental
arithmetic than a constitutional system.

The sheer complexity of the rules was delightful to Foscari's
devious mind. That the residual forty-one electors included
only nine dependable supporters did not unduly discourage
him. The actual election was almost, if not quite, as complicated as the choice of an elector and left ample scope for
political prestidigitation. Twenty-five votes were needed and
the mode of nomination tended to multiply the number of
candidates, especially when (as Mocenigo had pointed out in
this case) there was a wealth of talent. Foscari used his nine
sympathizers with skill. As each candidate was discussed and
voted upon, they concealed their preference for Foscari but
threw their united strength against the name proposed. One
by one Loredan and the others failed to get the necessary
majority. At the tenth ballot Foscari became doge. He was

already in his fifties. No one suspected that the reign now beginning was to last thirty-four years.

Mocenigo's forebodings were in part justified. Foscari's reign brought three wars with Milan and reduced the financial reserves of the republic by two-thirds. The struggle was prolonged and fluctuating. Foscari began with a characteristic stroke, buying over Carmagnola, the chief *condottiere* in the service of Milan, and making him captain-general of the Venetian army. After capturing Brescia from his former employer, Carmagnola became suspiciously dilatory and, though Foscari was still inclined to trust him, he was lured into a trap by the Council of Ten, tortured, convicted of treason, and beheaded between the granite columns in front of San Marco. Stimulated by this example, subsequent commanders displayed more zeal. Thus, when Brescia was besieged by the Milanese, the Venetians took thirty ships up the swiftly flowing Adige, dragged them overland in mid-winter, lowered them down the precipitous slopes of Monte Baldo, and launched them on Lake Garda, to the understandable chagrin of their incredulous foes.

On the whole the mainland policy succeeded, expensive though it was. Venice expanded westwards as far as Bergamo, whose distinguished son, Bartolommeo Colleoni, fought with equal brilliance on both sides and finished the war as captain-general of Venice, amply earning the well-known statue which Verrochio executed in his memory. Venice proved a popular mistress. Her new dependants kept their local autonomy and way of life, there was no purging of unreliable elements, and the overlordship was exercised with fairness and tact.

To the humbler citizens Foscari's reign was an era of pomp and pageantry unsurpassed even in Venice's colourful annals. Watching those tournaments and carnivals and regattas, those processions of scarlet-robed senators and white-clad ambassadors on horses draped in snowy taffeta, the doge himself gliding up the Grand Canal in *Bucentaur*, all red silk and gold, who could doubt that the Most Serene Republic was herself sailing upon the crest of the wave? Yet some certainly did. Hard-headed men frowned over the intelligence reports. They saw beyond the cloth-of-gold, the jewelled shoes and caps, the slashed sleeves and silken ribbons. They could hear, behind fanfare and serenade, the grumble of the Turkish cannon, the heaviest guns yet made, which were soon to demolish the ramparts of Constantinople.

So, in the council chamber and in the palatial loneliness to which the law condemned a doge, Foscari's triumph lost much sweetness with the passing years. His enemies remained implacable. Jacopo Loredan made the entry in his ledger: *'The Doge Foscari: my debtor for the death of my father and my uncle.'* More than once Foscari tried to resign his burdensome office, but there were never enough votes to enable his resignation to be accepted. His family life was tragic. Four sons died young, struck down by plague. The sole survivor was the apple of his father's eye. His wedding festivities became a legend even in that opulent period. People long remembered the decorated bridge of barges spanning the Grand Canal, and the hundreds of cavaliers who rode over it to the piazza for the tournament. The young man's interests lay rather in classical scholarship and book-collecting than in politics, but it was his bad luck to be his father's most vulnerable spot. When another of the Loredani gained a leading place in the Council of Ten, young Foscari was accused of treasonable contacts with Milan and was sent into exile. The last twelve years of the old doge's life were made miserable by the successive reconsiderations of the case, with recall, renewed charges, fresh hearings, and repeated banishment. This last phase was treated by Byron, with characteristic freedom, in *The Two Foscari*. The son died in Crete, an exile and a prisoner. Jacopo Loredan brought the father an ultimatum from the Council of Ten. He must resign and quit his palace in eight days, in which case he would receive a pension, or he would be evicted and his property confiscated. With a flash of his old spirit the eighty-five-year-old doge quoted the constitution which had prevented his voluntary retirement before and now made his forced abdication illegal. Then, yielding to the inevitable, he walked down the palace steps to his waiting gondola. A week later he died, and Jacopo Loredan wrote in his ledger, *'Paid.'*

.   .   .   .

Filippo Maria Visconti, Duke of Milan, was spared those problems of party management which attended the rise both of the Medici and of Foscari. He was the younger son of the redoubtable Gian Galeazzo who had conquered so much of northern Italy. Filippo inherited the dukedom in 1412, a decade after his father's death, a decade filled with the anarchy of disobedient *condottieri* and resurgent local barons, aggravated by the fantastic excesses of his elder brother, Giovanni. When the leading *condottiere*, Facino Cane, died and Giovanni was murdered, Filippo shrewdly contrived to take the places of both. He married the general's widow, thus gaining control of his troops and treasure-chest of half-a-million florins.

Giovanni must have been almost insane. Filippo was merely neurotic, a recluse haunted by the fear of assassination. Like the emblematic viper of his dynasty, he lurked in the recesses of the massive stronghold which loured over the city. Security was a mania. His staff were screened and then for ever afterwards suspected, spied upon, and checked by each other. Filippo believed that the best service was obtained by keeping every man jealous of his colleagues, and that, by pairing a dependable man with a rogue, the sharp wits of the latter could be combined with the fidelity of the former. Sometimes it must have worked. His administration was on the whole good. He kept his finances solvent and nourished industry, paid regularly, controlled his underlings, and looked after the peasants. It mattered little to them that for years on end his ugly features and bloated figure were never seen in the streets of his capital or that he travelled to his country villas by barge along specially dug canals rather than trust himself to the dangers of the open road. It might be whispered that no artist was ever permitted to paint his picture, that his marriage had never been consummated, that it was forbidden to look out of a castle window on suspicion of signalling to conspirators outside, and that his chamber had double walls because he was frightened of thunder. The fact remains that no one tried to scotch the viper, and that for thirty-five years he held the power of Milan together against such formidable enemies as the Florence of the Medici and the Venice of Foscari.

In 1435 Filippo entertained another of his remarkable contemporaries, Alfonso of Aragon. Joanna II of Naples had died at last and the fight was on. The succession was disputed by Alfonso, already ruler of Sicily, whom Joanna had long ago adopted as her heir, and by René of Provence, represent-

ing the Angevin connection, to whom she had switched her
favour after a quarrel with Alfonso. The Spaniard, though
nicknamed 'the Magnanimous', was not prepared to forgo
his claim. He set sail for Naples but was defeated and captured
by the Genoese, under instructions from Filippo, who had
decided to back the Angevin side. Alfonso was sent to Milan,
where a curious thing happened.

He charmed Filippo. This was an achievement even for
Alfonso, one of the more attractive Renaissance princes,
kindly, cultured, unaffected and approachable. It is hard to
imagine that he had much in common with the neurotic of
Milan, beyond an interest in the classics. With Alfonso this
was a passion. His coat-of-arms displayed an open book and
he travelled nowhere without his copies of Livy and Caesar.
Filippo, who had inherited a magnificent library from his
father, was also fond of the ancient authors.

Clearly they must have discussed more topical questions,
for Alfonso soon persuaded his captor that a French domination of Naples would be far more dangerous than an Aragonese. Filippo executed a prompt volte-face, threw over the
Angevin claimant, released Alfonso without ransom, and
became his ally. The first result was that he lost Genoa. His
Genoese subjects were infuriated that their victory had gone
for nothing and that they were now expected to be friends
with their traditional enemies, the Catalans. They rose in
revolt, threw out the Milanese, and set up a doge of their
own again.

Alfonso took another six years to drive René out of Naples
and reunite that kingdom with Sicily. The actual entrance
to the besieged capital was effected through an aqueduct
which perforated the east wall. Later Alfonso himself entered
with more dignity through a specially-made breach forty
yards wide, riding in a gilded chariot behind four white
horses, like the antique heroes he so much admired. The
scene is commemorated in the graceful triumphal arch which,
some time afterwards, was so incongruously squeezed between
the plain cylindrical towers of the Castel Nuovo. The Neapolitans were fortunate that, after the first few rough hours of
victory, Alfonso's success found expression so harmlessly. He
was a clement conqueror. There was an amnesty for Angevin
supporters and a distribution of titles which doubled the

aristocracy. Henceforth he kept his court in Naples and the city entered upon a brilliant period.

The antithesis of his late host at Milan, Alfonso walked fearlessly through the streets, accessible and popular, combining natural dignity with democratic manners. His government was good: he simplified taxation, administered justice in person, and formed a militia to make the kingdom less dependent on *condottieri*. But learning, both pagan and Christian, was his real passion, and he was never so happy as when seated at the library window of his castle, with the famous panorama of the Bay spread below and his treasured volumes ranked on their shelves within. Nor was he the type of book-lover who, while exalting the ancient authors, despises the living. The writers employed in his service cost him 20,000 gold florins a year. Bartolommeo Facio, retained to write the chronicle of his wars, received a bonus of three years' salary when the book was completed. 'It is not given to pay you,' cried Alfonso, who knew the proper way to talk to writers, 'for your work would not be paid for if I gave you the fairest of my cities.' When Constantinople fell to the Turks, and refugee scholars came streaming into Italy, Alfonso gave them a generous welcome in Naples, created academic posts for them, and went himself on foot to hear them lecture. We must hope that this appealing person found in such intellectual pursuits an adequate compensation for his less satisfactory family life. He was separated from his wife, Margaret of Castile, who had taken exception to one of his mistresses and had her strangled. Alfonso then turned for consolation to Lucrezia d'Anagno, an aristocratic Neapolitan, who, to his chagrin, was as virtuous as she was beautiful. She was clearly a remarkable woman, for she contrived to preserve both that virtue and the devotion of her king. Alfonso lived until 1458, when the two kingdoms separated once more, and the brief golden age of Naples faded with the succession of Ferrante, his son by his murdered mistress.

·   ·   ·   ·   ·   ·   ·

During Alfonso's six-year struggle for Naples, Pope Eugenius in his Florentine refuge had actively backed the Angevins. When Alfonso triumphed, he changed sides and joined the Milan-Aragon association. This meant deserting his Florentine hosts and returning to Rome, where the short memory of the citizens enabled him to be welcomed with all the customary show of delight. He died a few years later, expressing regret that he had ever left the monastery where his true vocation lay.

Six months later, death (which he had forbidden to be mentioned in his hearing) claimed the despot of Milan. Filippo Visconti left no son. On his death-bed he nominated Alfonso as his heir. The soundest hereditary claim was that of Gian Galeazzo's grandson, the Duke of Orleans — that Charles who married the widow of Richard II, was captured at Agincourt, and spent the next twenty-five years as a prisoner in England. During the seven years since his release he had been the centre of a literary circle at Blois, where his sensitive poetry was deservedly appreciated. Besides his literary talent he had, what was rather more relevant to his prospects in Milan, the support of the French king. Apart from these two well-bred intellectuals there was a formidable mongrel in the field, Francesco Sforza.

Sforza was the bastard son of an eminent though peasant-born *condottiere*, that 'Sforza' Attendolo (Sforza being quite strictly a *nom de guerre*) who had served Pope John against Ladislaus earlier in the century. The son had in due course outshone the father. It is interesting to contrast the paternal advice in this case with that given to Cosimo de' Medici. Attendolo laid down three golden rules. 'Let other men's wives alone. Never strike one of your men — and, if you do, transfer him to a distance. Don't ride a hard-mouthed horse or one that drops his shoes.' Thanks to this counsel, and partly also no doubt to exceptional qualities as a general, Francesco Sforza was by this time at the top of his profession.

He was a young forty-six, dynamic in action, princely in bearing. He had fought in turn for Milan, Venice, Florence and the papacy — and against them too. He had fought for the Angevins against Alfonso. But he was not content to remain a *condottiere*. His aim was to carve out a state for himself. Long ago, Filippo Visconti had tried to hold his allegiance by promising him his illegitimate daughter Bianca as a bride, but fulfilment of the promise had been continually deferred until Sforza in disgust had gone over to the Venetian-Florentine alliance. In 1441 Filippo had bought him back with the long-withheld Bianca and the city of Cremona as dowry. Filippo's death, six years later, opened wider horizons.

To the people of Milan, however, the end of the male Visconti seemed an excellent opportunity to try a more liberal regime. Invoking the name of their patron saint, they proclaimed the 'Golden Ambrosian Republic'. It was not an auspicious moment for internal reorganization: the Venetian army was threatening the city and there were French forces in Piedmont (then part of Savoy) waiting to intervene on behalf of Charles of Orleans if it seemed opportune. The idealists of the Golden Ambrosian Republic had no Danton to improvise an army for the defence of the infant revolution. They sought instead the solution natural to their period: they engaged Sforza to do it for them. He promised to drive back the Venetians and to hand over all liberated territory to his employers, except the town of Brescia which he might retain if he could occupy it. Such a contract was far too straightforward to appeal to any of the parties concerned. After one year Sforza changed sides, and after another two years the Venetians made a deal with the Milanese behind his back. Sforza was undismayed. His troops tightened their grip round Milan. In the city, he knew, the disillusioned republicans were already split by strife. In the background was the friendship of Cosimo de' Medici, who believed in his political future and would back him. Cosimo's estimate was sound. One February day in 1450 there was a popular demonstration in Milan, denouncing the Venetian alliance and demanding Sforza. On the morrow, delegates rode off to his camp, and on the day after that the *condottiere* made his triumphal entry, the hysterical crowd drawing him, still mounted on his charger, through the great doors of the cathedral.

So, through Bianca, the Visconti blood was perpetuated in the new line of Sforza. It took some years of fighting and negotiation before the succession was recognized by everyone as part of a wider settlement. But the saner elements in every Italian state were beginning to see that these perpetual inter-regional contests benefited nobody but the foreigner. In Venice Foscari was by then an unhappy old man, widely criticized for his mainland policy: the fall of Constantinople, shocking to all Christendom, forced the Venetians in particular to an urgent re-examination of their position. Nicholas V was striving energetically to restore the prestige of the papacy: he too had powerful motives for seeking peace in Italy and unity against the Turks. Cosimo de' Medici had favoured Sforza all along. The hardest nut to crack was Alfonso the Magnanimous, who had a special repugnance to any negotiations with the former *condottiere*. Not only did he regard himself as the rightful ruler of Milan, nominated by his old ally, Filippo, on his death-bed, but he alone of all the leaders concerned had known Sforza only as an enemy, never as an ally.

It is said that Alfonso's obduracy was overcome with characteristic tact by Cosimo, who sent him a rare manuscript of Livy. So at last, at the town of Lodi near Milan, that treaty was signed in 1454 which established an agreed balance of power between the five great states of the peninsula.

14. Quattrocento Continued

THE 1454 settlement wore well for twenty years, which was not bad for any international pact designed for permanent peace. As a move to unite Italy against the Turks it was sterile. Though successive Popes preached Crusades for the liberation of Constantinople, only the Venetians, with their own unspiritual motives, made any real attempt to plug the Turkish infiltration of Eastern Europe, and that without conspicuous success. The rest of Italy got on with its own business. The gorgeous *Quattrocento* rolled on to a new high-water level of cultural achievement. Few noticed that Italy was losing her leadership, that the economic basis of her prosperity was weakening. Just as, for Venice, the caravan routes across Central Asia to the Levant were now like so many severed veins, so Florence and the other textile cities began to experience a slow draining of vitality as the English and Flemish learnt to compete. But it was an age as innocent of statistics as of medical science, so that Italy, lacking experts to inform her that she was dying, continued to enjoy life with a zest unsurpassed in human history.

Rome in these decades was reborn. From an acreage of ruin comparable with the Warsaw of 1945 a Renaissance city rose to rival Florence herself. On his election in 1447, Nicholas V had set out to restore the prestige of the papacy. This, in the *Quattrocento*, meant making Rome the capital of a first-class state and the pontiff himself a temporal ruler who could talk on equal terms with a king. But Nicholas was also a book-lover and an amateur of the arts, a graduate of the Medici circle. His new Rome must be no hasty assemblage of 'prestige' architecture, but a garden in which all the choice flowers of the Renaissance should grow.

He began by rebuilding the walls and churches. The Vatican and St. Peter's were taken in hand, the Castel Sant' Angelo and its adjoining bridge repaired. The finest architects and artists were commissioned. Abundant material, perhaps unfortunately, lay ready to hand. The shattered Colosseum was a quarry from which, in one single year, his builders took 2,300 wagon-loads of marble. Ironically enough, these years saw the birth of archaeology. As the excavations proceeded, any piece of antique sculpture was seized upon with uncritical reverence. A cluster of art-lovers might stand gaping at some mediocre torso while behind them, unheeded, the lumbering wagon-train removed evidence invaluable to later students.

Nicholas' passion for classical literature deserves unqualified gratitude. This was a critical moment. In Germany the first clumsy experiments were being made with printing but a few years would pass before its wide adoption made the complete loss of an author's work virtually impossible. Meanwhile the Turkish advance threatened, along with so much else, the survival of books existing sometimes only in single manuscript copies, forgotten and disregarded in Byzantine monasteries. For many years Italian collectors had been rescuing such books from the risk of fire, mice, ravaging Turks and illiterate monks, the last being not the least dangerous, since they were quite capable of ripping up unique pages of Euripides and selling them to pious pilgrims as amulets. But for men like Guarino da Verona, who personally brought back fifty-four manuscripts in 1408, the world would now possess an even smaller fraction of classical literature than it does.

Nicholas flung the papal resources into this rescue-work when it was most urgent. He bought manuscripts, employed hundreds of scholars and copyists to work on them, and founded the Vatican Library, with a nucleus of five thousand books, splendid in red velvet bindings with clasps of silver. Nor was his concern for scholarship limited to Rome. It extended to the very fringe of Christendom. His papal bull of 1450 founded the University of Glasgow.

He died in 1455 and was succeeded by Calixtus, an aged Spaniard, chiefly notable as the first of the Borgia family to enter Italian history. He was quickly followed by another enthusiastic humanist, Pius II, that Aeneas Sylvius whose pictorial biography, painted by Pinturicchio in tactfully selected episodes, still adorns the cathedral library in his native Siena. We see there depicted some of his numerous diplomatic appearances — at the Council of Basle, at the court of the emperor, even as ambassador to James II of Scotland against a fanciful background more Italianate than Caledonian — but we should never guess by what cynical, careerist zigzags the future pontiff climbed the lower slopes of fame. Nor does the fresco devoted to his coronation as a poet emphasize that his literary reputation rests on a bawdy novel in the manner of Boccaccio (*Lucretia and Euryalus*), an amusing but improper play (*Chrysis*), and the autobiographical *Commentaries* which are so much more revealing than all the ten pictures put together.

Aeneas Sylvius was a kind of literary *condottiere* in his early days, serving as private secretary to a succession of eminent masters and using his pen ably in their support until a better offer drew him elsewhere. He had charm and taste. In many fields he had even sincerity — in his love of books, Rome and the countryside. As Pope he carried the new pastime of archaeology far beyond the city. Even when crippled by gout he was zestful in tracing the course of ancient roads and aqueducts, travelling out to Tivoli and Ostia by litter. But, as a true Renaissance man, he exalted the written word above all else. '*Literature,*' he instructed the boy king of Hungary, '*is our key to the true significance of the past, to a correct assessment of the present, to a reliable forecast of the future. Where letters die, darkness covers the land. A ruler who cannot read the lessons of history is defenceless against flattery and deception.*' He emphasized also the importance of military training, for '*it will be your destiny to protect Christendom against the Turks.*' He took the Cross himself though ill and nearing fifty-nine. On his way to Venice, to embark with the fleet, he caught fever and died.

Paul II — a Venetian of strong will amounting to arrogance — sought to re-establish papal domination over the cardinals. He felt that a too indiscriminate admiration of pagan antiquity was a threat to the faith and he repressed some of the extremer manifestations of humanism, such as the Academy. Scholars must be Christian scholars, he pointedly rebuked the Curia and the Sacred College. Though slandered as illiterate, he continued most of his predecessors' cultural schemes and his reign saw Rome's first printing-press. He built what is now the Palazzo Venezia and liked to watch from its loggia the races down the Corso, which he instituted, along with the annual carnival and other junketings, to entertain the populace and disguise their loss of independence. With a similar aim, perhaps, he decreed a more magnificent costume for the cardinals, whom he had stripped of some of their constitutional powers.

He was followed by a Genoese Franciscan of poor parentage, Sixtus IV, a name commemorated in the Sistine Chapel, built by Dolci, with frescoes by Botticelli, Signorelli, and others. His nephew, Julius II, completed the work by commissioning Michelangelo to decorate the barrel-vaulted ceiling. It would have been well if Sixtus had confined himself to art and architecture, continuing (as he did) the admirable road-widening, bridge-building, and housing development which were making Rome once more a city of grandeur. He might even have been pardoned those towering citadels of confectionery, munitioned with sweetmeats, which, together with storks and stags, peacocks, cranes, and other exotic delicacies, lent his dinner-parties a ridiculous and vulgar ostentation of Trimalchio's. Unfortunately, he was not content to make up for his earlier poverty by gluttony and immorality, to recreate not only the glories but the orgies of imperial Rome. He wished his numerous nephews to start life with the advantages he himself had lacked. Six he made cardinals. Another, Girolamo Riario, he decided to turn into an aristocrat, by betrothing him to an illegitimate daughter of Galeazzo Maria Sforza, the formidable Caterina, and by establishing him lord of Imola, a small Romagnan town. This part of his plan conflicted with Florentine interests and touched off a train of events destined to destroy the balance achieved at Lodi. It is time, therefore, to turn back to affairs in Florence.

.   .   .   .

Cosimo died in 1464. When, latterly, his wife taxed him with his long silences, he reminded her gently of her own elaborate preparations for even a short journey to the country. Surely he, with a far longer journey before him, had a right to look thoughtful? He died at his Careggi villa, seventy-five, his mind troubled for the future of his family, but for himself consoled by the Platonic philosophy he loved. The Florentines gave him the title *Pater Patriae*, 'Father of his Country', and it was not undeserved.

One by one the peacemakers of Lodi were passing from the stage: first Nicholas, Foscari in 1457, Alfonso in 1458, and the last, Francesco Sforza, in 1466. A new generation assumed control. In Milan Galeazzo Maria Sforza took over that minatory fortress which his father had raised and which still looms over the level city. Galeazzo's passion was for pageants, tournaments and extravagance of every kind. Especially he loved vocal music and by attracting fine singers to his court established the great tradition of Milan. He also loved his courtiers' wives and forgot his grandfather's excellent advice to his father in that connection. In Naples Alfonso's bastard son, Ferrante, took over the mainland kingdom, while Sicily, once more separated, went to Aragon under a Spanish viceroy. Ferrante, though not without constructive policies, was not big enough to cope with a country still backward relative to the rest of Italy, still a land of quarrelsome barons rather than a progressive bourgeoisie. His long reign lasted until 1494 and grew darker as, in old age, he came increasingly under his son's domination. For if Ferrante was a mixed character with a pronounced streak of savagery, Alfonso II was a savage with few redeeming features at all.

Only in Florence did a great man find a great successor, not in his quite estimable but ailing son Piero, but in his grandson, Lorenzo. Gozzoli's crowded, colourful fresco in the family chapel, ostensibly depicting the journey of the Magi, shows the three generations. In front, on a splendidly caparisoned white horse, rides the boy, glorious in the golden tunic, spiked crown and scarlet hose which he wore for an Oriental fiesta when he was eleven. Pageantry was always one of his delights. May Day revels and miracle plays, torchlight and fireworks, processions and masquerades, he loved and raised to new levels of elaboration. The very helmets, parade-shields and other devices were works of art, as the David-and-Goliath shield painted by Castagno bears witness. Lorenzo's own bent being literary, he composed carnival songs of daring impropriety, while in other moods, anticipating the Salvation Army, he wrote verses of impeccable piety to the same tunes. At nineteen he was the star performer in a tournament staged in the Piazza Santa Croce to celebrate his impending marriage to the aristocratic Clarice Orsini of Rome. The wedding itself was not popular, for the Medici had always married locally, and when the red-haired bride reached Florence a few months later she had to overcome a good deal of prejudice.

By the end of the following year Lorenzo's father was dead and within two days, so well-oiled was the party machine, a deputation was on the young man's doorstep offering him the reins of power. 'I accepted reluctantly,' he said afterwards, 'and only to safeguard my friends and our family interests. It is awkward for a wealthy person in Florence if he has no control over the government.' The gilded child of Gozzoli's fresco had become the rugged realist of Verrocchio's terra-cotta head.

Swarthy, nasal-voiced, Lorenzo was no Prince Charming. He blended, to a degree unsurpassed even in that age, the ruthless statesman, the acute intellectual, the virile sportsman, the sensitive art patron, the ebullient impresario. He loved to ride out with his falcons, but equally he loved to catch the beauty of the countryside and distil it in a poem. He delighted in the exquisite illumination of some unique manuscript, but helped Bernardo Cennini establish one of the new-fangled printing-presses which many bibliophiles despised. He never stood on his dignity. He deferred to men older than himself; otherwise his friends sat down at his table just as they arrived, without protocol. His garden and library were always open to them and to distinguished strangers. The still-extant register signed by those using his books is like a roll-call of Renaissance scholarship.

Veneration for the classics penetrated even to the nursery. Once when Clarice was teaching her children the Psalms she was upbraided by Angelo Poliziano, the eminent poet engaged as tutor, for contaminating their taste with the unclassical Latin of the Vulgate. But this rigidity was extreme. Poliziano himself attacked the idea that everyone should ape Cicero, and wrote his own impassioned lyrics in the youthful language of Tuscany. Leonardo da Vinci was almost unique in his violent reaction against the literary approach which he was not educated to share. He took himself off eventually to Lodovico Sforza's court at Milan where, to speak fairly, though there was more encouragement for his technical ingenuity, there was no more real understanding of his scientific attitude. Other artists, like Botticelli and the young Michelangelo, Filippino Lippi, Perugino, Domenico Ghirlandaio, and Antonio Pollaiulo, found the Medici ambience congenial enough. So did the scientist Paolo Toscanelli, with his mathematically convincing theory of sailing westwards to find India. It is said that he was in correspondence with Columbus. Certainly there was one young man working in the Medici bank, Amerigo Vespucci, who not only went on some of the early voyages but had his name almost casually attached to the new continent.

Lorenzo had been controlling Florence for five years when Pope Sixtus approached him for the forty thousand ducats needed to establish Riario as lord of Imola. Disliking the idea on political grounds, Lorenzo refused. But his bank, great as it was, had thirty-two competitors in Florence, prominent among them being that of the Pazzi. Francesco Pazzi, head of their Rome branch, offered to accommodate the Pope, who gratefully transferred his whole account. So, twenty years after Lodi, the entente began to crack. Lorenzo pointed out to Galeazzo Sforza and to the Venetians that Sixtus' avuncular affection might infringe the interest of all not fortunate enough to be his nephews. They formed a triple alliance. The Pope, turning hastily to Naples, secured the only partner left in the game.

For a while nothing dramatic occurred. In 1476 the unpleasant young Sforza was assassinated, but, as the assorted motives of his assassins made clear, he had given so many good reasons for the deed that it was probably devoid of political significance. This may not, however, have been universally appreciated at the time. The episode set other people thinking.

Riario consulted with Francesco Pazzi, who was becoming increasingly antagonistic to the Medici. If a Sforza could be removed, why not Lorenzo? At first expulsion was discussed, with bloodshed only as a last resort. But by degrees the plan became one for the simultaneous murder of Lorenzo and his young brother Giuliano, who would otherwise succeed him just as Galeazzo's eight-year-old son had, with a regent, replaced his murdered father in Milan.

A *condottiere*, Montesecco, enlisted to arrange the practical details, had scruples which must have been a handicap in his profession. According to his own account, they were over-

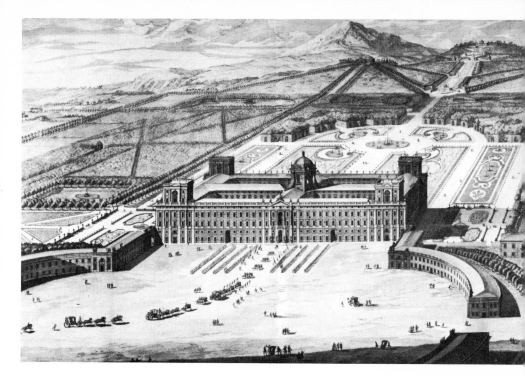

'At Caserta Vanvitelli built a Mediterranean Versailles' for the first Bourbon King of Naples. Vanvitelli's own engraving.

Castel Sant' Angelo and its bridge over the Tiber, storm-centre for innumerable historical events since it was first built as Hadrian's Mausoleum, depicted here by the 18-century artist, Claude Joseph Vernet.

Garibaldi, 'magnetic genius', 'romantic, chivalrous soldier', on his Sardinian islet of Caprera.

Mussolini, 'the fulminating, prognathous Duce, who used to harangue his hypnotized followers from the balcony of the Palazzo Venezia.'

come only after a personal interview with Sixtus, who assured him that the elimination of the brothers was justifiable on the highest grounds. As a further contribution to the scheme Sixtus gave the archbishopric of Pisa to another enemy of the Medici, Salviati, who now joined the conspiracy. Francesco meantime won over the head of his family in Florence, whither, in April, 1478, the scene moved.

The urbanity of Florentine society was such that, although Riario could scarcely show himself in the city, the other plotters were all able to join Lorenzo for supper at his villa one Saturday night. To their vexation Giuliano did not turn up and the assassination had to be postponed, but only to the next morning, when the brothers would be in the cathedral together for High Mass. Francesco Pazzi would stab Giuliano and Montesecco would account for Lorenzo.

Now, though, the tiresome *condottiere* developed scruples again. Homicide of one's host at supper was one thing, murder in the cathedral quite another. Luckily two priests were found who had no such conscientious objections, and on the principle that two amateurs equalled one professional both were deputed to perform Montesecco's share.

When Mass began there was another hitch. Lorenzo was there but not his brother. Francesco and his partner Bandini hurried to the house, where they found Giuliano in bed with a bad knee. With desperate persuasiveness they got him to accompany them to the cathedral, and, as they helped him along, satisfied themselves that he had no armour under his clothing. Sweating with apprehension they got him to the altar in time for the elevation of the Host, planned as the signal for the assassination.

The moment came. The cardinal held up the Host, the sacring-bell rang out, every head was bent except those of the conspirators. Bandini stabbed Giuliano in the chest, and, as he lurched over, Francesco attacked him with the febrile savagery of a frightened man, stabbing him again and again and even, in his panic, wounding himself deeply in the leg. Giuliano collapsed with nineteen wounds.

Lorenzo was luckier. His attackers bungled it. One stroke gashed his neck, then he was on his feet, his own dagger out, his cloak wrapped shield-wise round his left arm. He had no means of knowing the strength of the enemy. Sensibly he let his friends hustle him into the sacristy. Poliziano slammed the great bronze doors and barred them.

Terror seized the city for a brief hour. Archbishop Salviati had been deputed to take over the Palazzo Vecchio and proclaim the revolution, but his men muddled things and got themselves locked up in the chancery downstairs. The Archbishop, finding himself alone, suffered an understandable loss of confidence. The Gonfalonier of Justice, with a decisiveness rare on that confused Sunday morning, seized him and without more ado hanged him from an upper window. Meantime the conspirators were rallying their supporters on the streets. '*Popolo e Libertà!*' chanted the revolutionaries, to which the Medici supporters roared back: '*Palle!*' Francesco was caught and hanged beside the Archbishop. Soon more of their confederates were dangling like onions against the massive wall of the Palazzo Vecchio. Others were hunted down and hacked to death in the streets. Savage reprisals continued for days, during which hundreds of Pazzi supporters and suspects were wiped out. There was no more opposition to the Medici. In the next few years Lorenzo pushed through constitutional changes which still further secured his position.

In Rome the news was received with pious indignation. Sacrilege had been committed, not by the murder of Giuliano at High Mass, but by the summary hanging of an archbishop on a Sunday morning in full view of the vulgar populace. Lorenzo was excommunicated, an interdict laid upon the whole city. Papal forces crossed the border, supported by troops from Naples under the king's son, Alfonso.

Vainly Lorenzo appealed to his allies. Venice was nearing the end of a calamitous single-handed struggle with the Turks, about to surrender Euboea, Lemnos, part of the Morea, and other valuable territories. In Milan Lodovico Sforza, nicknamed 'the Moor', was manoeuvring against his brother's widow to displace her as regent for her unpromising child. Neither Venice nor Milan did much to help Lorenzo in his troubles. To add to them, plague broke out in Florence. Even the financial empire of the Medici was not as healthy as it had been. That year they closed their London branch.

With his back to the wall Lorenzo showed cunning and courage. Somehow he must neutralize Ferrante. Taking his life in his hands he went to Naples. It was a giant-killing enterprise, for he knew Ferrante all too well, though the king had not yet sunk to the depths of his later years. The Medici eloquence worked. Ferrante was talked round, and Lorenzo went home in triumph. It is possible that he had taken out a little reinsurance against the failure of his mission and that it was by no mere coincidence that the Turks, who had built up a powerful navy in recent years, chose this moment to descend upon the Apulian coast and storm Otranto. Alfonso, at all events, brought his troops hurrying back from Tuscany more quickly than he might otherwise have done, and Sixtus gave Lorenzo a grudging pardon in return for his equipping of fifteen galleys against the infidel. With this help the Turks were thrown out of Otranto after a year.

By now the old balance was thoroughly upset. Venice, offended by the Florentine-Neapolitan friendship, lined up with Sixtus, and they combined to attack Ferrara, a secondary but by no means negligible state sandwiched between their territories. Ferrara, long ruled by the great house of Este, resisted with spirit. Naples supported her, and so did Lorenzo and Lodovico il Moro, who was now the effective ruler of Milan, with no intention of handing over power to his inconsiderable nephew. The Ferrara war exemplified the disunity into which Italy was relapsing. It ended when Sixtus died in 1484.

His successor made no noteworthy contribution except to the population. He established a precedent as the first pontiff to acknowledge his illegitimate offspring. He chose the inappropriate name of Innocent VIII, which at once made him a sitting target for ribald epigram. '*Octo Nocens*—' began one such, the Latin lending itself to a pun—'Eight boys he begat in sin and just as many girls: well may Rome call him Father.' One of these sons the philoprogenitive pontiff married to Lorenzo's daughter, Maddalena, a demonstration of the policy-reversal which now restored the former happy Florentine-Papal relationship. Lorenzo, though glad enough of this new political turn, could have had few illusions about the man who had succeeded the implacable Sixtus. 'You are now to reside in Rome, that sink of iniquity,' he told his son Giovanni, when the boy, created a cardinal at thirteen, had completed his studies at Pisa and was ready to take up his duties. 'You will probably meet people who will make special efforts to corrupt you and tempt you to vice.' Twenty-four years later Giovanni attained the papacy itself as Leo X, and though he had never in the meantime taken priestly orders, the omission was quickly rectified in three ceremonies at forty-eight-hourly intervals, which ordained him priest, consecrated him bishop, and enthroned him Pope.

The Rome-Florence rapprochement left Naples disgruntled. Her relations with the papacy deteriorated. One could always harass her Aragonese ruler by mentioning the Angevin claim, which had now passed to the French king himself. On the least encouragement unruly barons would defy the man they still regarded as a usurper. Innocent gave that encouragement. In 1485, while English feudalism had its last fling at Bosworth, the Apulian barons rose in revolt. Unable to defeat them, Ferrante resentfully promised an amnesty. One rebel, the Duke of Salerno, distrusted this uncharacteristic gesture. He disguised himself as a muleteer, wrote over his gateway the relevant proverb, *'An old sparrow does not enter the cage'*, and departed inconspicuously for France.

His associates were more naïve. Shortly afterwards receiving invitations to a royal wedding in the Castel Nuovo, they accepted with alacrity. Ferrante (or rather, perhaps, his now-dominant son, Alfonso) used the occasion for the wholesale massacre of the opposition. At the height of the celebrations soldiers rushed into the hall, seized men, women and children, and hustled them away to the dungeons. Few were seen again. Those who reappeared, like the bridegroom's father, did so only to be publicly executed in front of the castle. At last Ferrante and Alfonso felt safe.

So the fourteen-eighties rolled on. In 1489 Alfonso's daughter, Isabella, married Gian Galeazzo Sforza, who, though now twenty-one, was still docile under Lodovico's steely hand. Isabella, a girl of spirit, was less likely to accept her husband's perpetual subordination: was he not rightful Duke of Milan? Lodovico would have prevented the marriage if possible, but the engagement had lasted ten years and to break it now would have been an insult to Naples.

It is hard, in contemplating Lodovico il Moro, to escape some obvious comparisons with his English contemporary, Richard III. Both had outstanding administrative ability, strong will, subtle intelligence, infinite ambition, and young nephews with a better legal title than their own, though in Richard's case even this is arguable. Both were determined not to relinquish power.

Lodovico combined a fervent faith in astrology with a practical approach to everyday life. He developed trade, canals, rice-growing, and other agricultural innovations. He may not have had much use for Leonardo's more premature inventions, such manifestly crazy notions as parachutes and helicopters, central heating and mechanical excavators, but he saw his immediate possibilities as a military engineer. Among others at his court were Franchino Fafori, the outstanding musical theorist of the day, and Fra Luca Pacioli, the mathematician, whose double-entry system earned him the title of 'father of book-keeping'. The Medici had no monopoly of talent.

Indeed, this is a fitting moment to remind ourselves that, though political power had become concentrated in the 'big five' cities, culture had not. At Urbino, Piero della Francesca, Pisanello, and half a dozen other eminent artists worked for the enlightened Duke Federigo. Mantua saw Europe's first lyric drama staged in 1471, Poliziano's *Orfeo,* despite its author's favoured position in Florence. Ferrara pioneered elaborate productions of Plautus and Terence in Italian. There was even a tiny but culturally influential court at Asolo, where the lovely and intelligent Caterina Cornaro, widowed Queen of Cyprus but by birth a Venetian, surrounded herself with writers and painters, including Bembo and Titian. Another sort of intellectual stimulus was created in Padua by the influx of Greek medical students. The Turks themselves had few doctors and there were golden opportunities in their territories. Padua became a magnet for the ambitious young Greek. Usually he studied philosophy as well which, in the current state of medicine, made an appropriate combination.

To return to Lodovico: in 1489 the inescapable marriage between his nephew and Isabella of Naples was celebrated. But the uncle still kept political control, helped by Gian Galeazzo's mental and physical feebleness. There was not much the duchess could do. In 1491 the forty-year-old Lodovico married her beautiful and vivacious cousin, Beatrice d'Este—an arrangement he at first accepted apathetically, for diplomatic reasons, only to find himself captivated by her wit. Now the situation developed a new piquancy, for besides strong uncle and weak nephew there were two young wives, who loved each other no better for being cousins and equal in looks and spirit. Nor did the common interest of maternity bring them any closer, when each produced a son and heir. 'Heir to what?' was the unspoken but unforgettable question.

Stresses of a different kind were developing in Florence: a financial crisis, currency depreciation, the shadow of national bankruptcy. Lorenzo salvaged his private fortune by methods which, while reasonable for an individual, did not increase his popularity as head of the state. Among his critics was the new Prior of San Marco.

Girolamo Savonarola came from Ferrara. His father was an insignificant member of the elegant Este court. Savonarola despised fashion and frivolity, distrusted even the higher manifestations of Renaissance culture. He preferred solitary tramps beside the River Po. An 'angry young man' from the beginning, foretelling doom in his juvenile treatise, *Contempt for the World,* he was confirmed in his attitude by an unhappy love-affair, when he was rejected on snobbish grounds by the daughter of a Florentine exile, one of the aristocratic Strozzi. At twenty-two he heard one of those life-changing sermons which made him throw up his medical studies and join the Dominicans.

It was soon his turn, as a preaching friar, to change countless other lives. No mere ranting revivalist, he could sway the intelligentsia no less than the mob. He challenged the Renaissance and all its pagan vanities, from Botticelli's naked Venus to the Platonic Academy. 'An old woman knows more of faith than your Plato!' he thundered unanswerably. Botticelli himself was converted. Lorenzo was less impressionable, but he tried unsuccessfully to make friends with this fascinating adversary. Lorenzo, however, died in 1492, only forty-three and still too young to hold office as Gonfalonier. His son Piero was twenty-one, sport-loving, extravagant, but with few of his father's greater qualities. Under his weak rule Savonarola's influence grew.

The friar was attacking, and most effectively, on two fronts. While denouncing humanism and exalting the Faith, he

blistered the Church with criticism. There was abundant evil
to expose. In 1493 Innocent died and Rodrigo Borgia, by
bribing all but five of the cardinals, became Pope Alexander
VI. His immorality was already a byword, though his famous
Ballet of the Chestnuts (when he threw hot chestnuts among
the naked dancing-girls) was a pleasure still to come. His love
of women was equalled only by his love for the children they
bore him. Best remembered are Cesare and Lucrezia, two of
the four born to his mistress Vanozza. Cesare, at this date a
sixteen-year-old student at Pisa, was promptly made archbishop of his father's native city, Valencia. Lucrezia had a
socially inferior marriage annulled so that she could marry
Giovanni Sforza, Lord of Pesaro; but when this ceased to suit
her father's diplomatic needs it was briskly annulled on the
grounds of Sforza's impotence, so that she could marry
Alfonso of Naples' bastard son, the Duke of Bisceglie. Before
long this third husband was murdered by Cesare. At twenty-
two, young in years but mature in experience, she married
the heir to the Duke of Ferrara and thereafter enjoyed a less
sensational existence, bearing five children and entertaining
such distinguished guests as Ariosto, Titian, and that admirable Venetian publisher, Aldus Manutius.

It was not long after his election that her father clashed
with Savonarola. The year 1494 saw the bloodless overthrow
of the Medici, when as a symbol of the people's triumph over
the 'tyrants' Donatello's *Judith and Holofernes* was removed
from the palace to the piazza. Savonarola, though he accepted
no office, was the theoretician of the new order. A constitution
was worked out on Venetian lines, with a Grand Council of
3,200 citizens but no doge. In fact, Savonarola's personal
domination left less scope for democratic discussion than there
had been under the Medici. 'He divides all men into two
groups,' Machiavelli told a friend. 'The ones made for God
—himself and his party. The others, ripe for Hell, are the
opposition.' Machiavelli took a clerkship in the chancery.
He did not love the Medici, but his cool intelligence was
equally proof against the propaganda of their successor.

The political change was only a beginning. Savonarola
swept on to the moral revolution which really interested him.
A Puritan hysteria seized the population. There was a public
'burning of the vanities', a holocaust of pictures and books

which portrayed too persuasively the beauties of this world. Clothing became depressingly utilitarian. Fasts were decreed for half the days of the year — a measure which drove a large number of butchers into the ranks of the opposition. Carnality of another sort was denounced with such unanswerable eloquence that married couples broke up their marriages and rushed impulsively into the appropriate monastic institutions. When the impulse was not mutual, fresh opponents of Savonarola's policies were no doubt created. With the shrewd instinct of a dictator, he organized the boys into an emotional youth movement.

Rome had never smiled on enthusiasm of this type. The worldly Spaniard in the Vatican was completely out of sympathy and watched with satisfaction the swift growth of resistance in Florence. Savonarola, getting more and more above himself, began to hear voices and see visions. The hypnosis of Florence weakened. Once, just before he preached, it was found that someone had driven nails, point uppermost, through the woodwork he was wont to bang for emphasis.

When the dangled bribe of a cardinal's hat failed to silence Savonarola, the Pope tried excommunication. The irrepressible friar replied with even more scarifying exposures of papal wickedness. Alexander put Florence under an interdict. Savonarola circularized the princes of Christendom, proposing a general conference to depose so unworthy a pontiff. Lodovico intercepted one of these letters and sent it to Alexander. Rome rose in fury, and it was made plain to the Florentines that Savonarola must go, or condign punishment would descend upon their city. The friar had already made many enemies. Now his monastery was stormed and he was made captive, though with traditional independence the Florentines refused to surrender him even to the Pope: they would deal with him themselves. How they did so is a familiar but ever-tragic story. After forty days of imprisonment, interrogation and torture, Savonarola and his two particular associates were sentenced as heretics, ceremonially degraded by a bishop and prior of their own Order, hanged, and burnt in the piazza outside the Palazzo Vecchio.

.   .   .   .

One of Savonarola's early prophecies, which had helped to

build up his reputation, had spoken of 'the sword of the Lord upon the earth, soon and speedily'. It was interpreted, especially afterwards, as referring to the French invasion of 1494, which helped to sweep the Medici from power.

That eventful year began with the death at last of Ferrante, and the succession of the sanguinary Alfonso. This was the signal for an immediate revival of the Angevin claim, now held by Charles VIII of France. In March he mobilized an army at Lyons for use against Naples.

Charles was a romantic young fool, whose mediocre abilities did not match his dreams. King at thirteen, he had only recently asserted himself at twenty-two. His head was now filled with a conception of conquest like that of the earlier and abler Charles frustrated by the Sicilian Vespers two hundred years before. He too dreamed of an Angevin army sweeping into Constantinople, an Angevin monarch reviving the glories of the Eastern Empire. Naples was to be a mere stepping-stone.

It was pretentious, but circumstances gave Charles a flying start. Lodovico Sforza was glad of any diversion which would occupy Alfonso. Lorenzo de' Medici had just died and Florence was drifting, with his son's weak hands upon the tiller. The Pope, barely settled on his newly acquired throne, was hedging and — while recognizing Alfonso — gave Charles permission to visit Rome 'on his way to the East'. The Frenchman had certain practical assets too. His court had long been the refuge of those Angevin barons who had survived the purge in Naples and if he entered Southern Italy many humbler people would come over to his side. Finally, his own lack of military experience was offset by the quality of his army. The French took war seriously. They fought for victory, not like the Italian *condottieri*, for ransom and security of employment. They had no chivalric prejudice against artillery, and were ungentlemanly enough to use iron cannon-balls which battered down castles instead of stone ones which splintered and bounced off.

In September Charles led this army through Piedmont. Lodovico welcomed him at Asti and they rode on to Pavia together. Here news reached them that young Gian Galeazzo had suddenly died. Lodovico's responsibility, if any, remains as debatable as Richard III's in a similar family bereavement.

At any rate, the sorrowing uncle excused himself, hastened to Milan, and proclaimed himself duke, ignoring the infant heir. Charles went on into Tuscany and was peppering the first Florentine fortresses with his alarming new cannon-balls when young Piero de' Medici came scuttling out to meet him, his nerve gone, offering to hand over not only the forts but Pisa and Leghorn into the bargain. This spineless behaviour, combined with much genuine pro-French sentiment in Florence, encouraged the rising against the Medici, and Savonarola was one of those who were soon officially welcoming Charles to the city. It was not long, though, before the exorbitant demands of the occupying army turned people against them. 'We shall blow our trumpets,' the French threatened darkly when their requirements were refused. 'Then we shall ring our bells!' retorted the magistrates. Even the tough French had no appetite for a street fight against the entire population. They prudently passed on their way, and entered Rome on New Year's Eve.

In Naples Alfonso was seized with panic. He had made too many enemies to have any hope of rallying the country. He abdicated and fled to Sicily. There was just a chance that his son Ferrantino, young and relatively popular, might be able to tip the scales. But Ferrantino was driven back step by step, from Capua to Naples, from the city itself to the Castel Nuovo, from the castle to the offshore island of Ischia. The exultant Angevins seemed irresistible.

Then the situation took a new turn. Lodovico Sforza, now duke in name as well as fact, began to regret his passive acceptance of the French invasion. Others, too, had misgivings about Charles' triumphant progress down the peninsula. An anti-French league was hastily formed to cut the young king's communications with home. Milan, Venice and the Pope joined with the king of Spain and the newly-elected Emperor Maximilian, who had an additional reason for disliking Charles: Charles having married Anne, Duchess of Brittany, in spite of that young lady's existing engagement to Maximilian himself. The pact against Charles was signed secretly at Venice, in the doge's bedchamber, on 31st March. So swiftly were events moving.

No less swiftly the news reached Naples. Charles could not ignore the threat to his rear. He at once began to withdraw.

Ferrantino borrowed some ships from Venice and some troops from Spain, under the 'Great Captain', Gonsalvo de Cordova, landed in Calabria, and reoccupied his kingdom. The French retreated northwards and an allied force, commanded by Gonzaga, Marquis of Mantua, prepared to bar their emergence from the Apennines. They fought at Fornovo, the honours (or dishonours) being equally divided. The French lost their baggage-train: the Italians, superior in numbers but deficient in determination, allowed them to escape.

So Charles got back to France, with little more to show for his expedition than the expert Italian gardener who proceeded to create for him, at his beloved château of Amboise, a typical Italian garden without any flowers in it. But Charles would not abandon his dreams. He was planning a second campaign when, hurrying to the tennis-court, he struck his silly head on a low doorway and died.

15. French and Spaniards

THE NEW king of France, Louis XII, had served with the Italian expedition and was more than ready to take over the unfinished business. On accession he promptly styled himself also King of Naples and Duke of Milan.

Pope Alexander, consistent only in furthering his children's interests, was quite willing to switch alliances: Louis could help Cesare. The young Borgia, a cardinal since eighteen, had just asked permission to renounce his holy orders, which his father had granted the more readily since it was an essential step in his own scheme to found a dynasty.

Another essential was territory to rule. This was to be found in the Romagna, which had reverted to anarchy once more under a host of petty local tyrants, called by courtesy 'papal vicars' though they paid not a scrap of attention to their impotent overlord. Cesare was to snuff out these insubordinate lordlings, unify the country, and become Duke of the Romagna. Alexander saw nothing wrong in distributing papal lands as though they were family estates. In a single document he assigned twenty-eight towns and castles to Lucrezia's little son and thirty-six more to a just-legitimized three-year-old who is confusingly described in one bull as his own son and in another as Cesare's. In the current conditions of Roman society the uncertainty was understandable, for he had made Rome more than ever a 'sink of iniquity', crowded with courtesans, adventurers and assassins.

There was a third essential step before Cesare could found a dynasty: he must marry well. Louis could help both in this and in the conquest of the Romagna. Louis would, for there were two comparable matters in which the Pope could reciprocate. First the king wanted his own marriage annulled so that he could marry Charles' widow and keep control of her dowry, the duchy of Brittany. Second, he wanted to overthrow Sforza. So a deal was done. Louis got his annulment, the Pope got his royal daughter-in-law, the King of Navarre's sister. Once Louis held Milan, he would lend Cesare troops to subdue the Romagna.

Lodovico Sforza now found himself isolated. All his late allies against Charles seemed strangely reluctant to move against Louis. Even the Emperor Maximilian did not send the help he promised. In Milan itself there was unrest, the head tax-collector was murdered, and Lodovico felt that he could no longer count on holding the city. Deciding to appeal to the emperor in person, he set off northwards, leaving his great fortress strongly garrisoned under a trusted officer. But so low had his stock fallen that, as soon as the French occupied the city, the castle surrendered without firing a shot. Within a month Louis himself entered Milan, and Italian supporters, Cesare Borgia among them, came flapping down like vultures on all sides.

Cesare got his troops and set about the town-by-town reduction of the Romagna, a task most congenial to his bloodthirsty character. He took time off, however, to accompany the French on their southward march, and shared in their pitiless sack of Capua. Naples was saved similar horrors by the retirement of the humane King Federigo to Ischia. Louis's plan was to partition the South with Spain, whose general, Gonsalvo de Cordova, held Apulia and Calabria.

Now, however, Lodovico came back across the Alps with ten thousand Germans and Swiss supplied by the emperor. Triumphantly he rode into Como, Pavia, Parma, Milan itself. Then the French rallied and penned him in Novara. His Swiss mercenaries refused to fight the Swiss in Louis' army. Lodovico tried to slip away in disguise but was betrayed. Louis combined a gentle attitude towards his own countrymen with a hatred of Italians, and Lodovico spent the remaining eight years of his life in a French dungeon.

By 1503 Cesare had made considerable progress in the conquest of the Romagna, despite sundry setbacks overcome by treachery, murder and French assistance. In Rome his father was eliminating awkward cardinals and taking over their wealth for his own purposes. Cesare knew, though, that this happy family partnership could not last for ever. Alexander, for all his phenomenal vitality — he had been described as 'a magnet for women' — was now over seventy. Cesare told Machiavelli afterwards how he had tried to foresee every possible contingency, so as to ensure, when the time came, a new pontiff favourable to himself.

Meantime in the South the French had run into trouble and Alexander was pondering another change of sides. France and Spain could not agree on the partition of the Regno, and in Gonsalvo the French had found their most formidable adversary. His men were trained in mountain guerrilla-warfare, ideal for Calabria. Fighting in flying columns of light cavalry, crossbowmen, arquebusiers and swordsmen, often helped by local partisans, they made rings round the heavily armoured French and their Swiss pikemen under their Scots general, Stuart d'Aubigny. Yet, when forced to fight in the open, Gonsalvo could adapt himself, building up a solid centre armed with the pike, and using his mobile troops on the wing. He was the creator of those disciplined Spanish pikemen who became the finest infantry in Europe and the trainer of countless young officers who led them to victory in the decades which followed.

Gonsalvo defeated the French at Cerignola, bottled them up in Gaeta, and entered Naples. Alexander told Louis that he would continue his support only if Cesare were given the kingdom of Naples in exchange for the Romagna. Simultaneously he offered the Spaniards his help if they aided Cesare in taking over Tuscany.

It was midsummer. A fine French army was riding south to relieve Gaeta, Gonsalvo was preparing to hold the line of the Garigliano against them, Alexander was still trying to predict the ultimate winner. Then, in the August heat, malaria struck him down, and in five days he was dead. Cesare himself was at death's door. This simultaneous incapacitation was the one contingency he had never foreseen. He was unable to rig the papal election. Strangely enough, the new Pope lived only twenty-six days, but the second election came too soon for the convalescent Cesare. The dangerous Giuliano della Rovere assumed the tiara as Julius II. A bargain was struck, but the two men had little in common except distrust.

During these electoral intrigues the outnumbered Spaniards doggedly held the French along the Garigliano. Reinforced at last, Gonsalvo slipped across the river one dark December night. Surprised, the French fell back in panic. On New

Year's Day, 1504, Gaeta surrendered to him, and the long
Angevin adventure was over at last. Thereafter the kingdom
of Naples was a dominion of the Spanish crown, ruled like
Sicily by a viceroy.

.   .   .   .

The new Pope resembled Alexander only in his brimming
vitality. But whereas it had made Alexander voluptuous it
made Julius an aggressive campaigner, a blunt statesman, and
a bold town-planner, decisive in destruction and ambitious
in design. He it was who pulled down St. Peter's and commissioned the present basilica from Bramante, and set Raphael
to obliterate the masterpieces of his predecessors. For many
years he had been Borgia's bitter rival, and, when the latter
had become Pope, he had watched with increasing horror the
distribution of Church possessions. Sixty when at last the
chance came to reverse the trend, he flung himself into the
task with the energy of a young man.

First, the Romagna must be recovered. Cesare was seized
and forced to surrender his castles. He then fled to Naples,
where Gonsalvo arrested him again as a menace to Italian
peace. After two years' detention in Spain, he escaped to his
brother-in-law's court in Navarre, and his career ended only
six months later, on an obscure campaign in the Pyrenees.
His historical importance never quite matched the legend
which grew up around him, as the incredibly wicked and
cynical young Spaniard, certainly murderous, treacherous
and lecherous, and possibly incestuous into the bargain.

Other papal cities had still to be regained. Perugia and
Bologna were under formidable local despots: Julius rode
forth and brought them to submission. Faenza and Rimini
had been occupied by the Venetians. Unable to take on Venice
by himself, Julius formed an alliance with Louis and Maximilian, soon to be joined by Ferdinand of Spain, all of whom
had their own reasons for disliking the Republic. Louis sent
an army through the Alps, Julius issued a bull of excommunication. This did not unduly disturb the Venetians,
traditionally contemptuous of papal authority, but the
French advance was different. The Venetian forces were
routed near Cremona, and for a few months the future of the
Republic looked sombre. She must do something quickly to

break up the alliance. The obvious partner to detach was the Pope, a fellow Italian, with a common interest in resisting foreign penetration of the peninsula. Julius lent a willing ear to her ambassador. 'These Frenchmen,' he admitted, 'have robbed me of sleep and appetite. I spent last night pacing my room.' A deal was done. Venice gave him back Faenza and Rimini, together with Ravenna and Cervia. Julius discovered a new mission for himself, the expulsion of 'the barbarians' from Italy, to be achieved with Swiss mercenaries.

The bellicose pontiff, now sixty-seven, was thoroughly enjoying himself, riding with the troops, joking and cursing with them, sharing the crudities of active service, even in the depth of winter. At Bologna he was nearly taken prisoner but was saved by his new allies. In the following year the French advanced again and sent him flying for safety to Ravenna. But by autumn he had got the Spanish king to change sides, forming with Venice the 'Holy League', their joint forces being commanded by Raymond de Cardona, Gonsalvo's pupil and successor as viceroy in Naples. By one of those coincidences so frequent in the society of the time, Cardona's opponent was his master's brother-in-law. On Isabella's death, King Ferdinand had married Germaine de Foix, and her brilliant young brother, Gaston de Foix, deservedly nicknamed 'the Thunderbolt of Italy', now took over the French command in Lombardy. With his dashing cavaliers, among whom the romantic Bayard was conspicuous, Gaston waged mobile war across the great plain. He seized Bologna, then galloped to Brescia (which had revolted in support of Venice), and put the town to sack. Only Bayard, lying badly wounded, raised his voice to restrain the soldiers. Gaston next threw himself against Cardona's motley army of Spaniards, Swiss, Venetians and papal troops, forcing them back to the marshes near Ravenna. There on the banks of the Ronco they stood at bay. The Spanish pikemen held firm and the French cavaliers swerved from their glittering points, but the other allied forces broke in confusion. Gaston, in the moment of victory, saw the road open to Rome, to Naples even, and the recovery of the Angevin inheritance. But in the next moment the vision faded, for he was struck down as he harried the fugitives, and with him died the opportunity.

The very genius of Gaston was the undoing of the French: nobody could even pretend to take his place. While they dithered, awaiting instructions from France, the allies pulled themselves together. Julius, with his flair for splitting hostile formations, drew Maximilian over to the Holy League. Lodovico's young son, Massimiliano Sforza, who had spent the last ten years in German exile, was brought out of store and proclaimed Duke of Milan. Twenty thousand Swiss pikemen came swinging down the road to Verona, where they linked up with the Venetians and began to push the French out of Lombardy. By the end of the year the French were out and the young Sforza was in.

Restoration was in the air. Since Savonarola, Florence had been decently and quietly governed by Piero Soderini, who had been elected Gonfalonier for life. Now the exiled Medici stirred. Florence, though inactive in recent campaigns, had been consistently friendly to France. She had offended Julius by allowing a conference of opposition cardinals at Pisa, while prominent among the majority supporting him was that very son of Lorenzo the Magnificent who had been a member of the Sacred College since adolescence. With Gaston dead and the French once more beyond the Alps, the day of reckoning had arrived. Cardona's support for the Medici was bought with ten thousand ducats and his Spanish columns began to wind down through the Apennines. Florence defied them. The militia were sent to stop them at Prato, eleven miles away — the militia which Machiavelli, a staunch supporter of Soderini, so fervently held to be the answer to mercenaries. The Spaniards, neither militia nor mercenaries, but a disciplined, professional, national army, stormed the little Tuscan town and for three weeks subjected its people to appalling atrocities. The lesson was not lost on Florence. There was a bloodless revolution, Soderini exiled to Siena, the Medici restored in the person of Lorenzo's gentle second son, Giuliano, and Florence brought into the Holy League.

A few months later Julius died, having achieved much in his ten-year papacy of what he had set out to do. The rejoicings of the Medici were redoubled when the news came that Cardinal Giovanni de' Medici had been chosen to become Pope Leo X.

. . . .

'As God has given us the papacy, let us enjoy it,' Leo is supposed to have said to his brother. The remark was at least in character. His florid complexion and heavy jowl belied both his thirty-eight years and the refinement of his intelligence. Lorenzo had rated him, of his three sons, 'the clever one', and in that informal household the impressionable boy had met the foremost artists and intellectuals of the day. What more natural than to strive now to recreate in the Vatican the remembered delights of the Medici? In the morning he listened to music. Then the poets crowded in upon him, pursuing him with their proffered dedications even in his garden and his private rooms. And so the day went on, from the consideration of one cultural project to that of another. A Greek printing-press, another in Hebrew for the Jews, the expansion of the university, Raphael's appointment as keeper of classical antiquities, the grandiose rebuilding of St. Peter's — it is small wonder that he sometimes sought relief from these weighty preoccupations and took delight in masques and comedies, even in the knockabout humour of jesters and buffoons. Books were his great love. 'The great writers,' he said, 'are a rule of life and a consolation in misfortune. One of my highest aims has always been to assist scholars and obtain books of excellence.' He found work for writers of every type, from the classicist Bembo, whom he made his secretary, to the Dominican Bandello, whose scabrous novelettes later provided plots for *The Duchess of Malfi* and other Elizabethan plays.

Unfortunately Leo could not devote himself entirely to making Rome a new Florence — or even to discharging his religious responsibilities, in which he was indeed reasonably zealous. Like other Popes, he had to walk the political tightrope. Nor was he without ambition for his relatives, his unaggressive brother Giuliano, and his nephew Lorenzo whom he installed by force in Urbino and married to a French princess. Their daughter was Catherine de' Medici, the future Queen of France.

Leo had always to consider two most powerful sovereigns whose accession closely followed his own.

First, in 1515, came the twenty-year-old Francis I, '*Le Roi Grand Nez*' whose otherwise not unhandsome face, with its neat horseshoe of beard and narrow moustache, its sly eyes under the slanting, feathered bonnet, is most familiar from Clouet's portrait in the Louvre. Though too much must not be made of the gold brocade and the enormous sleeves, since all Renaissance rulers were *ex officio* resplendent, Francis was a dandy even by contemporary standards, and his clothes did in truth reflect the superficial brilliance of the man beneath. A lively conversationalist, fluent versifier, and amateur of the arts, he had also a passion for physical exercise, whether tennis or tournaments or the chase. Some of his early amours provided his sister, Marguerite of Navarre, with material for the *Heptameron*. Himself reared on the romances of the Round Table, the young knight lost no time in seeking chivalrous adventure. Italy was the obvious field. Everyone knew that the French had not been driven out three years before: they had simply faded away 'like mist' (as a Florentine had put it) when Gaston's death paralysed the leadership. Bayard and his fellow paladins were eager to expunge the embarrassing memory. Six months after his accession, Francis led them forth in all their highly-polished glory.

Italy met them, as usual, disunited. Each member of the Holy League was trying to limit his liabilities, each looking nervously over his shoulder in the wry-necked attitude made habitual by the impermanence of political friendships. The Venetians had long ago reverted to their French alliance and Cardona's army was tied down near Verona, watching them. Young Lorenzo, commanding the papal forces for his uncle, had orders not to advance beyond Piacenza. Milan stood isolated in the path of the French, her main defenders the stalwart Swiss. They waited at Susa, ready to stop Francis whether he came over the Mont Cenis Pass or the Mont Genèvre. But Francis, though young, inexperienced and indeed never much of a general himself, had veterans to advise him. Following an Alpine track regarded as impracticable for armies, the French flowed down like a glacier of steel between the foothills of Piedmont.

A tremendous battle ensued at Marignano, ten miles from Milan. As usual the armies formed up on either side of a stream which offered, football-fashion, a convenient dividing line. The French put their famous cannon in front: it was useless, at that stage of artillery development, to put them anywhere else. Behind them, Francis sat his horse with the

marshalled chivalry of France. His arquebusiers held the
right wing, and the rest of his host, mainly French and Rhineland mercenary pikemen, the new *landsknechts* or *lansquenets,* were massed in three divisions. The Swiss, who had neither
cavalry nor guns, put their faith in the sheer weight of their
columns, solid and disciplined as a Macedonian phalanx. With
three such columns they opened the battle that September
afternoon, making straight for their hated professional rivals,
the *lansquenets,* who were beginning to threaten Switzerland's vital export trade in mercenaries.

The French artillery, still something of a dreadful novelty
in open warfare, drilled deep holes in the advancing masses.
The arquebusiers poured in their shot, the armoured knights
charged again and again, and, as the opposing infantry masses
interlocked in hand-to-hand struggle, the pike had often to
be abandoned for the sword. Even dusk brought no ending.
The harvest moon hung over the Lombard plain and by its
light the slaughter continued till nearly midnight. Then the
armies drew apart and the next few hours were spent in grim
reorganization, the hasty gulping down of what food and drink
were available, uneasy cat-naps on the trampled ground.
Francis himself stayed with his outposts and did not unarm.
At sunrise the undaunted Swiss came back for more punishment. All that day the struggle raged. Towards evening,
twenty-eight hours after it began, the king's Venetian allies
arrived and only then did the surviving Swiss turn in flight,
wading through flooded ditches across the darkening countryside. They lost about twenty thousand killed and wounded,
the French barely half that number. Bayard, with mingled
pride and embarrassment, obeyed his young king's order to
knight him on the field.

Francis made his state entry into Milan a month later.
Massimiliano Sforza accepted a pension and went to live in
France, but his brother, Francesco, retired to Trent, which
with the Brenner as back-door was a healthy observation-post.
Leo quickly sought an *entente* with the conqueror. It looked
as though this time the French had come to stay.

Now, though, the other new sovereign took the stage. In
the following January, 1516, a pale, thin-faced, conscientious
boy from the Netherlands succeeded his grandfather, Ferdin-
and, as King of Spain, the Two Sicilies, and dominions yet

undemarcated in the New World. Three years later, still only nineteen, he was elected to succeed his other grandfather, Maximilian, as Holy Roman Emperor, Francis being one of the defeated candidates and Henry VIII of England another. So, in the person of Charles V, the papacy saw the old Hohenstaufen threat reborn, Central Europe and Southern Italy under one crown, not to mention Spain and the American colonies.

Leo, however, took the short view. He decided to change partners again. He met Charles at Bologna, and made an agreement. Charles would liberate Milan, where French governors like the arrogant Constable de Bourbon had made themselves vastly unpopular, and install Francesco Sforza. Leo lived just long enough to see this done. He was succeeded after a brief interlude by Clement VII, another Medici, son of that Giuliano murdered by the Pazzi long ago.

In spite of the first sweeping imperial successes, the Franco-Spanish struggle for Lombardy dragged on for four years, during which Milan changed hands, the Constable de Bourbon changed sides, and the heroic Bayard was killed by a shot from an arquebus. Francis, with characteristic vanity, thought he could do better than his commanders. He returned to Italy and was besieging Pavia in February 1525, when his camp was surprised at dawn by the relieving army of the Empire. The garrison, in which citizens had fought shoulder to shoulder with German mercenaries, made a simultaneous sortie. Francis fought courageously but could not save the situation. He was knocked off his horse, made prisoner, and sent to Madrid. '*Nothing is left,*' he wrote to his mother, '*but life and honour, which is safe.*' It was an unusually simple and accurate estimate of the situation. Francis and (for many a long day) France were finished in Italy. When peace was made and the royal captive released, he had to content himself with little corners of Italian culture in his own châteaux, created for him by Leonardo da Vinci, Andrea del Sarto, Benvenuto Cellini, and the other artists whom at one time or another he had tempted into his service.

.   .   .   .

Effective as a cardinal, Clement was disastrous as a Pope. Continuing his cousin's policies, he put family interests first and ignored the bigger issues in a world changing with vertiginous speed. This was the age of Luther: it was Clement who refused Henry VIII his divorce and precipitated the English Reformation. The Spaniards and Portuguese were penetrating into the immeasurable territories of America and Asia, while the Turks, at their zenith under Suleiman the Magnificent, were thrusting forward through the heart of Europe. Gunpowder, the printing-press, the flood of gold and silver from the New World — in every sphere of life at once there was revolution, technical, ideological, economic. All served to diminish the relative importance of Italy.

Lacking our hindsight, Clement could not even see that the French were no longer the side to back. He continued to look wistfully towards them and to emulate Leo's diplomatic duplicity. Two years of this resulted in the 'Sack of Rome' in 1527, so termed, despite all the innumerable other occasions, because of its particularly memorable horror.

That spring, a great imperial army composed of Spaniards, German *landsknechts*, and Italians marched south from Piacenza. The Germans were mainly Lutherans, with a genuine hatred of the papacy, though, being also mercenaries with pay perpetually in arrears, they had a frank interest in loot. Many of the Italians were supporters of the Colonna family, with whom Clement was conducting a bitter feud: they wanted revenge for the Colonna villages burnt by his men. The commander of this unruly horde was the renegade Frenchman, the Constable de Bourbon. The emperor, far away in Spain, knew nothing of what was happening and could have done little had he known. His viceroy in Naples did in fact hurry northwards, but he could not give the men their back pay and they laughed at his authority. They swept on, Bourbon, like the driver of a runaway team, just hoping to reduce the crash.

In the golden mist of a May morning they fell upon a city deluded until the last moment that this thing could never happen. Out of the fog the startled defenders saw the ladders reared up against the low walls hemming the Vatican Hill. Benvenuto Cellini's memoirs give vivid glimpses of what followed, though with disproportionate emphasis on his own skill with arquebus and culverin. Inevitably, being Cellini, he claims that it was his shot which killed Bourbon. Whoever fired it, it was a truly fatal shot, for it removed the only man with any power to mitigate the subsequent atrocities.

All was panic as the tide of invaders washed over the defences of the papal suburb. Clement heard the news in chapel. He fled down the long fortified corridor connecting the Vatican with the Castel Sant' Angelo, his page holding up his train, his courtiers panting at his heels. Cellini was among the last of the fortunate three thousand who squeezed inside the castle before the portcullis came down. Two cardinals arrived late: one was hauled in through a window, the other pulled up to the battlements in a basket. Meanwhile the imperial troops began to pillage and massacre. The main part of the city could still have escaped if the authorities had blown up the Tiber bridges. But they could not nerve themselves to anything so drastic, and so, to save three beautiful bridges, they sacrificed the whole glory of Renaissance Rome. The invaders surged over, mad with greed, drink, lust, and bigotry. The Lutherans sacked churches, dragged naked cardinals through the streets, and lurched about in Church vestments, parodying the ceremonies they abhorred. If their Spanish and Italian comrades did not join in their blasphemies, it was only to devote themselves the more wholeheartedly to the ransacking of the city and the murder, torture or rape of its inhabitants.

This lasted for eight days. The Pope meantime stayed safe in Sant' Angelo. Cellini, when not performing prodigies of gunnery or remonstrating with cardinals, ' *because those red caps of theirs were marks for the enemy*', occupied himself professionally on the Pope's instructions, melting down gold and breaking up jewels, so that ' *each could be rolled up in a small piece of paper and stitched into the linings of the Pope's garments.*' No help came. The Duke of Urbion, who had shadowed the enemy throughout their march, retired now without attempting more than he had already done, which was precisely nothing. Venice and Ferrara soon exploited the Pope's predicament to occupy corners of territory, Florence threw out the Medici again.

Once satisfied that his position was hopeless but that enough discipline had been restored to make his person safe from outrage, Clement came to terms. Some months were spent in frantic efforts to raise at least part of his ransom, which was done by persuading three ambitious bishops to pay ten thousand ducats each for advancement to cardinal. In September the impatient *landsknechts,* who had evacuated the city during the fever season, swarmed back and went over it again for any surviving articles of value. At the finish, two houses out of three were blackened shells, eighty years of tireless and inspired development had been blotted out, and Rome was once more the desolate wilderness which Nicholas V had found. At last, one December evening, Clement slipped out and rode away to Orvieto, dressed as a simple merchant, with only a few attendants.

'*We are waiting to know how Your Majesty intends the city of Rome to be administered,*' wrote the emperor's envoy to his master, '*whether it is to be some sort of apostolic seat or not.*' He pointed out shrewdly that, if the status of Rome were completely destroyed, the kings of England, France and other lands would merely set up national patriarchs. So '*the opinion of Your Majesty's servants is that it would be best to keep the apostolic seat, but so subordinate that Your Majesty can always control it.*'

That was very much the course followed. The Italian settlement was tied up with a great many other matters, political and ecclesiastical, and it suited emperor and Pope to make friends. By the Treaty of Cambrai Francis I gave up his claim to Milan, which Charles left for the moment to be ruled by the last Sforza; on his death, childless, Milan came under a Spanish viceroy. For the rest, Charles was content to leave Venice alone — she was always a hard nut to crack — to confirm the Este family in their duchy of Modena and Reggio, combined with Ferrara, and to promote the Marquis of Mantua to a dukedom. Clement regained the papal territories intact and was promised imperial troops to restore his relatives in Florence, which was accomplished after some desperate fighting. The new friendship between Charles and Clement was sealed by the latter's coronation of the former at Bologna, Rome being in no condition for such solemnities. Never again, indeed, was a Holy Roman Emperor to be crowned there.

Italian politics, fluid for so long, were now fast congealing into the flabby condition which they maintained for generations. Alessandro de' Medici ruled Florence until he was murdered, and replaced by a new young Cosimo, whom Charles made a duke. The Medici, soon still further ennobled as Grand-dukes of Tuscany, produced no more great historical figures. Clement's successor as Pope was Alessandro Farnese, whose early progress in the Church had owed much to his sister Giulia, mistress of Alexander VI. He too obtained a duchy for his family, by making over Parma and Piacenza to his son. It was the third Duke of Parma, formidable as general, diplomatist, and Spanish viceroy in the Netherlands, of whom Elizabeth thought 'foul scorn' in her Tilbury speech.

Charles V abdicated in 1556, to spend his last year or two in retirement. The imperial crown was not his to assign, but that of Spain went to his son Philip, already King of the Two Sicilies, Duke of Milan, and husband of the English Queen Mary, though specifically excluded from any authority in her country. Now, for the last time, the old French claim to Naples flickered into life, fanned by a new and virulently anti-Spanish Pope, Paul IV. An expedition was led by the Duke of Guise, a general who in other circumstances could have been dangerous. But he had no sooner scored some minor successes than he was called home to defend France against a Spanish attack from the Netherlands. In Italy the French threat had no chance to develop, and faded from notice as the war went on. After the Treaty of Câteau-Cambrésis in 1559, no one challenged Spain's domination of Italy.

16. The Age of the Grand Tour

WHAT SINGLE phrase can designate the two and a half centuries of Italian subjection, first to Spain, then to Austria? To call this chapter the 'stagnant' or the 'servile centuries' would be unjust to Venice and Savoy, as well as to countless individuals elsewhere, ranging from popular rebels to the more enlightened Popes and princes, who struggled against circumstances too strong for them. Also it would unduly emphasize the purely political and military, obscuring progress in other fields. For Italy remained the school of Europe, the magnet of the cultivated man. Thither went Inigo Jones to study landscape drawing at the end of Elizabeth's reign, there his eyes were opened to the delights of architecture and there he began his development into 'the English Palladio'. Thither travelled Milton and Evelyn just before the Civil War. Thither, in the seventeen-sixties, went Gibbon, Smollett and Boswell. Earlier and later, artists and architects, writers and musicians, scholars and schoolboys, Englishmen and others flocked to Italy like pilgrims to Mecca. As poor Johnson, who never managed the journey, declared with feeling, 'A man who has not been in Italy is always conscious of an inferiority.' So, for want of a better title, the long period between Cateau-Cambrésis and Napoleon may be termed the Age of the Grand Tour.

Naturally the antiquities were a potent attraction but Italy was not living on her cultural reserves. Much was being achieved in many fields. Renaissance architecture was giving place to florid and flamboyant baroque. Rome was being transformed by that alliterative trio, Barozzi, Bernini and Borromini. Barozzi, better known as Da Vignola, was already in his prime when, in 1568, he began the famous Jesuit church of Gesù, setting the pattern of ecclesiastical architecture for two centuries. He was followed by two keen rivals and exact contemporaries: the Neapolitan Bernini (1598-

1667), more than any other individual the creator of the Rome we see today, whose countless memorials range from the Triton Fountain to the vast colonnaded piazza in front of St. Peter's; and that uneven, unhappy genius Borromini (1599-1667) who contributed the Falconieri Palace and a number of churches before he committed suicide. Baroque swept the country from Turin to Palermo, often with interesting regional variations. Rococo never widely established itself outside Venice, though in Rome the Spanish Steps and the Fountain of Trevi border upon it. In the late eighteenth century native architects were overshadowed by the French Valadier and the half-Flemish Vanvitelli.

In painting, despite an inevitable decline from the zenith of the Renaissance, the output was not inconsiderable, particularly in Venice. Tintoretto and Veronese belong to the beginning of this epoch, Tiepolo and Canaletto to the end. The seventeenth century saw the great days of Neapolitan painting, inaugurated by two outsiders, the raffish Lombard labourer Caravaggio, who fled to Naples to escape the consequences of his crimes, and the more respectable Spaniard, Ribera, who came as court painter to the viceroy but thoroughly acclimatized himself in Italy.

Musically, this was a rich period. Palestrina, throughout the later sixteenth century, was creating the new church music of the Counter-Reformation. Monteverdi, forty years his junior, added to it and at the same time laid the foundations of Italian opera. His *Orfeo* in 1607 was the first opera of significance, yet so quickly did the new art-form catch on that Venice alone soon had four different opera-houses which he supplied during the thirty years from 1613 when he was also in charge of the music at San Marco. Soon followed the Scarlattis, Alessandro born at Palermo in 1659, Domenico in Naples in 1685. Alessandro's long record of productions in Rome, Naples, Florence and elsewhere indicates the demand throughout the peninsula, while his son's preference for the harpischord shows that development was not confined to one form.

Despite the growth of censorship writers maintained a gush of words which Bernini's fountains might have envied — plays and poetry, histories and romances, books on science and religion, manners and morals. Countless they may be, but at least someone has counted the Italian works translated and published in England during the first hundred years of this period: the number is 383, tiny perhaps compared with the horrific statistics of modern publishing but evidence of a formidable total output. In quality it was not perhaps a great era, but, though the poets in general declined into artificiality, it included some notable names. It begins with Tasso, the hapless, unbalanced author of the epic *Jerusalem Delivered* and the pastoral play *Aminta*. It ends with the lyrical Metastasio, so popular as a librettist not only with his countryman Scarlatti but with Handel, Gluck, J. C. Bach, and others; and the picturesque Piedmontese adventurer, Alfieri, who combined the writing of classical tragedies with the conduct of romantic affairs, including one with the wife of the Young Pretender. In prose-drama there was Goldoni, who delighted Venice with his Molière-style comedies until, in 1761, he departed to the Italian Theatre in Paris. Outside the strict limits of literature was the *commedia dell' arte,* which had held the stage for the two centuries before him, as unwritten as the improvised jazz of our own era and as wide in its influence, which ranged from Shakespeare and Molière to the harlequinade in the Victorian pantomime. It used stock characters — a quartet of young lovers, a boastful soldier, a Venetian merchant (Pantalone), and so forth, with supporting clowns and zanies. Though the dialogue was impromptu, eight hundred different scenarios survive.

Science was hampered but not stifled by the Inquisition: though our period opens with the burning of Giordano Bruno and the intimidation of Galileo, it ends with the electrical discoveries of Alessandro Volta. The authoritarian climate could not blight the buds of political speculation. Liberal ideas were not only published, as in Cesare Beccaria's book on penal reform in 1764, but won some acceptance. Italians were specially active as Orientalists, philologists, geographers and botanists. Always to the fore in distant travel, whether as navigators, traders or missionaries, they now gave the world of scholarship the by-products of their adventures. Between them they mastered Persian and Chinese, detected the link between Sanskrit and the European languages, reported on the social life of India, and recorded everything from their impressions of Peru to the possible value of drugs new to European pharmacy.

In short, then, though nineteenth-century nationalists might look back with shame at what they felt to be the ignoble period separating them from past glories, it did in fact contain a wealth of achievement, of which any people could have been proud.

.   .   .   .

The first, and larger, part of this period (1559-1713) was the era of Spanish domination, exercised either by viceroys in Milan, Naples and Palermo, with strong Spanish garrisons to overawe the people from new-built fortresses and barracks dotted about the land, or indirectly through the rulers of the satellite territories. The Spanish officials milked their provinces rather as the ancient Romans had milked theirs in the corrupt republican period. Hearth-taxes, salt-taxes, market-tolls, and innumerable other payments were extracted from people who did not even receive efficient government in return and, impoverished and discouraged, sank ever lower. In the South, conditions were further worsened by the interplay of deforestation, erosion, malaria, and depopulation, factors which even the most enlightened government at that date could scarcely have understood and removed.

Violence was common. '*Revenge is a kind of wild justice,*' wrote Francis Bacon, and he might well have had contemporary Italy in mind. There was little real justice to be found in the courts, so men sought it for themselves. The rich employed the *bravo* or professional thug; the poor formed companies of *banditti*, which, though started as co-operative efforts for self-protection, degenerated into criminal gangs, like the Mafia.

From time to time there was an impulsive riot or more serious rebellion, usually quenched by a whiff of musketry. In Naples, however, in 1647, a new tax on fruit touched off an explosion of popular indignation, which found a leader in a fisherman from Amalfi, Masaniello. The viceroy took refuge from the angry demonstrators in the Castel Nuovo and issued soothing promises which Masaniello was too shrewd to accept without proper guarantes. He had a flair for organization and kept his followers under control in those feverish July days. He was clearly a dangerous man and the viceroy acted accordingly: he took a solemn oath to make good his promises and then sent his *bravi* to murder Masaniello in the cathedral precincts.

The fisherman's death did not end the insurrection, which found fresh leaders and spread throughout the countryside. A punitive force, urgently summoned from Spain, was chased back to its ships after two days of the ferocious street-fighting to which the city so admirably lent itself. The people proclaimed a republic, but then, with a fatal lack of self-confidence, invited a French prince to be their general. After a few months of incompatibility and misunderstanding the revolutionary impetus petered out and the Spaniards were welcomed back, having made solemn promises which they promptly dishonoured.

Tuscany and the papal states presented many similar features: severe taxation and repression, corruption, lawlessness and economic decay. But the picture was less consistently sombre. There were long interludes of reform, when *bravi* and *banditti* were firmly dealt with, and the groaning taxpayer saw at least some return for his money.

Cosimo de' Medici, first Grand-duke of Tuscany, had come to power in 1537, a forceful eighteen-year-old not unworthy of his forebears. He ruled as a despot until his death thirty-seven years later, taking the people by the scruff of the neck and impelling them forward for their own good. He taxed them heavily, was remorseless to opponents, and maintained a strong police force and ubiquitous spies. In exchange he provided order and justice, absorbed the traditional enemy, Siena, revived the port of Pisa and gave that city a university, and in Florence tried to stimulate the textile trades. Midsixteenth-century Italy might have been better for more such autocrats. Subsequent Medici dukes lacked his character and their degenerate line became extinct in 1737.

In Rome too there was improvement — at a price. It was the period of the Counter-Reformation launched by the Council of Trent, of the new Jesuit Order, the Index, the Inquisition, and other manifestations of a religious zeal long overdue but not always happy in its effects. There was still plenty of corruption under the new fashionable veneer of piety, but a real effort was made to discipline the clergy, cleanse the papal court, and reduce nepotism. Popes and cardinals were, on the whole, better men than their predecessors. One Pope, Sixtus V, was an autocrat of truly remarkable vision and vigour. Queen Elizabeth said of him, slyly: 'I know of but one man who is worthy of my hand, and that man is Sixtus V.' In his five-year reign he suppressed the hordes of brigands in the Romagna and turned a financial deficit into a handsome surplus, while carrying through an immense programme of public works. The consequent level of taxation may be imagined. Some of this expenditure was justifiable, some less so. Not content with new streets and squares and an aqueduct, with completing the dome of St. Peter's and continuing the new summer palace of the Quirinal, he had a passion for erecting obelisks and perching saints' statues on top of Trajan's Column and such-like pagan monuments.

That, however, was one of the more innocuous manifestations of the Counter-Reformation, which caused an earlier pontiff to order the draping of the nudes in Michelangelo's *Last Judgment,* threatened Galileo with torture, and by its censorship drove many Venetian and Florentine publishers out of business. Milton himself, visiting Rome in 1639, ran into trouble with the police for airing his religious views too freely. Still, the Roman Inquisition was milder than the Spanish, and was reluctantly accepted in Naples as the lesser evil. Outside his own territory the Pope's authority was viewed with differing degrees of respect, notably by the indomitable Venetians, whose critical attitude to the Jesuits (stimulated by the independent-minded monk Paolo Sarpi) brought the city under an interdict in 1607.

After Sixtus the Popes relapsed into family favouritism, heaping perquisites on their respective relatives, the Barberini, the Borghese, and the rest. Corruption and disorder returned. What could not be arranged by whispered intrigue and bribery was accomplished with the *bravo*'s dagger, even in the open street. Two such *bravi* were commissioned by the Cenci to murder their father in his bed, and supplementary assassins were paid to silence the first pair when the work was done. The latter half of the scheme was only partially successful. The story came out. The resultant *cause célèbre* shocked even the Rome of 1599, and the English Lord

Chamberlain rather later when Shelley dramatized it. The Cenci were publicly executed, the two women involved by a species of guillotine, and their estates confiscated by the Pope.

While the wealthy and the aristocratic busied themselves thus, the common people rotted. The population fell. The boys found no work, the girls no dowries. As a result, the Venetian ambassador reported to his government, the priesthood and the religious orders were filled with reluctant and unsuitable recruits. It was not the best foundation on which to rebuild the Church. Luckily the end of the century brought, in the nick of time, a Pope who finally destroyed the conception of the office as a God-given opportunity for the assistance of relatives. Innocent XII was seventy-six when elected, but for nine years he tackled the cleansing of the Augean Stable with irresistible energy. When he died in 1700 he had done his work so well that, whatever the human weaknesses of later pontiffs and their attendant bureaucracy, the Church leadership would never again fall below a certain standard of morality.

In all other respects the eighteenth century saw the papacy decline in influence. There was a movement everywhere to destroy the old favoured position of the Church. When the Pope was compelled to suppress the Jesuit Order in 1773, it was merely one episode in a long struggle raging not only throughout Italy but all over Catholic Europe. Internationally, papal prestige was at a low ebb, and treaties were signed with little regard for the interests of Rome. Within the peninsula, the old territorial rights of the papacy were barely respected and its nominal overlordship of other regions was ignored. The papal states themselves decayed, lacking any of that reformative impulse which from time to time revitalized the others. The farmlands of the Campagna deteriorated. The administration was continually haunted by bankruptcy. Pope Clement XII, in the seventeen-thirties, was reduced to running a state lottery to raise revenue, and to pronouncing excommunication against those unpatriotic subjects who preferred a flutter with the rival lotteries of Naples and Genoa. Only the city herself contrived somehow to produce a few fresh flowers of culture, the Trevi Fountain, the Spanish Steps, a rococo palace or villa here and there.

.   .   .   .

Two states were still truly independent: Venice and Savoy, henceforth Italian rather than French. Savoy, straddling the Alpine wall from Geneva to the Mediterranean, had suffered many vicissitudes, though one family had ruled her since the eleventh century. After the Treaty of Câteau-Cambrésis the duchy was taken firmly in hand by Emmanuel Filibert, who set up an extremely efficient despotism and, by skilful diplomacy and exchange of territory, shifted the centre of gravity into Piedmont, on the Italian side of the mountains. In 1562 he entered Turin, which the French had held for over fifty years, and made it his capital. His son, Charles Emmanuel I, reigned from 1580 to 1630, losing no opportunity to weed out French influence in the peninsula and aligning himself with Spain against the common enemy. The rivalry of foreign powers continued to ravage Northern Italy in these years, and Mantua especially never recovered from the sack of 1630, when the castle, so elegantly decorated by Isabella d'Este, was wantonly pillaged by the Austrians.

Soon after these two strong dukes, there was a long regency under the Duchess Christine, herself a French princess. With a masterful neighbour like Louis XIV it would have been strange indeed if Savoy had not drifted back under French influence. The reign of her son, Charles Emmanuel II, saw the duchy once more the battleground of France and Spain, and the scene of an inhuman massacre of the Waldensian sect, Milton's 'slaughtered saints', who had previously found toleration in the Alpine valleys. A second massacre was perpetrated by the next duke, Victor Amadeus II, under pressure from Versailles.

Victor Amadeus was anxious, however, to reassert his duchy's independence. He embarked upon the political tight-rope, nimbly shifting his weight from side to side, leaning first away from Louis towards William of Orange, then back to Louis, then away again as Marlborough's victories altered the outlook. In 1706 the French besieged Turin. He drove them off with the aid of the gallant Eugène, Marlborough's close comrade-in-arms and his own distant kinsman. When the War of the Spanish Succession ended in the Treaty of Utrecht, he got Sicily and a slice of Milanese territory, though seven years later he had to exchange Sicily for Sardinia. Thus it was as Kings of Sardinia that the House of Savoy continued until the Risorgimento. Turin remained their capital, architecturally ennobled by Guarino Guarini and Filippo Juvara, but otherwise a somewhat cheerless place of church bells and military parades, with 'little of the pleasures and less of the sins' of other Italian cities.

Eastwards across the Lombard plain, the Most Serene Republic of Venice kept up a show of serenity which her well-informed government must often have been far from feeling. The opening of the world's oceans had reduced the Mediterranean to a large salt lake, but the Venetians refused to see themselves as mere coastal carriers. Their quays were still lined with carracks and stacked with goods, their trade with Central Europe tremendous. The city was prosperous and orderly, thanks to the firm grip of the Council of Ten and their new colleagues, the Three Inquisitors of State. New baroque churches and *palazzi* proliferated like exotic fungi. The great dome of Longhena's masterpiece, Santa Maria della Salute, rose up across the Grand Canal to rival San Marco. The carnivals and regattas went on, theatres and operahouses were thronged, and when relief from all this vibrant gaiety was needed the wealthy citizens could retire to elegant Palladian villas spaced along green silent waterways in the green silent countryside.

Life was pleasant too in Padua, Verona and the other dependent cities of Venetia. Taxation was relatively light and the revenue mostly spent in the district, not transmitted overseas as tribute or diverted into the pockets of corrupt officials. These towns were left free to govern themselves and create their own culture. If we doubt that they did so, or that it was a vital culture, we have only to think of Palladio's own little town of Vicenza, which he and his follower Scamozzi almost completely rebuilt, and to picture the glittering scene at the opening of their Teatro Olimpico in 1585 when the local Academy presented Sophocles' *Oedipus Rex* in the first permanent playhouse erected since classical days.

All this time the Venetians refused to accept their loss of the Aegean. They continued to fight the Turks, usually single-handed and with more hindrance than help from their occasional allies. Their struggle to keep Cyprus ended in August, 1571, with the loss of Famagusta through the dilatory behaviour of their Spanish comrades under the Genoese admiral, Doria. In October there was indeed the spectacular victory at Lepanto, at the mouth of the Gulf of Corinth, when their navy combined with Spanish, papal and Tuscan forces under the emperor's bastard son, Don John of Austria. But in the long run the victory was less effective than Chesterton's verses about it. Though it discouraged Turkish advances into Western waters the Christian allies did not follow it up, and the Venetians were too much weakened to do so alone.

> 'Cervantes on his galley sets the sword back in the sheath,
>   (*Don John of Austria rides homeward with a wreath*).'

That was just the trouble. Two years later Venice had to sign away Cyprus to the Turks.

Two generations later it was the turn of Crete, which Venice had held since 1204. The war dragged on from 1645 to 1669. At sea the Venetians held their own and won numerous engagements near the Dardanelles, but when the Turks besieged Candia things went less well. The garrison fought doggedly and Francesco Morosini, one of the great commanders in Venetian history, took out a relieving force in 1667. The Turks were not to be driven off. They were determined to capture the city. Morosini directed the defence until 1669, when he was forced to surrender on honourable terms. Back in Venice he was impeached for this, but the state's reputation for justice was maintained and he was acquitted. When the struggle was resumed in 1684 (following Sobieski's historic defeat of the Turkish land-forces at Vienna), the sixty-six-year-old veteran was reappointed commander-in-chief. He was brilliantly successful, reconquering both the Morea and Athens, but the most lasting result of his campaign was the destruction of the Parthenon when a Venetian bomb landed on the Turkish powder-magazine.

His election as doge (at seventy) might reasonably have marked a transfer to more sedentary service, but five years later he was once more sailing eastwards, like Dandolo five centuries before, in personal command of the fleet. Like Dandolo he never returned. The Turks avoided action, so alarming was his reputation, for in those days the victorious commanders of the latest war gained rather than lost respect as the years went by. Morosini wintered in the harbour of Nauplia and died there in the shadow of Fort Palamidi, whose rock-clinging battlements still recall the days when the Lion of St. Mark glared inland towards the lions of Mycenae. Those days soon passed. Morosini's triumphs were transient. By 1718 the overseas empire of Venice had shrunk to the Ionian Islands, Istria, and the coastal fringe of Dalmatia.

.   .   .   .

Now within a decade or two the lines of Italian history run together as though into a railway-junction, and 'All change! ' is the cry. In 1713 the Utrecht treaty ended Spanish domination. Austria took Naples, Milan and Sardinia, exchanging the last for Sicily with Savoy in 1720. The seventeen-thirties brought war over the Polish succession: net result for Italy, the adventurous Don Carlos of Bourbon marched on Naples with a small army of Spaniards, ejected the Austrians and founded an independent Bourbon dynasty for the Kingdom of the Two Sicilies. 1737 completed the reshuffle: the last Medici died and Tuscany passed to Francis of Lorraine, a Habsburg connection who had just married the formidable Maria Theresa. Now we have the pattern familiar to the English milords who made the Grand Tour in the later eighteenth century: Bourbons in the South, an Austrian viceroy in Lombardy, an Austrian Grand-duke in Tuscany, Venice and Rome under the same old management but increasingly enfeebled, Piedmont with Sardinia the unsuspected seed-pod of a national dynasty to come. Corsica, long the neglected appendage of Genoa (herself still surviving as one of the minor Italian states), was sold to France in 1768, just in time to make Napoleon French. He was born in the following year.

Some of these changes brought a new impetus to progress. Carlos started well in Naples, aided by his minister, Tanucci, a professor of law from Tuscany with immense reforming zeal. It was needed. In that corrupt feudal country half the land belonged to the Church, half to two per cent of the population. The other ninety-eight per cent, declared a contemporary, 'had not enough to be buried in'. A population of five millions supported twenty-one archbishops, one hundred and sixty-five bishops and abbots, and a hundred thousand priests, monks and nuns, not to mention the feudal landowners.

Carlos and Tanucci did what they could. They aimed at halving the number of clergy, but got nowhere near their target. They expelled the Jesuits and clashed continually with the Pope, withholding the money-tribute and symbolic white horse which had been sent him yearly since Norman days. They tried to free the peasants from humiliating feudal services, allowed them to sell their produce in the open market, and gave them the right to appeal from the verdict of the manorial court. Too often it meant only that, if the poor men could afford the long journey and escape the intimidation of their lord's armed retainers, they had the satisfaction of hearing their appeal dismissed by judges drawn from his own class. Tanucci was no more successful in his attempt to codify Neapolitan law, a gallimaufry of eleven different systems accumulated over two thousand years of ever-changing regimes.

Carlos, himself half-Italian through his Farnese mother, was determined to make Naples a cultured capital. He established the royal library and commissioned the Teatro San Carlo, still the largest opera-house in Italy. The art collections of the Farnese family were brought down from Parma and the first finds from Pompeii and Herculaneum became the nucleus of the national museum. Twenty miles away, at Caserta, Vanvitelli built him a Mediterranean Versailles, six-storeyed, with twenty-six staircases, twelve hundred rooms, and a park with cascades, vistas, and an artificial river.

In 1759 Carlos inherited the throne of Spain and departed, leaving Tanucci to govern for his eight-year-old son Ferdinando. Ferdinando grew up to marry Maria Carolina, whose powerful personality echoed that of her mother, Maria Theresa. Maria got rid of the veteran Tanucci after forty-three years in office, and replaced him with John Acton, a distinguished naval officer formerly in the service of Tuscany, who had been called in originally to reorganize the Neapolitan fleet but was advanced step by step to chief minister. Working closely with Sir William Hamilton, the amiable dilettante who was British ambassador from 1764 to 1800, Sir John (who had meanwhile come into an English baronetcy) helped the queen to switch Neapolitan policy away from Spain towards Austria and Britain. That was the situation which Emma Hamilton found when she moved into the embassy—a Naples in which British influence was popular in ruling circles and disliked by the liberal reformers.

The Austrians similarly began well in Lombardy, where intensified cultivation made the countryside prosperous. Maria Theresa believed in letting the Italians largely govern themselves. She kept a viceroy in Milan and a few high-ranking Austrians in key positions, but that was all. As there was no military service for the inhabitants an unobtrusive minimum of imperial troops sufficed to maintain her authority. Her successor, Joseph II, had an unfortunate passion for centralization and reversed this tactful policy. He did away with the local senate, filled the offices with Austrians, and treated Lombardy as a mere province of the Empire. All his good works, his endowment of hospitals and Pavia University from the proceeds of suppressing a hundred super-fluous monasteries, could not make up for the affront to Italian pride.

Just as Naples lost her Bourbon ruler on his promotion to the throne of Spain, so Tuscany was, for the Habsburg Grand-dukes, a stage on the road to Vienna and the imperial crown. The first of them, Francis, became emperor in 1745 (in effect he was Maria Theresa's conscientious secretary) and there-after Tuscany was governed for twenty years by a series of officials who, though an improvement on the later Medici, treated the country mainly as a source of revenue for Austrian needs. After the death of Francis, however, the Grand Duchy was bequeathed to his second son, Leopold, who took up his residence in the Pitti Palace, recruited Tuscans in place of foreigners, and worked with Teutonic efficiency to revitalize the country. Marshes were drained, agriculture stimulated, the Inquisition suppressed, clerical privileges pruned, the criminal code revised, and free trade and disarmament sub-stituted for torture and the death penalty. He was more successful than the kings of Naples, but, like our own prince-consort, Leopold was not appreciated by his people. He was a foreigner, with notions too far ahead of his time. He had once been intended for the priesthood, but his preliminary training had, if anything, given him an anti-clerical bias, which provoked opposition in some influential quarters.

In 1790, when his elder brother Joseph died childless, he succeeded to the imperial throne. The demand for a serious opera to celebrate his coronation distracted Mozart's last year of life and might easily have cost us *The Magic Flute*. But the new emperor had things to distract him too. Every dispatch from Paris brought worse news, and his sister, Marie Antoinette, was now virtually a prisoner in the Tuileries.

17. Napoleon and Italy

THE FRENCH REVOLUTION had perhaps more violent side-effects in Italy than in any other European country.

The rulers were, as elsewhere, appalled. In the first year or two the French attack on feudal and Church privileges was only a more business-like version of what several Italian states had long been attempting, but there was a difference between the decrees of a benevolent despot and the voting of a horde of deputies. That difference was accentuated as the months went by. As Louis and Marie Antoinette drifted nearer to the guillotine, it became more and more a personal issue. They were not merely two royal individuals treated in a manner which struck at the sanctity of crowns. They were close relatives, by blood, marriage, or both, of all the ruling houses in the peninsula. The kings of Naples and Sardinia, the Grand-duke of Tuscany, the emperor, all were brothers-in-law or cousins to the hapless Louis.

For equally obvious reasons the politically conscious middle class found inspiration in the news from Paris. The French seemed to be doing something for themselves which the most progressive of Italy's foreign autocrats had failed to accomplish. The Italian liberals had never been asked to help. As in pre-Revolutionary France they had been slighted, their energies given no political outlet. This was the more resented because Italy's past glories had been so largely created by the middle class. What scope would there have been, they wondered, for Lorenzo the Magnificent in 1780? In Piedmont, for instance, would not snobbery have debarred Sforza even from a commission in the army? Though the bourgeoisie had no legitimate party organization, they possessed in Free-masonry a ready-made channel for the transmission of political ideas. The first lodge had been started in Florence in 1733 by the Duke of Middlesex — and condemned by the Pope in the same year. In due course the movement, originally a harmless English importation supported by the aristocracy, fell under the disfavour of the various governments. By driving it underground, they transformed it in half a century into something really dangerous, a secret society no longer aristocratic but bourgeois, no longer primarily social but political. By 1792 the network of lodges helped not only the circulation of news and manifestoes but the actual movement of Jacobin agents.

When war came between the Revolution and the kings of Europe, the French tried to detach Piedmont from her alliances, so that they could get at the Austrians in Lombardy. Victor Amadeus refused even the bribe of Lombard territory. He prided himself upon his army with its gorgeous uniforms and precise parade evolutions, which was almost the only effective Italian fighting-force then in existence. Hostilities broke out in September and, even as the main revolutionary army was doggedly withstanding the Prussian bayonets at Valmy, other French forces invaded Nice and Savoy. After this their progress became slow, hampered by counter-revolutionary risings behind them in Provence, by the lack of good supply-routes on land, and by British frigates and Sardinian corsairs which prevented their using coastal transport. By late 1795 there was stalemate. They had pushed along the Genoese littoral as far as Savona but the mountain crests were held by Piedmontese and Austrians. Then, in the following spring, the situation was transformed.

Napoleon Bonaparte was now twenty-six and in his short career remarkable responsibilities had already alternated with dismissals for unreliability. He knew the Italian front, had imaginative ideas for breaking the deadlock, and got them accepted by the Directory. Late in March, a few weeks after his marrying Josephine, he arrived in Nice to take over the dispirited army. Soon they were under his spell.

' Soldiers! ' he harangued them. ' You are half-starved and half-naked. The Government can do nothing for you. But I will lead you into the most fertile plains in the world. You will find honour, glory and riches! '

He then struck hard at the obvious place, where the Piedmontese line hinged on the Austrian. It took just eleven days of tough mountain warfare to split the allies and defeat them separately. By May Victor Amadeus was out of the war.

Napoleon swept across Piedmont, surprised the Austrians by crossing the Po at Piacenza, fell upon their rearguard at the bridge of Lodi, and, wheeling back, made a triumphal entry into Milan.

Everywhere the tricolour was welcomed with frenetic enthusiasm. But before long the liberated Lombards noted a discrepancy between the slogans of the Revolution and the behaviour of its soldiers, whose personal plundering was matched by a policy of ruthless exploitation at the higher levels. Napoleon had already begun his collection of foreign art treasures for the Louvre, but it was the seizing of the people's savings-banks that stirred ordinary men to fury. Frenchmen were murdered. Napoleon ordered savage reprisals. Binasco, near Milan, was burnt and its able-bodied men executed, Pavia given up to looting and massacre, hostages deported to France.

Meantime the main Austrian forces had been pushed over the mountains into the Tyrol, and the Italian princes, having no effective armies of their own, hastened to make terms with the invader. Only the great fortress of Mantua withstood the flood of French victory. The Austrians sent three successive armies to relieve it, all to be defeated by the brilliant young Corsican. After six months Mantua surrendered. The rot began to spread beyond the province: Bologna threw off her papal government, Reggio and Modena their duke; even in Venetia there were murmurs against the light yoke of the ancient oligarchy. Despite widespread exploitation and occasional terrorism by the French, the *Marseillaise* still fell on most Italian ears as the promise of liberty.

Napoleon settled the affairs of the peninsula with a highly individual interpretation of his instructions from Paris. A flying visit to Carinthia — in force — frightened the exhausted Austrians out of the war. By the Treaty of Campo-Formio they surrendered Lombardy in exchange for Venice and the easterly half of Venetia. To make this possible, Napoleon picked a quarrel with the Republic, though she had leant over backwards in her timorous attempts to remain neutral. He violated her mainland territory, disarmed her garrisons, and affected indignation when his own soldiers were attacked in Verona. Venice had neither the spirit nor the resources to resist such a man. On 14th May, 1797, Manin, the last of a hundred and twenty doges, voted with his Grand Council for the liquidation of the state. Two days later the first conquerors ever to occupy the city in eleven centuries were ferried across the lagoon (ultimate indignity, in Venetian craft) and the doge handed his official biretta to his servant, saying: 'Take it away, we shall not need it again.' The bronze horses of Byzantium went on their travels once more — to Paris. Thus, ironically, was Wordsworth's 'eldest child of Liberty' numbered among the victims of the Revolution.

Having extinguished one ancient republic, Napoleon proceeded to create several new ones. Genoa was permitted a precarious independence as the Ligurian Republic. Two experimental units, the Cispadane and Transpadane Republics ('this side of the Po' and the 'other side'), were quickly amalgamated as the Cisalpine, which combined Lombardy, Emilia, Romagna and western Venetia. He then sailed for Egypt, the next move towards the ultimate defeat of Britain. That was his objective from the start. It was in his mind when he seized the Venetian navy and annexed for France, of all Venetian territories, only the Ionian Islands; and when, using as excuse the murder of a French general in Rome, he ordered his chief of staff, Berthier, to occupy the city. *In sending me to Rome,* wrote Berthier, *you make me treasurer to the expedition against England. I will do my best to fill the exchequer.*

Until then, Napoleon had ignored his government's instructions to destroy the Pope's temporal power. He had been satisfied to humiliate the eighty-year-old Pius VI, robbing him of the Romagna and the ancient Avignon territory, and extracting a huge cash tribute together with a hundred works of art. Now, under the protection of Berthier's bayonets, a mass demonstration in the Forum repudiated papal authority and proclaimed a republic, with all the antiquarian apparatus of praetors and quaestors then fashionable. Pius refused to abdicate, but soon French troops escorted him, protesting, to the Tuscan border. After a brief sojourn in Siena and Florence, he was removed to France, where he shortly afterwards died. The Grand-duke Ferdinand next received his expulsion order with only twenty-four hours' notice to leave his duchy: an Etruscan republic replaced him. Even the newly-proclaimed Victor Emmanuel I was driven into retirement in Sardinia, leaving Piedmont to the French.

Only one ruler in Italy now defied them, the ridiculous and hen-pecked Ferdinand of Naples, whose teeming brood of little Bourbons are a classic example of the difference between paternity and virility. Pushed on by his masterful queen, Marie Antoinette's sister, together with the English baronet, Acton, his prime minister, and the ever-acquiescent British ambassador, Hamilton, Ferdinand signed a secret pact with Austria. Soon he was encouraged by the arrival of an experienced Austrian general, Mack, and Nelson, flushed from Aboukir. This was all too intoxicating for one of the weakest of crowned heads. Ferdinand sent an ultimatum to the young French general, Championnet, to evacuate Rome. Championnet did in fact retire about twenty miles to the north of the city, for his army was under strength and he had not a cartridge to waste. Ferdinand made a triumphal entry with his resplendent but unreliable regiments, and declared pompously to the world: 'The kings are awake.' He was in fact in a dream, from which he was rudely awakened a few days later. Championnet attacked, broke the Neapolitan army, and chased them along the road to Naples, Ferdinand's personal leadership being never more conspicuous. Nelson had a warship waiting. Ferdinand scrambled aboard. His queen, his dozen children and his more negotiable treasures were bundled after him, along with the Actons and Hamiltons, and all set sail for Palermo.

In his deserted capital there were divided counsels: those aristocrats who had not fled wished to buy off the French, while the liberal middle class wanted to hang out the flags of welcome — until the ignorant masses, in an incomprehensible enthusiasm for their royal family, began to murder everyone suspected of democratic sympathies. It was the mob, the *lazzaroni*, who put up the only resistance to Championnet. Heroic but ill-organized, they were beaten down in blood and yet another republic proclaimed, called the Parthenopean from the earliest Greek settlement on that site, in turn named after the siren Parthenope. Outside Naples, the French patrols were murderously harried by peasant guerrillas under the bellicose Cardinal Ruffo, a Neapolitan aristocrat who was never in fact ordained. Elsewhere, French power was unchallenged. Italy was a string of satellite republics.

After a few months the czar entered the anti-French alliance. His warships joined the British off Naples; his brilliant general, Count Suvorov, led an Austro-Russian invasion across the Adige with an energy which belied his sixty-nine years, and bundled the French out of Northern Italy. Napoleon was away in Egypt and no one else could stop Suvorov. The French army in Naples hurried back, but was lucky to escape destruction. It joined Masséna's forces in Genoa, which, by midsummer, was about the only corner still held by France. Elsewhere the satellite republics were swamped by reaction. In Piedmont the bishops led forth the peasants to wipe out the surviving French garrisons, in Tuscany the peasants found their own leaders, and in Lombardy the Austrians made a point of exterminating the native republicans. In the South, Cardinal Ruffo went from strength to strength, his fanatical 'Army of the Faith' stiffened by notorious bandits like Fra Diavolo, a detachment of British regulars (presumably, as always, overwhelmingly recruited from the Church of England) and another of Turks. In mid-June these variegated crusaders entered Naples and began two days of barbarous massacre and looting, from which no one was safe but their real opponents, the republican government and its soldiers, who had retired into the castles.

Ruffo came out of the affair better than some. He managed to restore order and arranged for the besieged republicans to surrender on honourable terms, with safe-conduct by sea to France. The instrument of surrender was signed also by the officers commanding the foreign troops in his army and by Captain Foote of H.M.S. *Seahorse*. Transports were being got ready when Nelson arrived with his squadron. Furious at Ruffo's clemency, fanatical in his devotion to Lady Hamilton's royal friends, he could still hardly countermand the agreement. He detailed officers to superintend the embarkation, which had no sooner taken place than dispatches arrived from Palermo insisting on exemplary vengeance. Not unaffected, we may suppose, by Lady Hamilton's persuasive presence on board, he convinced himself that he was now justified in tearing up the agreement. The elderly Prince Caracciolo, a Neapolitan admiral who had gone over to the republican side, was court-martialled aboard the British flagship and hanged from the yard-arm of a Neapolitan frigate before the interested eyes of Emma Hamilton. The previous massacre by the brutish irregulars was now matched by the counter-revolutionary tribunals. About a hundred leading liberals, including two women, were executed, two hundred and twenty sent to the galleys for life, hundreds of others given long sentences or exiled.

This reversal of circumstances was no more sudden than the one which followed. In October Napoleon wrote off his Egyptian scheme and slipped back to France. In November a *coup d'état* removed the discredited government of the Directory and left him all-powerful as First Consul. In the New Year, 1800, he turned to the urgent problem of Italy. Mid-May saw his famous crossing of the Great St. Bernard Pass, his precious artillery painfully hauled on sledges. He had no Suvorov to worry about (that excellent general was on his death-bed in St. Petersburg, ignored by an ungrateful czar) but there was no lack of other problems. He decided against relieving Genoa, where Masséna was starved into surrender on 6th June. On the 14th, much to his surprise (his information was faulty and he had sent off two separate columns in search of the enemy), he found himself face to face with the main Austrian army on the plain of Marengo. '*Come back in God's name!*' was the tersely scribbled message sent off by his gallopers to recall the reconnaissance columns. It reached only one of them, which, by forced marching, arrived on the battlefield between four and five o'clock. By this time Napoleon's depleted forces had been badly mauled and the Austrian commander, calmly assuming victory, had handed over to his chief of staff and ridden back to his headquarters for dinner. The French rallied. Thanks less to Napoleon than to his generals, Desaix, Kellermann, and the rest, the muddle was converted into a decisive triumph. After some more fighting on the Mincio, the Austrians surrendered Lombardy, and the Cisalpine Republic was recreated as the Italian Republic. Napoleon himself accepted the presidency, with a Milanese nobleman as vice-president.

Now, year by year, he proceeded to consolidate his power over the peninsula and to delegate it to trusted relatives. The revolutionary era was over. Hard on his proclamation as Emperor of the French followed his announcement that the

'Kingdom' of Italy was henceforth to be hereditary in his family, and on 26th May, 1805, he placed the Iron Crown of Lombardy on his own head in Milan cathedral. His stepson, Eugène Beauharnais, was appointed viceroy, his sister Eliza Bacciocchi was, with her husband, presented with Lucca and shortly afterwards Tuscany, while Genoa and the Ligurian Republic were annexed to France. Early in 1806, with the defeat of the Austrians at Austerlitz, their half of Venetia was added to the new Italian kingdom.

Naples had, for the past three years, clung to independence by deserting her former protectors: British and Turkish ships had been banned from her harbours, while Brindisi, Taranto and Otranto had been occupied by French garrisons. Napoleon now calmly announced that the Bourbons had 'ceased to reign' in the Two Sicilies. They took his word for it, so far as the mainland was concerned, packed with the efficiency born of practice, and sailed across to their island to enjoy once more the protection of the British Navy.

Britain made one or two gestures in their support. A naval squadron seized Capri and a military force landed in Calabria to beat the French at Maida, a victory now commemorated only in the name of a London district. Napoleon's brother, Joseph, became King of Naples and in two years proved himself the best ruler she had ever had. When in 1808 he was promoted to the senior Bourbon throne in Spain, he was succeeded by Napoleon's handsome and charming brother-in-law, Murat, who at times displayed excessive individuality, sternly discouraged by the emperor as 'monkey tricks'.

Except for the two kings marooned on their respective islands of Sicily and Sardinia, there was now only one Italian ruler outside the Bonaparte family circle. This was the elderly Pius VII, who, while anxious enough to achieve some sort of *modus vivendi* with the emperor, was not prepared to be a mere puppet. Napoleon decided to cut him down to the status of a mere bishop. He announced from Vienna the annexation of the papal states. Pius retorted with excommunication. French troops then broke into the Quirinal at night and took him away to captivity at Savona, whence he was removed to Fontainebleau lest he be rescued by the British fleet. The old man obstinately withstood the ill-treatment of his jailers and lived to enjoy a triumphant restoration.

For the next few years Italy was governed with energy and efficiency. Here at last was a reforming autocrat strong enough to break down all obstacles. Feudalism was swept away, land-ownership extended. Even in the South, Joseph Bonaparte achieved more in two years than Don Carlos in twenty. Redundant bishoprics and monasteries were suppressed. New roads were driven across the country, breaking down the old regional isolation. In Dalmatia it was said of the great Adriatic coast road: 'The Austrians discussed the plans for eight years, Marmont got on his horse and when he got off the road was made.' It was the same in Italy, where the new works included routes over the Simplon and Mont Cenis. Bridges were built, canals dug. Even the long-incomplete Milan Cathedral was finished on Napoleon's instructions, though his insistence on economy prevented it from ranking among his major achievements. Taxation was heavy but fair. So was the hand of justice. The Code Napoléon was clapped firmly upon the whole country, with no sentimental regrets for the quaint survivals of forgotten regimes. And there were no brigands on the fine new roads.

Napoleon's contribution to Italy was not confined to these material benefits. There was a quickening of the spirit. Ulti-mately, the Italian was as much the subject of a foreign ruler as he had been under Austrians and Spaniards, but at least he was taught to think of himself *as* an Italian, not as a Tuscan, Neapolitan or Milanese. Napoleon gave him a national identity and even a national flag, the tricolour originally devised by the Bolognese rebels of 1794 when they combined the green of liberty with the papal red and white. Napoleon taught him to fight, if only for Napoleon, and long-lost martial qualities were rediscovered by Italian regiments on the steppes of Russia and the sierras of Spain. It was brusque treatment that the emperor gave his Italian subjects, the treatment of an old-style sergeant-major kicking, cursing and shaking his recruits into life, but he made men of them.

By 1813 his power in Europe was on the wane. Murat, nervous for his Neapolitan throne, wrote asking for a free hand in Italy. The emperor did not even reply. Murat then deserted him and made an alliance with the Austrians. By

May, 1814, Napoleon was sailing to Elba in an English warship, the Pope was back in Rome, and all the kinglets and
grand-dukes, Bourbon, Habsburg or Savoyard, were preparing their several triumphal returns. The Napoleonic nightmare was to be forgotten. As Victor Emmanuel I proclaimed
on his arrival in Turin: *'Disregarding all other laws whatso-
ever, the public will, from this date, observe the royal ordin-
ances of 1770, together with all other decrees issued up to
23rd June, 1800. . . .'* Over the whole peninsula hung a
strong odour of moth-balls.

Even Victor Emmanuel did not insist on restoring the
status quo in every respect. He felt it unnecessary to revive
the Republic of Genoa, which for tidiness was now merged
with his own kingdom. Nor did Liberty regain her 'eldest
child': Austria thought it better to keep Venice in the
kingdom of Lombardy-Venetia, ruled by an archducal viceroy on behalf of her own emperor. There was long diplomatic
debate over the Two Sicilies. Some felt that Murat should stay
in Naples as a reward for deserting Napoleon. The Bourbons'
main advocate was the British envoy in Palermo, now Lord
William Bentinck, a very different man from Hamilton. He
had put in a lot of hard work persuading Ferdinand to grant
a constitution on British lines and made such progress that
the indignant queen had flounced off to Vienna, there to
die of apoplexy. The situation was still in doubt when
Napoleon escaped from Elba in March.

Murat acted quickly, whether from remorse for his past
betrayal or from shrewd calculation of his own prospects.
Gathering his troops, he marched north. On 30th March
he issued a proclamation at Rimini: *'Italians! Providence
has called you at last to be an independent nation. . . .'*
Bentinck had already warned Castlereagh from his observation of the country and the people's mood that *'there is not
a doubt that under the standard of Italian independence the
whole of Italy will rally'*, and he doubted if the whole force
of Austria would be enough to expel Murat. In this he was
over-pessimistic. Murat's forces were routed by the Austrians
on 2nd May. He fled to France and offered his services to
Napoleon, who snubbed him. For a week or two he hid near
Toulon, a price on his head. On 6th June King Ferdinand
was back in Naples, on the 19th came Waterloo. The

Napoleonic era was over, but Murat did not know. Refusing the offer of asylum in England, he plotted to recover his kingdom from the Bourbons. He landed in Calabria with a mere thirty followers, a storm having scattered the rest of his miniature armada, and found to his chagrin that the local people would not spring to arms. He was taken prisoner and summarily tried in the medieval castle of Pizzo; there in the courtyard the pathetic little adventure was ended by the firing-squad. Meanwhile in Naples King Ferdinand forgot, in his Bourbon fashion, all his promises to rule like a constitutional British sovereign, and swept away even the reforms Bentinck had induced him to make in Sicily; while the British government was, as so often, too apathetic to insist on the honouring of past promises.

18. Risorgimento

THE ITALY to which Byron and Shelley hastened after the Napoleonic wars was a beautiful but melancholy country, sick-hearted with hopes indefinitely deferred. Austria — and that meant Metternich — controlled almost every corner of the land. Even where there was no white-coated garrison, no black-and-yellow flag fluttering on the tower, the nominal rulers glanced over their shoulders at Vienna, and either through Austrian wives or Austrian ambassadors were instructed in the reactionary policy it would pay them to follow. Metternich, struggling to hold together the Habsburg Empire, dared not let any province or satellite explore the dizzy paths of progress. The Italians especially must not play with dangerous ideas picked up from the Bonapartists. He did not imagine that he could turn them into Teutons; the peoples were, he told his wife, 'as different as chalk from cheese'. But, while recognizing Italians, he saw Italy as 'a mere geographical expression'. Even in 1847, when the new railways were linking region with region, he still held that to talk of an Italian nation was a delusion. 'A Milanese,' he told Cobden, 'won't place a mortgage in Padua or Cremona. He can't see their steeples!'

The only unifying influence permitted was Austrian policy. Frontiers were forgotten when he wished to send troops across them, to bolster an unpopular government. Thus, in 1820, the elderly Ferdinand of Naples was frightened into 'granting a constitution', that panacea of early liberalism, and standing before the altar he invoked 'Almighty God, Who lookest into the heart of man and canst discern the future: if I lie or if one day I shall prove false to my oath, do Thou at this moment strike me dead'. Metternich was having no constitutions. He sent in Austrian troops. Ferdinand broke his oath and began a vindictive persecution of the reformers, with executions, public floggings and rigorous

261

imprisonment on remote islets. Despite his unwise invitation
to the Deity, he lived another four years and bequeathed his
tarnished crown to three more generations of Bourbons.

Elsewhere, though the efficacy of administration might
vary, there was the same suppression of human liberties.
Opposition went underground. The most active secret movement was now that of the Carbonari or 'Charcoal-burners',
with whom Byron had dealings. Metternich hunted down
their leaders in Lombardy and immured them for long years
in Austrian dungeons. His repression was matched by that of
the Church, and sometimes combined with it. Thus in Piedmont, where the Jesuits had been readmitted, no Waldensian
could hold office and in Turin itself no Protestant sect could
even build a chapel. The queen was Austrian, and, for all the
little kingdom's boasted independence, it was Austrian troops
who were invited in to quell the short-lived revolt of 1821.
Pius VII, aided by the skilful diplomacy of Cardinal Consalvi,
tried hard to restore the political identity of the papal territories, but when trouble really came with the widespread
insurrection of 1831 he had to bring in the white-coats. After
that, he enlisted more Swiss and formed companies of
Centurioni, Italian irregulars whose undisciplined brutality
was worse than the systematic repression of the Austrian
jackboot.

For a time enlightenment flickered on in the little state
of Parma, which had been assigned to Napoleon's ex-empress
as a sort of political dower-house. Marie-Louise had refused
to accompany her husband to St. Helena and seemed determined to forget the whole unhappy episode, including their
offspring, so briefly titled 'King of Rome'. She had a lover,
Count von Neipperg, whom she lost no time in marrying
when Napoleon died, and to whom she bore several children.
Though an Austrian princess, backed in the last resort by the
Austrian garrison at Piacenza, she allowed the Napoleonic
reforms to survive in the duchy. But she too, in the 1831
rising, had to shelter under the imperial flag, and, having
lost her second husband and come under the influence
of the less liberal Baron Werklein, she grew increasingly
reactionary.

Tuscany was different. Here alone had the restoration of
the grand-duke been widely welcomed, thanks to his pro-

RISORGIMENTO

LOMBARDY VENETIA
(Austrian) (Austrian)
1859 1866

Piedmont

PARMA
1860

MODENA
1860

STATES

of

TUSCANY the
1860 CHURCH
1860

CORSICA
(French)

PAPAL
STATE
1870

KINGDOM of SARDINIA (House of Savoy)

SARDINIA

1860

KINGDOM
of the
TWO SICILIES
(Bourbon)

1860

W.B.

Miles 0   100   200

gressive views, which made his duchy an invaluable sanctuary for persecuted radicals.

Such, then, was the Italy of the eighteen-twenties and thirties, the Italy which Stendhal illuminates with his irony in *The Charterhouse of Parma*, and in which three young men were growing up:

> *Who blew the breath of life into her frame:*
> *Cavour, Mazzini, Garibaldi: Three:*
> *Her Brain, her Soul, her Sword; and set her free. . . .*

Meredith's commemorative verses label them with useful vividness and more historical truth than such rhetoric usually achieves.

All three were born in the Napoleonic era: Mazzini at Genoa in 1805, son of a professor of medicine; Garibaldi, a fisherman's son, two years later at Nice, still an Italian town; Cavour at Turin in 1810, younger son of a Piedmontese nobleman. Mazzini, unable to face the practical anatomy classes, forsook his father's faculty to graduate in law, after which he embarked without conscious inconsistency on a life of illegal activity and the fomenting of bloody revolution. Garibaldi went to sea and soon was master of a brig. Cavour attended the Military Academy in Turin and was commissioned in the engineers, but left the army at twenty-one to travel and pursue his true interests, which were sociological and agricultural. His political views became increasingly inspired by England, where the Reform Bill had just been pushed through Parliament. Mazzini travelled too but with government encouragement: after six months in prison without trial, for activity in the Carbonari, he withdrew to Marseilles, where he launched his *Young Italy* movement, was expelled by the French police, and moved on to Switzerland. Garibaldi was the last to enter politics. In 1833 he met Mazzini and caught fire from his idealism. The next year Mazzini, always confident that he had only to wave the torch of freedom and the whole of Italy would go up in flames, organized one of his abortive little revolutions. He re-entered Piedmont with an international brigade of Germans, Poles and Italians, while Garibaldi, who had joined the Sardinian navy with no other objective, plotted to seize a frigate and occupy the arsenal

at Genoa. The combined operation ended in fiasco. Mazzini
fled back to Switzerland, and thence to London, a few years
before Marx. Garibaldi escaped to South America with a
death-sentence hanging over him, and in the revolutions of
that continent soon acquired the guerrilla experience which
made his later achievements possible. There, too, he met and
eloped with his future wife, Anita.

All three future leaders came from the same Italian state,
all three realized its special importance as the nucleus of
national independence. Cavour, the realist, saw that the ruling
House of Savoy was no less important. The only native
monarchy in the peninsula, neither Austrian nor Spanish
Bourbon, it was the only form of government capable of
uniting all classes and all regions. Mazzini, the republican
idealist, was unwilling to compromise. Garibaldi, the romantic, chivalrous soldier, leaned heavily to the republican view
but was prepared to serve king or Pope if the objective,
Italian unity, could be achieved with honour.

Mazzini's great contribution was made in those years.
While Cavour quietly studied to become a statesman, while
Garibaldi had breathless adventures on the pampas and learnt
to become a military liberator, Mazzini, a lonely and
impoverished exile, was preparing the ground with his tireless propaganda from London. There at least he could write
freely. In Italy notions of progress and national unity had to
be subtly wrapped up so as to hoodwink the censor. The
scientific and trade journals of Piedmont were one medium
for the delicate insinuation of the idea that change might be
a good thing or that lessons might be learnt from abroad. The
historical novel, too, achieved a vogue not solely attributable
to Sir Walter Scott. Cavour grumbled that there were 'too
many songs about freeing Italy'. One of his blindest followers
in the years to come, Verdi, was using the opera as a vehicle
for patriotic sentiment. *I Lombardi* was staged in 1843.
Ernani, a year later, led to political demonstrations in the
theatre. *La Battiglia di Legnano* and *Simon Boccanegra* were
openly nationalistic. Even *Rigoletto* and *Un Ballo in Maschera*
involved the composer in prolonged disputes with the censorship. The last opera was banned in Rome because it portrayed
not only a dissolute ruler but his successful assassination.
The censor allowed it only when the scene was transferred,

somewhat improbably, to Boston, Mass. In those later years the slogan, *VIVA VERDI*, clandestinely chalked on walls, implied even more than support for a popular composer. All knew that the *graffiti* were to be read also as *VIVA V(ittorio) E(mmanuel) R(e) D(') I(talia)*.

But that is anticipating. Victor Emmanuel II was not even King of Sardinia until 1849. Meantime, from the thirties to the mid-forties, reaction remained in the ascendant, and the brightest interlude, though brief, was provided by Sicily. The unspeakable Ferdinand of Naples had died at last in 1825, to be followed first by an elderly son and then, in 1830, by his no less odious grandson, Ferdinand II, later to earn the disapproval of Mr. Gladstone and the nickname 'Bomba' for his indiscriminate artillery-fire against his own subjects. On his accession, however, he was thought to have liberal sympathies. His popular younger brother, Count Leopold, certainly had, and when he was made viceroy of Sicily the islanders welcomed him with joy. Leopold managed to secure some concessions for them, but soon his very popularity made the king jealous. Leopold was replaced, the old tyranny returned, and hard on its heels came an appalling plague of cholera which, though affecting most parts of Europe, was particularly virulent in Sicily. Seventy thousand people died. Ignorance and superstition goaded the miserable inhabitants into violence against the authorities, which was no less violently repressed. Thus cholera and Bourbon brutality, strangely bracketed with the idealism of Mazzini, worked for the eventual triumph of Garibaldi over twenty years later.

.   .   .   .

By the mid-eighteen-forties the wind was changing all over Europe. It was the decade of desperation and of wild new hopes — of the Hungry Forties, the Chartists, the *Communist Manifesto*, the overthrow of Louis-Philippe, revolutions and rumoured revolutions everywhere. Nowhere blew the wind more freshly than in Italy.

In 1846 a new Pope was elected, Pius IX, that 'Pio Nono' who was to reign thirty-two years and play so memorable a part in the nineteenth-century evolution of the Papacy. Personally charming and impressive, he was welcomed as a man of liberal sympathies. A change was badly needed after a regime which had repressed its subjects with wholesale imprisonment, espionage and the undisciplined thuggery of the irregulars. Pius proclaimed an amnesty for the thousand liberals who were either in the cells or in exile. Hopes soared. Choruses in *Ernani* were re-worded as topical tributes to the new pontiff. Garibaldi wrote from South America, offering his support. But Pius, for all his benevolent intentions, was the head of an ancient institution, stately and at times unwieldy, which could not change course quickly like one of the newfangled steamships. Caution was imposed upon him by his immense responsibilities. He must move slowly, carrying his cardinals with him, and it was not fast enough for some. He nudged gently forward, an ice-breaker (to change our nautical comparison) against the long-frozen mentality of the papal bureaucrats. The people forced him to go faster than he wished, but not nearly so fast as they hoped. Soon, with a relaxation of the censorship, newspapers burgeoned like springtime leaves. Rome was allowed to form a civic guard, the traditional guarantee of popular liberty against military domination and a warning light to Metternich, who hastily moved his white-coats into the papal city of Ferrara.

Spring was indeed in the air, politically. Soon not only newspapers but constitutions unfurled their perilous leaves. The liberal Grand-duke of Tuscany, piqued by papal competition, accelerated his own reforms. In 1847 Cavour founded a weekly in Turin to disseminate his political ideas and in calling it *Il Risorgimento*, 'The Resurrection', christened the whole national movement now boiling up in the peninsula. Not for him the life of conspiratorial exile. He worked through the top stratum of society, winning acceptance for his ideas even in the royal family. In 1848 Charles Albert reluctantly granted his subjects a constitution, and the dismissal of his reactionary prime minister brought near the day when Cavour would pass from propaganda to participation in the government.

Admirable, all these developments, but not fast enough for events. The political spring turned with unpredictable suddenness into feverish summer. All Europe in 1848 seemed on the brink of revolution. In February Paris rose: Louis-Philippe departed hastily to end his days in Surrey. In March it was Vienna's turn, the university students leading the riots:

Metternich retired to Brighton, and his departure was the signal for Hungarians and Czechs to rise against the tottering Empire. In Milan there had been riots in January, savagely quelled by old Marshal Radetzky: the news of the Vienna rising came like a match to an oil-soaked rag. Up went the barricades. Radetzky, unwilling to take on a whole population even with fifteen thousand soldiers, backed out of Milan into the famous Quadrilateral, the four fortresses of Mantua, Verona, Peschiera and Legnano, protecting the Brenner and the road to Austria. In Venice the people stormed the jail and released their leader, Daniele Manin, not in fact a blood-relative of the unfortunate last doge but the son of a converted Jew befriended by the ancient Manin family. Worthily he made up for the recent humiliation of that name. Under his inspiration the Venetians ejected the Austrian garrison with only a single fatal casualty, and set up a provisional government committed to Italian unity. Meanwhile, in the South, Sicily celebrated the royal birthday with an armed rebellion which gained control of the entire island, and proclaimed the affectionately remembered 'British constitution' which Bentinck had drafted thirty-six years before.

Sicily apart — and Sicily was almost always apart — everything depended on the attitude of the Sardinian king. Only his trained Piedmontese army could give the revolutionaries the professional stiffening needed against the Austrians. Charles Albert wavered. He was ready to accept an enlarged kingdom by heading the anti-Austrian movement, but reluctant to receive it from liberals who openly preferred a republic. His brief hesitation gave Radetzky invaluable time to regroup.

When the king entered Lombardy all Italy felt that a crusade had been launched. The duchies of Parma and Modena voted for political union with Piedmont. Detachments set out to join him. Others started from Tuscany, Rome and even Naples. Garibaldi, who had long been planning his return from South America, arrived in June and offered his sword, which the embarrassed monarch ignored, since its owner was an unpardoned rebel under sentence of death. Garibaldi was not to be discouraged by formalities. He obtained a commission from the provisional government in Milan and raised his own army of three thousand men.

He was too late. After some initial successes the tide had turned against Charles Albert. Radetzky received reinforcements. The king on the other hand lost the support of seventeen thousand volunteers from Rome when the Pope insisted on remaining strictly neutral, and most of the Neapolitans, whom Ferdinand recalled as soon as he dared. Late in July the old Austrian marshal smashed the heavily outnumbered Italians at Custoza, south-east of Lake Garda. By early August he was back in Milan — and Charles Albert was in full retreat across the Piedmontese frontier, his marching columns fringed with pathetic refugees. Only in two places did the struggle continue. Garibaldi kept it up, guerrilla-fashion, in the hills round Lake Maggiore until it became useless and he slipped over the Swiss border. Venice, refusing to surrender her independence, hurled defiance at Radetzky and appeals at Palmerston from the dubious safety of her lagoons.

'The kings' war is over, the peoples' war is just beginning,' declared Mazzini, who had fought under Garibaldi. The military disaster was everywhere bringing Left-wing parties to the fore. All shared a belief in republican institutions and some form of association between as many Italian states as possible, even if it meant renewing the war.

In Rome the Pope was striving to reconcile two incompatible functions, as temporal sovereign, with all the inescapable responsibilities, including military defence, and as the Church's leader, with implied neutrality between Catholic powers. His minister, Count Rossi, was one of those doctrinaire intellectuals who win the dislike of the very people they wish to serve. He was working on a federal scheme, as an alternative to the proposals of the extremists, when he was stabbed as he went up the steps to open the first session of the new Chamber of Deputies. Several wild days followed, with mass demonstrations outside the Quirinal Palace and an attempt to burn it, stopped by the Swiss Guards. Pius bowed to the storm. He accepted the extremist ministers pressed upon him, and then, realizing that he could never condone their policy, he disguised himself as an ordinary priest and took a carriage across the Neapolitan frontier to Gaeta.

It was much the same tale in Tuscany. The moderate government was replaced by one of the Left-wing, and by January, 1849, the Grand-duke's own position was untenable.

He too fled to Gaeta. Ferdinand had by now dealt with his own troubles in Sicily and was in a position to welcome both illustrious fugitives.

In Piedmont there had been much recrimination, military and political. The shadow of Austrian invasion hung over the country, for the Empire had staggered to its feet again, dangerous as ever. The rebellious Czechs had been blasted into submission and the dim-witted emperor had abdicated in favour of his eighteen-year-old nephew, Francis Joseph, fresh from military service under Radetzky. That Piedmont escaped Austrian occupation was due to French and British diplomacy. Turin now had a government almost as Left-wing as those in Rome and Florence, and when the armistice expired in March Charles Albert was pushed into a foredoomed renewal of the war. He took the field again in person, though the campaign was really directed by a Polish general, Chrzanowsky. Radetzky took exactly six days to outwit them, defeat them at Novara between Turin and Milan, and enforce surrender. Charles Albert apologized emotionally to his staff for having failed 'to find death on the battlefield' and abdicated in favour of his son, Victor Emmanuel. He then passed unrecognized through the Austrian lines and travelled to Portugal, where he died four months later. Piedmont had to give up some territory, pay an indemnity, disband her volunteers from outside, recall her fleet from the defence of Venice, and evacuate the duchies. These were thereupon occupied by the Austrians, who also in the course of the summer overran the Marches, stormed into Leghorn, and restored the Grand-duke of Tuscany to an unresisting Florence. Rome remained to be dealt with.

After the Pope's flight, the assembly there had voted, 131 to 5, for 'a pure democracy with the glorious title of the Roman Republic'. Pius promptly issued an appeal to all Catholic nations for armed intervention to restore him. A race began. Though favourites, the Austrians had some way to come down the peninsula and a good deal to do. The Spaniards landed five thousand men at Gaeta, King 'Bomba' himself started out from Naples with sixteen thousand, and the French shipped eight thousand under Oudinot to Civitavecchia, only thirty-five miles from Rome.

The onset of these converging armies was awaited by the

infant republic with an almost Spartan fortitude. Mazzini was there, one of its elected Triumvirs, galvanizing the assembly with his eloquence. Garibaldi and his men were there, with numerous other volunteers just dismissed from the Piedmontese service under the armistice, including a battalion of Lombard sharpshooters, the Bersaglieri. When Oudinot made an optimistic advance against the city in late April, he received a surprise. Garibaldi led the resistance, a romantic figure. long-haired and golden-bearded, with red shirt, white South American poncho, and black ostrich plume. Though wounded early on, he spent the whole night in the saddle. Shaken, the French withdrew to Civita-vecchia. There they waited a whole month for reinforcements, while the diplomat, De Lesseps, patiently tried to bring the two sides together, with much less success than he subsequently had with the Mediterranean and the Red Sea. Garibaldi meantime slipped away to deal with the Neapolitans, and, though outnumbered five or six to one, routed them at Palestrina and Velletri. Then he hurried back to Rome, where Oudinot, now immensely reinforced and equipped with siege-guns and scaling-ladders, was ready to disown De Lesseps' negotiations and storm the city.

The attack opened on 3rd June. All through that torrid month the French cannon thundered, the red-and-blue figures crept remorselessly forward. On 1st July Mazzini was still demanding resistance to the last, but Garibaldi, of all romantic heroes the most realistic, declared bluntly that it was useless. Two days later Oudinot marched into a battle-scarred city and pronounced the demise of the republic. Garibaldi was not there to surrender his sword. He had gone into the mountains with his wife and several thousand followers. There was nothing left to do in Rome, where a committee of cardinals was already arranging the Pope's return. But Venice still held out, last island of Italian independence, and the Garibaldians meant to cut their way through to join in her defence.

It was a forlorn, chivalrous adventure. Thanks to their leader's genius it nearly came off. They escaped French, Spaniards, Neapolitans. Zigzagging through the sun-scorched Apennines they side-stepped three Austrian columns. On the last day of July they limped into San Marino, whose ancient neutrality offered sanctuary from the hunters. Garibaldi himself, however, still meant to reach Venice. He mustered a fleet of fishing-boats sufficient to hold the two hundred men still with him. They sailed on 1st August, were overhauled by Austrian patrol-boats in the moonlight, and had to run ashore in the desolate lagoon country near Ravenna. Many were shot or captured. Garibaldi and Anita struggled on until, exhausted and ailing, she collapsed and died in his arms. He then made his way across country, helped by countless patriots, and escaped to America.

Three weeks later, with the Austrian guns firing into the heart of Venice, with cholera and typhus raging through the tortured city and only two days' rations left, Manin surrendered on honourable terms and the last spark of liberty went out. So the terrible year 1849 ended with Mazzini once more a conspiratorial journalist in London, while Manin supported his family in Paris by giving Italian lessons and Garibaldi worked in New York as a chandler. But Cavour, who had never compromised himself, remained in Turin, and now his hour had come.

.   .   .   .

To the clear, subtle mind of Cavour several points were now unarguable. The Austrians could not be ejected by cloak-and-dagger plots, revolutionary barricades, or the small army of Piedmont. Some great ally must be enlisted. The obvious choice was France, where Louis Napoleon had just seized power and was about to revive the Empire. The goodwill of Britain was important too, but he could hardly hope to see her army invading Lombardy. Both these governments would be more sympathetic if the Italian cause were headed by the King of Sardinia rather than by Mazzini's Left-wing republicans. Mazzini indeed could be a liability, frightening off foreign statesmen and the more conservative of the patriots. After he had fomented another abortive revolt in Milan in 1853, thereby calling down the usual Austrian reprisals (including the public flogging of women), he lost many supporters and there was a swing towards Cavour's more practical policies.

Cavour went into the cabinet in 1850, differed quickly with the prime minister, resigned, and was recalled as prime minister himself in 1852. Circumstances were ideal for winning friends in the West. Feeling ran high in Britain. When the Austrian General Haynau visited London, preceded by an atrocious reputation for brutality, he was attacked and thrashed by the draymen of Barclay and Perkins' brewery. A more reasoned, but no less vehement, protest against the Neapolitan tyranny was made by Gladstone in his *Letters to Lord Aberdeen,* wherein he published the well-documented observations made during a private visit. Half the Neapolitan deputies were in jail for their opposition opinions. At least twenty thousand people had been imprisoned under the most barbarous conditions. Nor did the papal government stand up to scrutiny: Pio Nono's reforming zeal had been curbed by his reactionary cardinals, dominated by one Antonelli, whose nepotism, corruption, and scandalous personal life revived the worst memories of the Renaissance. Against these regimes Victor Emmanuel's progressive government could hardly fail to stand out attractively.

When the Crimean War broke out, the world was treated to the bizarre spectacle of the little Sardinian kingdom marching side by side with Britain, France and Turkey. What, people wondered, were these Italians doing in the Crimea when they could not free even their own peninsula? Cavour knew quite well. Participation meant recognition as a European power, put France and England under an obligation. Austria would probably come in on the Russian side. France would then be involved willy-nilly in the liberation of Italy. Here he forecast wrongly, but his troops did well in Russia, helping to win the battle of Chernaya, and his friendship with France and England matured accordingly.

In 1856 a new political movement was launched, the National Society, with the slogan *'Italy and Victor Emmanuel'.* Cavour gave it veiled encouragement: a prime minister had to preserve the diplomatic decencies. Garibaldi, back from America and living on a rocky islet off Sardinia, accepted the new policy as the best available. So did Manin. Only Mazzini would not swallow his republican principles.

Things were moving well. In the summer of 1858 Napoleon III invited Cavour to informal talks at Plombières. In the quiet health resort, surrounded by the forests of the Vosges and by invalids exchanging symptoms of internal disorders, the two statesmen discussed treatment for the chronic case of

Italy. The Austrians were to be driven out when the time was ripe. Piedmont was to take over Lombardy-Venetia and the adjacent duchies, and be associated with Tuscany, the papal states and Naples in a federation. France's reward was to be Savoy and perhaps Nice.

The war-clouds now began to thicken. Patriots swarmed into Piedmont. Garibaldi was secretly invited to Turin, taken up the back stairs to see Cavour, and commissioned to raise three thousand volunteers. Cavour was an early master of the timely 'leak': while not yet ready to give open sanction to these bellicose preparations, he had no wish to hide them from the Austrians, for if they could be goaded into aggression it would enable Napoleon to enter as the defender of gallant little Sardinia. The plan nearly failed. Napoleon began to hesitate, especially when Britain rushed in to oil the troubled waters with proposals for disarmament. Cavour, longing for war, had to convince the British and French public that he wanted only peace. He agreed to disarm if Austria would. But the Habsburg Empire was not to be treated on the same level as the little House of Savoy. Vienna sent an ultimatum to Turin. Disarm in three days or else. . . . Cavour's eyes must have glinted behind his undistinguished spectacles. The Austrians were running true to form. He had got what he wanted. Six days later, on 29th April, 1859, France declared war on Austria. By road and rail, and by steamer from Algeria, French troops poured into Piedmont.

It was soon over. The Austrian general, Gyulai, missed his chance to take Turin before the French arrived. Napoleon too showed no trace of his uncle's military genius. The one good general, Garibaldi, commanded only his three thousand volunteers, with whom he performed prodigies of commando-style valour among the lakes and hills of Como and Maggiore. *'I am living in a world of poetry,'* one of his lieutenants wrote home ecstatically. The lesser generals with the larger forces met on 4th June at Magenta, the little silk-town whose dye-works gave the world a new colour about this time. Napoleon and Victor Emmanuel defeated Gyulai and liberated Milan. By the end of the month they faced a regrouped Austrian army commanded by the young emperor in person, whom they defeated after twelve hours of ghastly slaughter at Solferino near Lake Garda. From the horror of that day was born the

International Red Cross. At this point Napoleon's wider pre-occupations (Prussia, the Pope, the clerical party at home) stopped him from exploiting his victory. He abandoned Cavour. The two emperors met at Villafranca and settled things between them. The promises made to Cavour the previous summer were whittled down. Piedmont gained only Lombardy and Parma. Austria was to keep Venetia and to reoccupy the other territories from which she had been temporarily expelled.

Cavour was staggered by the betrayal, for under his more conventional exterior beat a heart as patriotic as Garibaldi's or Mazzini's. He upbraided the helpless Victor Emmanuel for his acquiescence and handed in his resignation. Almost his last official act was to recall the Piedmontese commissioners in liberated Modena and Bologna. Simultaneously he sent them personal telegrams to stay where they were. For the next six months he was out of office, free from his usual necessity not to let his right hand know what his left hand was doing. He worked with both hands to nullify the Villafranca agreement. He knew that the Austrians could reoccupy their lost territories only by force, that he could regain Napoleon's support at a price, and that England's new Liberal government was pro-Italian. 'What is to become of us,' Pio Nono lamented to a nephew of Lord John Russell, 'with your uncle and Lord Palmerston at the head of affairs in England? And that Mr. Gladstone, who let himself be taken in about the Neapolitan prisoners?' In January, 1860, Cavour was back as prime minister. By mid-March he had engineered plebiscites in Emilia and Tuscany whereby those regions voted for union with the emergent Kingdom of Italy. Napoleon's approval was bought with Nice and Savoy — a painful and difficult sacrifice, for Nice was Garibaldi's birthplace and Savoy the king's ancestral home. Cavour managed it with his accustomed dexterity. Nice and Savoy were not 'surrendered', they were given the chance of a plebiscite, so that they could vote themselves out of Italy as freely as the other territories voted themselves in. To assist them in making up their minds, Napoleon occupied them with French troops, while, to avoid the least suggestion of intimidation, these troops were not sent from France but were 'withdrawn' from positions elsewhere in Italy. Garibaldi saw no beauty

in these subtle manoeuvres. He never forgave the abandon-
ment of Nice.

In that spring of 1860, however, he had much to distract
him. 'Bomba' had died. The new King of Naples, the weak-
minded Francis II, was in the hands of his reactionary
ministers, who, refusing all co-operation with Cavour, were
plotting armed intervention in the liberated provinces. The
Sicilians were boiling up to another of their periodical insur-
rections against this regime and begged Garibaldi to lead
them. He agreed, on condition that they showed themselves
in earnest by making the first move. Meanwhile he enrolled
volunteers at Genoa. Cavour as usual turned a blind eye. A
successful rising in Sicily would embarrass Naples. But open
approval would cost him the friendship of Napoleon, to
whom Garibaldi (since the defence of Rome) had been
anathema.

So, on the moonlit evening of 5th May, began the great
adventure of 'Garibaldi and the Thousand', which combined so much of the epic with more than a little of the
comic and almost farcical. The whole district knew what was
afoot. The volunteers had been gathering for days. Of the
total 1,089 about half were workers and half professional or
business men. There were authors, journalists, professors,
civil servants, artists, sculptors, and no less than a hundred
and fifty lawyers. Even Oxford University was represented by
the massive J. W. Peard, among a handful of non-Italians.
These men assembled at the rocky Bay of Quarto, near Genoa,
and were to put out in boats and embark in two little steamers,
hi-jacked from the port with the connivance of their owners'
agent. Still further along the coast other boats were to bring
out the ammunition.

Nearly everything went wrong. The ships, the *Lombardo*
and the *Piemonte,* were duly seized, but engine-trouble
prevented the *Lombardo* getting away, and in the end she
had to be towed out by her sister-ship when dawn was
perilously near. The volunteers got aboard safely with their
leader. Most of them then proceeded to be horribly seasick.
Worst of all, owing to the delay, the ammunition-boats missed
the rendezvous. It is doubtful if even Mr. Peard had ever
known a cause so manifestly lost from the beginning.

Garibaldi did not despair. Landing briefly in Tuscany, he

put on his Piedmontese general's uniform and persuaded a local garrison commander to supply him with some arms. The Thousand, who had utilized the welcome break ashore to organize themselves into military formations and do a little drill, then sailed forward more cheerfully to conquer Sicily. They had now about one hundred modern Enfield rifles and a fair number of muskets, though many had only ten rounds apiece. Their artillery would have graced any museum: it comprised two bronze cannon, 1802 vintage, a culverin, and two other venerable relics of the eighteenth century. The garrison at Palermo, their prime objective, numbered a mere twenty-four thousand men.

How this absurdity was transmuted into glory by the magnetic genius of Garibaldi and the heroism of his dedicated amateurs forms perhaps the most fascinating page in all the long Italian story. On the sixth day the expedition reached Marsala at the western tip of Sicily, closely pursued by Neapolitan warships. The *Lombardo* ran aground at the harbour entrance, which still further lengthened the disembarkation. The Neapolitans, commanded by a member of the Acton family so long identified with their navy, could have raked the mole as the volunteers hurried along it. But Captain Acton hesitated. Two British warships were anchored near by and though, as it proved, they behaved with scrupulous neutrality, Acton was afraid that they meant to intervene. He even mistook the red shirts worn by some of the volunteers for the tunics of British soldiers. Finally, the port being Marsala, the waterfront included the warehouses of British wine-shippers, and in 1860 it was a serious matter to damage British property. His gunfire was therefore belated, timid and ineffectual. Garibaldi got his troops and equipment ashore with only two casualties, one suffered by a dog and neither fatal.

Now began the march on Palermo. At Calatafimi the way was barred by a force of two thousand, who fought with (for Bourbon troops) unusual confidence and courage. The battle was decided with bayonets on the steep mountainside, and at last the Neapolitans broke and ran. Characteristically, many of the weary victors walked three miles the next day to admire the ruined Greek temple at Segesta. And so the fantastic story continued, too good to be spoilt by summarization.

How the Garibaldians reached Palermo with all too little help from the undisciplined *squadre* of the local rebels, and how they secured the capitulation and evacuation of regular soldiers outnumbering them twenty to one, demands the full-length treatment of a Trevelyan.

No less incredible was the sequel. Master of the whole island, Garibaldi prepared to march on Naples. Diplomatic considerations of the utmost delicacy now came into play. If he reached Naples — and who now dared to say he might not? — he would go on to Rome, and, with Napoleon still protecting the Pope, that would never do. Cavour waved his conjuror's hands, left, right, with the old mystifying dexterity. Garibaldi was met at Messina with a letter from his king, ordering him not to cross the straits — but another letter, also, in the king's writing, thrust under his nose but not into his grasp, told him to disregard the first. On 18th August the Red Shirts (it was now the Garibaldian uniform) crossed the water and began their long march, driving the enemy pell-mell before them, all the way up from the toe of Calabria to Naples itself. They got there on 7th September. The last of the Bourbons had fled the previous day.

While Garibaldi still fought hard to complete his conquest, Cavour warned Napoleon that, if the Red Shirts were not to appear in papal territory, they must be forestalled by the southward movement of regular Italian troops. The emperor agreed. While Rome and the surrounding region remained 'the Papal State' under French protection, the Marches and Umbria (often differentiated as 'the States of the Church') were quickly overrun by Victor Emmanuel's forces, the attempted resistance of the papal soldiers being rapidly crushed. Victor Emmanuel was thus able to reach Garibaldi while he was still on Neapolitan soil and ensure that he came no further. Garibaldi conducted his sovereign into Naples and the very next day, refusing any reward for having meta-phorically handed him the Two Sicilies on a plate, went quietly home to Caprera. He could not forget the bartering away of Nice.

Over that and other issues he had a heated scene with Cavour a few months later. It probably contributed to the fatal illness which seized the prime minister soon afterwards. 'Italy is made,' Cavour murmured on his death-bed, 'all is safe.' He was fortunate at least in having seen, at fifty, his patient life's work almost accomplished. The jigsaw was complete except for two pieces — Venetia and Rome — both destined to drop into place as the result of external events. Venetia came in 1866, after the Prussian defeat of Austria, though Italy's own share in that struggle was undistinguished by land and disastrous at sea. Rome, against which Garibaldi made two unsuccessful attacks on his own initiative in 1862 and 1867, fell in 1870 after Napoleon surrendered to the Prussians at Sedan. Victor Emmanuel, who had already transferred his capital from Turin to Florence in 1861, now felt able to establish it in Rome. The thing was to be done as decently as possible. No Garibaldi — he was kept under surveillance. No Mazzini — he was interned at Gaeta. For the Pope, deference, guaranteed religious independence, a pension, and extra-territorial privileges. Even so, Pius was not to be won over. The royal troops had to fight their way into Rome, where the Zouaves of the French garrison resisted bravely until ordered to give in. Pius then made a dignified retreat into the precincts of the Vatican, where his successors remained in self-imposed imprisonment until 1929, their sanctuary respected by the government they refused to recognize. Only their palace of the Quirinal, across the river, was taken over as the residence of the king.

19. The Age of Mussolini

AFTER THE heroics of the Risorgimento who could have prevented anti-climax? Italy had now to adjust herself to the hard facts of the nineteenth century, to live prose instead of poetry, to learn that (as Nurse Cavell said in a very different context) patriotism was not enough. In liberating themselves the Italians had also loosed a cageful of intractable problems, with which it was now their business, nobody else's, to deal.

A land repeatedly divided over fifteen centuries was not to be unified merely by erasing dotted lines from its map or hoisting an identical tricolour on every tower. There were deep local differences and jealousies, above all the perennial North-South animosity: progressive Piedmont and Lombardy realized that in backward, poverty-stricken Sicily and Naples they had tied two millstones round their necks, while those regions felt themselves Cinderellas, unjustly neglected. Even the North was a late starter in the industrial race: Britain, France and Germany were already vanishing down the track. Italy was deficient in technical skill and (until the hydro-electric age) in power.

Nor could a parliamentary democracy be created simply by admiring the institutions of Victorian England. Centuries of autocracy and foreign domination had produced apathy in the masses and a habit of illegality among the intelligentsia. Political responsibility had to be developed in a society in which illiteracy had been the rule for the majority and censorship for the rest. Regional prejudices were complicated by lingering sentimental loyalties to displaced regimes. The devout Catholic, especially, was placed in a dilemma by papal policy, which for a long time forbade him to use his vote. Doctrinaire republicans remained irreconcilable. 'Monarchy,' declared Mazzini, 'will never number me among its followers,' and he regarded his countrymen as deluded to accept it. He refused to come to terms with the new order and continued his propaganda from abroad. He was visiting Pisa incognito in 1872 when he was taken ill with pleurisy and died. Ironically, the Italian parliament paid a unanimous tribute to his work for the Risorgimento.

One by one the other chief characters in the drama left the stage, Pio Nono and Victor Emmanuel in 1878, and Garibaldi in 1882, dying at his home on Caprera, just short of his seventy-fifth birthday. Though strongly critical of the way in which things had turned out, he had been as always more practical than Mazzini, entering parliament and finally agreeing to accept a state pension for his services.

In the year he died, his country entered into an incongruous association, the Triple Alliance, with her hereditary enemy, Austria, and with Germany. The immediate reason was pique with France for the occupation of Tunis the previous year. The new friendship never went deep into the hearts of the people, and, no matter what efforts were made to strengthen economic and other links with the two Teutonic empires, there was still much goodwill for France and even more for Britain.

One year later, in 1883, a son was born to a blacksmith in the Romagna whose character and career vividly epitomize the subsequent history of his country. Benito Mussolini was named after a famous Mexican revolutionary, his father being active in the Socialist movement then surging up throughout Italy. The mother was a school-teacher and a pious churchwoman, and, like D. H. Lawrence's, the social superior of her husband. The boy was nourished on a mixed diet of Socialist theory and the marching songs of the Risorgimento. He never forgot seeing, at fifteen, the departure of nine local families emigrating under the stress of poverty to Brazil. It left him with an ineradicable determination to create an Italy rich enough to support her people either on her own soil or in colonies. Those nine families of neighbours represented eight million other Italians who, over a space of forty years, had to leave their homes for North or South America.

The Italy in which Mussolini grew up was one of strikes, unemployment and agitation. An opportunist and cynical prime minister, Agostino Depretis, with little faith in his country's future, had given place in 1887 to a swashbuckling

Sicilian, Francesco Crispi, Garibaldi's chief Sicilian lieutenant in the 1860 adventure. He was an intense individualist:
'What party do I belong to? I am Crispi!' A rabid anti-
clerical, he scarcely improved relations with the Papacy by
authorizing the erection in front of the Vatican of a statue
to Giordano Bruno on the exact spot where he had been
burnt as a heretic. None the less, he achieved an almost
dictatorial ascendancy over the people, foreshadowing that
of the little boy then growing up in the smithy at Predappio.
At home Crispi tried hard to stop the spread of the revolutionary trade union branches, the *fasci*. Abroad he saw the intensi-
fying international struggle for raw materials and markets,
and under him Italy joined, late again, in the scramble for
African colonies. By 1890 she had secured Somaliland and
Eritrea. An attempt to take over Ethiopia as well led to the
annihilation of the Italian forces at Adowa in 1896, when two
generals and about ten thousand men were killed, wounded
or captured by the despised Ethiopians. Crispi was broken
by this disaster, resigned, and disappeared into penurious
obscurity.

The turn of the century saw the assassination of King
Umberto by an anarchist. The diminutive and astute Victor
Emmanuel III assumed the crown he was to wear, if not quite
all his life, at least for the next forty-six years. Up to the First
World War the dominant politician was Giovanni Giolitti,
who had a Medicean grasp of the distinction between power
and office. His chief concern was to build up for himself the
maximum parliamentary following, so that he could move in
and out of the premiership at will. When trouble threatened
(and there was abundant trouble in the years before 1914)
he knew just when to resign and make way for some short-
sighted scapegoat, well aware that he retained the real control
and could return as soon as it was safe to do so.

In this period extreme poverty went hand in hand with
expanding prosperity. Foreign trade grew, electrical power
was multiplied, the traditional industries like silk and textiles
developed along with new ones like the manufacture of the
motor-car. As profits rose, so did proletarian and agrarian
unrest. Every year saw hundreds of strikes in the factories
and on the railways. Milan, in 1907, held the first general
strike. The class-war was conscious and intense. Soon indeed

there was a four-page weekly in circulation, entitled *La Lotta di Classe*, edited and entirely written by Mussolini.

These were formative years for the blacksmith's son. An aggressive, maladjusted boy at school, early using his knife on his fellows just as, a little later, he used it on his mistress, he was full of undigested self-education and intellectual pretensions, always parroting the opinions of the last book he had read, which was often by Nietzsche or some other inflammatory prophet of extreme individualism. In 1901 he took up a post as schoolmaster, a youth of eighteen 'with burning eyes, a drooping black bow tie, and a broad-brimmed black hat', finding relaxation from the classroom with the twenty-year-old wife of an absent soldier. It was not the first of the innumerable affairs which punctuated his career. Only ten years afterwards he could write in his *Autobiography* with smug sentimentalism: '*I have loved many women but by now the grey veil of oblivion covers these long-past loves.*' His attitude to women was crude and insensitive. As Claretta Petacci, the last and most permanent of his mistresses, recalled: 'He did not even take his boots off.'

These out-of-school activities, combined with his subversive opinions, were not calculated to advance him in the teaching profession, and it was not long before he left it. The next few years saw him in and out of trouble, at one time evading military service by slipping into Switzerland, at another serving his period in the Bersaglieri, sometimes doing manual work or even being unemployed (brief experiences subsequently exaggerated for propagandist reasons) but tending more and more towards Socialist and trade unionist agitation. When in 1911 Italy went to war with Turkey, a war which led to her acquisition of Libya, Cyrenaica, and the Dodecanese Islands, he made himself conspicuous in the violent popular demonstration against the campaign. He was arrested along with Pietro Nenni for inciting the people to insurrection and for sowing disaffection among the army reservists. Both received sentences of a year, reduced on appeal to five months. This modest martyrdom greatly increased his reputation in the Socialist movement, and it was not long before the party executive unanimously appointed as editor of their paper, *Avanti,* 'Professor Benito Mussolini', the title being accorded, Italian-fashion, to one who had passed successfully through a teachers' training college.

.   .   .   .

The outbreak of the First World War did not automatically involve Italy, for her partners in the Triple Alliance had not consulted her during the critical weeks following Sarajevo. When the conflict was not 'over by Christmas', both sides started to bargain for her goodwill. Austria wanted only her continued neutrality and was prepared to pay for it with territorial concessions. The Allies bid higher for active help. In April, 1915, Italy signed the secret Treaty of London with Britain, France and Russia, by which she was promised a defensible Alpine frontier extending to the Brenner, Trieste, Istria, a strip of the Dalmatian coast and various Adriatic islands, as well as recognition of her title to the Dodecanese. The open declaration of war on Austria followed just a month later.

It was by then a popular decision. Few Italians had any love for their age-old enemy. The only argument had been between Giolitti's neutralists, supported by big business, and the pro-Ally man-in-the-street, ranging from patriotic conservative to socialist. Mussolini was one of those who broke with his former comrades, veering round from neutralism to the policy of intervention. The four weeks between secret pact and public declaration were marked by disorderly meetings of ever-increasing ardour, demanding what the government had already decided to do.

The memory of the Caporetto debacle has tended unfairly to obscure the Italian achievement before and afterwards. Though ill-equipped and under-munitioned for twentieth-century warfare, the Italians took a calculated risk and launched their first offensive before mobilization was complete, thereby surprising the Austrians. For two and a half years they endured the rigours of the Alpine front, with ice and avalanche in place of Flemish mud, and, if their advances were not geographically impressive, at least they advanced. But their main contribution was to pin down large enemy forces.

In October, 1917, came disaster at Caporetto, a key-point on the Isonzo, now just inside Yugoslavia. A German-Austrian

offensive was planned by Ludendorff, using a massive con-
centration of troops and artillery just released from the
Eastern Front by the collapse of Russia. The first hammer-
stroke cracked two Italian corps which happened to be
especially demoralized by the now universal war-weariness.
They surrendered, and catastrophe followed by chain-reaction.
Four hundred thousand Italians took to their heels. Two
hundred thousand were captured, with fifteen hundred guns,
and in a few nightmare weeks the gains of two and a half
years were obliterated. At last the Italians stood at bay along
the flooded Piave, twenty-nine divisions against fifty, resisting
with a heroic ferocity which deserved to wipe out much of
the earlier humiliation. By the time French and British help
arrived, they had halted the enemy by their own efforts.

The offensive was not resumed until June, 1918, when the
Austrians, now deprived of German assistance, launched a
two-pronged attack, one in the mountains and the other where
the Piave enters the plain. Torrential rain washed away ten
of the fourteen bridges they threw across the river and they
had to fall back with nothing achieved. By October, with the
Austro-Hungarian Empire tottering, the time was ripe for a
counter-stroke. The Italians and their allies crossed the Piave,
a difficult operation in which the Tenth Army under the
British Lord Cavan played a decisive part, at a point where
the flooded river was a mile and a half wide. It was now the
turn of the Austrians to know the ignominy of rout and mass
surrenders. In the Battle of Vittorio Veneto they lost half a
million prisoners and five thousand guns. An armistice was
signed on 3rd November, a week before Germany too accepted
defeat.

.   .   .   .

When the cheering died away Italy was faced, more than
most countries, with disillusionment. The echoes of the
Soviet revolution were reverberating dangerously through
Europe. In Italy, as in Germany and Hungary, Communism
seemed a serious possibility. Victory had not yielded its
promised fruits: America had never signed the Pact of
London, Czarist Russia's signature was now an historical
curiosity, and Italy found herself cold-shouldered in the
conference-chamber. Though gaining the Trentino (South

Tyrol) and other territory, she was not after all to have Dalmatia. That coveted coastline was to go to the newfangled state of Yugoslavia. The action of the eccentric poet-patriot, d'Annunzio, in seizing the port of Fiume with a party of black-shirted volunteers, was a symptom of the general disorder.

'We, the survivors, we, the returned soldiers, shall urge our claims to govern Italy,' Mussolini had announced in a speech six months before the armistice. He spoke already as a returned soldier, having survived a trench mortar accident which had cut short his military career at the level of corporal and enabled him to resume the editorship of his new paper, *Il Popolo d'Italia.*

Now, on 23rd March, 1919, he called a small meeting in a business-men's club in Milan and founded the Milan Fighters' Fascio, from which sprang the whole movement of Fascismo. The vocabulary, the emblem of the rods and axes, and the outstretched-arm salute, were all inspired by ancient Rome. The black shirt and gangster tactics were soon imitated from d'Annunzio. The ideology was a hotchpotch with something to please every one. It was nationalistic, it professed to be neither capitalistic nor socialistic, and a too close analysis was discouraged by its motto, '*No discussion, only obedience*'. · Above all, the movement was anti-Communist, and if only for that reason it was viewed with sympathy by a wide variety of Italians, as indeed it was by some very eminent foreign statesmen.

In the hot-house atmosphere of anarchy, Fascism grew with incredible speed. In 1919 Mussolini stood for parliament and met with humiliating defeat. Two years later he was elected with two or three dozen supporters. In 1922, when a national general strike was proclaimed, the whole Fascist organization went into action, took over the essential services, and broke the strike within twenty-four hours. After that, recruits flooded in. Realizing their strength, a great party rally in Naples that October declared that if they were not given political power they would march on Rome and take it. The prime minister wished to proclaim martial law against them, but Victor Emmanuel refused to sign the proclamation. The next day the Fascists arrived in Rome unopposed. Mussolini himself, summoned by the king, made the legendary

'March' by sleeping-car from Milan, and assumed power as the head of a coalition government.

The next few years saw the gradual transformation of the top-hatted, be-spatted Signor Mussolini, as he appeared at the Lausanne Conference, into the fulminating, prognathous 'Duce', who used to harangue his hypnotized followers from the balcony of the Palazzo Venezia in moments of national hysteria. At first his position was anything but secure. He suffered crises of confidence and was always prepared to desert the sinking ship. The murder of the Socialist Matteotti, of which he always protested his innocence, none the less nearly brought his downfall. But he survived — it was for twenty years his good luck that he had to face no really determined opposition at home or abroad, and that, though many privately despised him, it suited their purposes that he should remain. Soon the coalition gave place to an all-Fascist government. Parliamentary democracy disappeared, along with freedom of the press and of association, to be replaced by the conception of the Corporative State, in which subservient trade unions were integrated with employers and Fascist Party representatives. In fact, the Duce became more and more a despot, avid for flattery, impatient of discussion, ridiculous in his personal vanities. Undoubtedly, order had returned to daily life. His admirers, none more than the foreign visitors, pointed to punctual trains and other amenities. He enjoyed world-wide popularity as the saviour of Italy from Communism, though his more knowledgeable critics argued, *sotto voce,* that Communism had been on the wane even before his coming to power, thanks to the subtler policies of Giolitti in his final, post-war ministry of 1920-21. Similarly it has been argued that some of his much-publicized constructive works, his marsh-draining and archaeological excavations, were either taken over from previous planners or were anyhow ill-advised. It is still a little early to see all the facts clear of prejudice. One act was indisputably his — the Lateran Treaty of 1929, which at last established an agreed relationship between the Papacy and the Kingdom of Italy, created the Vatican State, and freed the Popes from their self-imposed immurement.

When Hitler seized power in Germany, Mussolini at first maintained his alignment with the West. He was flattered by the German imitation of Fascism, but privately convinced that Teutons would ruin his ideas. Years earlier he had snubbed the still-struggling Nazi leader when he asked for his autograph. The two men, destined to be partners in tragedy, never achieved any deep measure of sympathy. On various occasions Mussolini described Hitler as a 'clown', a 'madman', and a 'horrible, sexually degenerate creature'. Recording their first meeting at Venice in 1934, he complained that 'instead of talking about concrete problems, Hitler only recited *Mein Kampf* from memory — that dreary book which I have never been able to read'. During a motor-boat trip Hitler had denounced all the Mediterranean peoples, including the Italians, on the score that they had Negro blood in their veins. Mussolini had no use for racial theories and particularly deplored the Nazis' anti-Semitism. Understanding was not helped by his becoming increasingly vain, as the years passed, of his command of the German language. Interpreters were injudiciously dispensed with, and genuine misconception was added to the inconsistency and duplicity with which the two leaders cloaked their respective purposes.

In 1934 the Austrian Nazis murdered their chancellor, Dollfuss. Mussolini sent two divisions to the Brenner, a clear warning to Hitler against any move into Austria. At Stresa, in the following April, he still showed himself the friend of the West: he agreed with Ramsay Macdonald, Sir John Simon, Laval and Flandin that the new German danger must be controlled. Rightly or wrongly, he came away with the impression that, if he lined up with them in Europe, they would condone his impending attack on Ethiopia. That attack, however, launched in October, 1935, produced a world-wide reaction which amazed the professional politicians. Baldwin, the new British prime minister, had to disown the Hoare-Laval Pact, which had coolly assigned half Ethiopia to the Italians, and its two red-faced authors had to resign. The League of Nations demonstrated moral disapproval by imposing various half-measures which infuriated Mussolini without stopping him. Italian troopships continued their unimpeded procession through the Suez Canal. Soon the warlike but medieval Ethiopians were overcome by modern tanks, artillery, and aeroplanes which, besides bombing and machine-gunning them, sprayed them with mustard gas.

Within a few months their emperor was in exile and his title assumed by Victor Emmanuel. The Italians were assured officially that the shame of Adowa had been expunged.

This was a turning-point in Mussolini's career. He had won the enlarged colonial empire which was part of his dream, but he had lost the friendship of the Western nations and was forced into an uncongenial association with Germany. In his own personality, too, megalomania was more evident, the poses and postures more ridiculous. He received callers in the immense, bare Mappomondo Room of the Palazzo Venezia, seeking to intimidate them by the long walk to his desk and the absence of a visitor's chair at the other end. One man, at least, remained unimpressed, a famous Sicilian comedian, who pointedly looked round for the missing seat and exclaimed in dialect, ' Oh, is this the bar? ' There were not many, though, who could afford to throw off such sparks of independence. Another of the dictator's tricks was to have the lights burning in his office until a late hour, to convey the impression that he was still working devotedly in the cause of the nation when he had in fact retired to his private suite. Here, from early afternoon onwards, the infatuated young Clara Petacci was always waiting for him. His wife and children were safe at home in the Villa Torlonia and it was only in 1943, after seven years, that Rachele Mussolini learnt of the association.

In 1936 the Spanish Civil War brought Hitler and Mussolini into open comradeship. Both sent troops, transparently disguised as ' volunteers ', to help the Spanish Nationalists overthrow their Left-wing government. Exiled Italian anti-Fascists fought their countrymen in the sierras and in the trenches outside Madrid. Those who later criticized the Italian people for not rebelling against their Duce might well ask themselves how much encouragement such rebels received from the Western democracies at the time. At Easter, 1939, emboldened by Hitler's successful aggressions elsewhere, Mussolini occupied Albania; but when the Polish crisis came in the late summer he was in a panic of indecision, at one moment declaring that Italy would march with Germany and at the next ' to let loose a war now would be folly '. In the event, the Second World War opened with Italy preserving her neutrality, which he preferred to call ' non-belligerence '.

In March, 1940, he met Hitler at the Brenner and promised his armed support. The dizzy sequence of Nazi triumphs during the next two or three months convinced him that he must enter the fray at once if he was to share in the winnings. When Badoglio, the conqueror of Ethiopia, told him that the Italian forces were totally unequipped for real warfare and that it was 'suicide', he retorted, 'Everything will be over by September. I only need a few thousand dead to give me a seat at the peace conference.' On 10th June, just a week after Dunkirk, Mussolini declared war on France and Britain. 'Like a jackal,' commented Churchill. And the well-drilled crowds outside the Palazzo Venezia chanted Italy's war-aims: '*Nice, Tunis, Corsica!*'

On 10th July, 1943, the Anglo-American forces shattered these illusions by invading Sicily. The intervening three years had brought Italy little but disaster. Despite powerful German help she had been swept out of North Africa. Her Ethiopian empire had fallen like a house of cards. Only more German help had saved her from ignominious defeat in Greece. Her navy had been crippled at Matapan and Taranto. Finally, ten divisions of unenthusiastic Italians had left their stiffening corpses on the Russian front. Now her home territory was attacked. Patton's American Seventh Army seized all their allotted beach-heads within three hours and swept forward rapidly. The British and at times the Canadians were less sensational in their progress, but in a little over a month resistance was finished and the island was in Allied hands.

The Duce's days were numbered. Opposition was developing along two separate and unrelated lines. There were his critics inside the Fascist Grand Council, including his son-in-law, Ciano, and there was the king—still the same little Victor Emmanuel, seventy-four now, unimpressive but far from negligible — with Badoglio and other generals. This second group had fixed 26th July for their coup, but the timing had to be hastily revised when at six o'clock in the morning on the 25th (a Sunday) the king was brought extraordinary news: at a stormy meeting of the Grand Council, lasting from the previous afternoon until after 2 a.m., Ciano and most of the other leaders had risen one after another to denounce Mussolini, finally voting two to one that he should surrender his powers.

Victor Emmanuel decided to put his own plan into operation a day sooner. Badoglio was warned to stand by. Mussolini, who had asked for an audience, was invited to come to
the Villa Savoia at five o'clock. The two men were alone in
the study for twenty minutes, which can be reconstructed
only from their somewhat differing recollections and from
what other persons observed at their parting. It would seem
that the king was completely inflexible and showed no outward sign of his emotion, while the Duce, when told of his
dismissal, was completely deflated, repeating: 'Then it's
all over. Then it's all over. And what'll happen to me? And
to my family?' He was shown out, livid in the face, shrunken
and old. He looked round dazedly for his car. A waiting officer
of the *carabinieri* saluted and said, 'His Majesty has ordered
me to go with you and protect you from the mob.' He let
himself be helped into an ambulance, which he found full of
armed guards, the door was slammed behind him, and he
was driven away to the barracks under arrest. His own bodyguard, sitting in cars drawn up along the kerb outside, knew
nothing until later that evening, when someone remembered
their existence and told them to go home.

Just before eleven the bald announcement was broadcast
that the king had accepted Mussolini's resignation and invited
Badoglio to form a government. Everybody knew what it
meant. Late as the hour was, the whole city reawoke to life.
The streets filled with crowds shouting: 'Down with Fascism!
Death to Mussolini!' and pulling down Fascist emblems
wherever they could be found. The regime had fallen without
the firing of a shot.

.   .   .   .

In one important respect these rejoicings were premature.
The Duce's fall did not mean, as simple folk assumed, the
end of the war. Old conventions of national honour inhibited
men like Victor Emmanuel and Badoglio from dropping the
sword too impulsively and in theory the alliance with Hitler
continued. The British and Americans, as usual least happy
in their conduct of political warfare, chose this moment for
intensified bombing of the Italian cities. On 8th September
Badoglio surrendered unconditionally, but even this, far
from marking the end of the agony, opened a new and terrible

phase, in which the Italian people became the helpless victims of their recent allies.

For Kesselring's Germans, who had been the backbone of resistance in Sicily and still occupied key-positions all over the mainland, were not going to give up the peninsula without a struggle. On 13th September a picked detachment of their parachutists rescued Mussolini from the remote clinic, six thousand feet up in the Abruzzi, where the Badoglio government held him prisoner. He was spirited away by light aeroplane and taken by stages to Munich, where Hitler harangued him unmercifully, and insisted that he should resume the leadership of the Italian people and his alliance with Germany. The Duce was in no condition to argue. He was fast going downhill, both physically and psychologically. He became Hitler's puppet for the remainder of the war.

Meanwhile the Allied Eighth Army was pushing up the toe of Italy and a simultaneous landing had been made at Salerno by the Fifth. Naples was taken on 1st October, and the great Bourbon palace at Caserta became the Allied headquarters, where eventually Field-Marshal Alexander received the German surrender. For a long time, however, the advance was stayed along a line cutting straight across the peninsula. The king and Badoglio's government, having prudently moved south of this line to Brindisi, declared war on the Germans on 13th October. This action exacerbated the ferocity of the Nazis, and those Italians who were north of the line now experienced the full force of their terrorism, with all the horrors of mass-executions and the concentration-camp. In reply, a partisan resistance developed in the country-side, fired with the spirit of Garibaldi though not always able, in the debased conditions of the twentieth century, to emulate his chivalry. Regular Italian troops, the Corpo Italiano di Liberazione, took over a sector on the Allied right wing.

Early in the New Year Alexander tried to outflank Kesselring by an Anglo-American landing at Anzio, just south of Rome, but the bridge-head was contained and the general deadlock continued until May. The difficulties were numerous throughout the campaign. German resistance was spirited and obstinate. Fortifications, land-mines, and demolitions obstructed the Allies at every step, and to these military devices were added the natural obstacles of mountain and river, together with some bitter wintry conditions and torrential rains. Finally, the Italian Front was regarded as of secondary importance in the war, and Alexander never had that superiority of men and material which could have produced a swift decision. His outstanding general, Montgomery, for example, had long ago been taken away to lead the invasion of Normandy. However, May brought the break-through, after a concentrated bombardment which for the fifth time in history demolished the monastery of Cassino, previously the victim of Lombards, Saracens, Normans, and earthquake. The main forces joined hands with the dogged defenders of the Anzio beach-head, and on 4th June Rome welcomed the latest of her liberators. The Germans fell back to their heavily fortified Gothic Line, running from Pisa across to Rimini. This in turn was broken by the end of the year. The advance was beginning to resemble an international crusade, as Siena fell to the French, Ancona to the Poles, Ravenna to the Greeks and Canadians. Indians, New Zealanders, and the Italians themselves were driving forward along with the soldiers of the United States and the United Kingdom.

Again there was a lull. A devitalized Mussolini went through the motions of governing his new but shrinking Italian Republic from a gloomy villa overlooking Lake Garda. At Verona, near by, Ciano and the other former leaders who had deserted him were strapped to chairs and executed by the firing-squad. But the Duce seemed to have no spirit left, even for revenge.

In the spring of 1945 the Allied advance was renewed. Much of the territory behind the Germans was now occupied by the partisans. The war began to assume the meaningless savagery of some monster's death-agony, full of spasmodic atrocity. City after city was captured: Spezia, Modena, Ferrara, Verona, Genoa in as many days. German resistance cracked as the news came of disaster on the home front. Mussolini, rejoined by Clara Petacci, was making panic-stricken efforts to escape into Switzerland, but all was confusion. There were partisans everywhere. He heard that his wife and children had been turned back by the Swiss, then that the Italian frontier guards had gone over to the Committee of Liberation and were seizing any Fascist who tried to leave the country. There followed a day or two of nightmare driving backwards and forwards through the Como countryside, its beauty now blanketed in rain. On 28th April he and Clara were stopped, recognized and arrested by partisans at Dongo. The next day they were put into a car, driven up a quiet lane, pushed against the ornamental gateway of the Villa Belmonte, and hurriedly shot, with no more ceremony than if they had been dogs.

That was the day Milan fell to the Fifth Army. On the morrow, while the victorious Allies were sweeping on into Turin, the bodies of the Duce, his mistress, and fifteen other prominent Fascists were loaded on to a lorry and taken into Milan. There they were displayed, dangling head-downwards, outside a garage on the Piazzale Loreto, where the Germans had shot fifteen Italian hostages the year before. Meanwhile, on that same 30th April, 1945, Hitler and Eva Braun were committing suicide in their Berlin shelter as the Red Army drew ever nearer.

A few days later the war in Europe was over. In Italy, as everywhere, the work of reconstruction began. Victor Emmanuel's anti-Fascism had come too late to save the discredited monarchy. He did his best by abdicating in favour of his son, Umberto, but the ensuing referendum led to the immediate proclamation of a republic, and the last sovereign of the House of Savoy departed to exile in Portugal.

Now the Italian people could turn the page and start the next chapter of their chequered story. All their faith was needed. The age-old problems remained, only intensified by the new ideologies and the accelerated changes of the modern world: ignorance and illiteracy, corruption and political immaturity, narrow regionalism, the historic rift between North and South, and that other rift, intolerable to men of the twentieth century, between the indecently rich and the abysmally poor. It is too early to write that next chapter, or even to sketch its shape. The politicians must deal with their daunting agenda before words are needed from the historians.

Short Bibliography

IT WOULD be pretentious, if not impossible, to list all the books consulted for a work of this kind. The following are those to which the author is particularly indebted.

Cecilia M. Ady. *Lorenzo dei Medici and Renaissance Italy.* 1955.

Raymond Bloch. *The Etruscans.* 1958.
   The Origins of Rome. 1960.

Oscar Browning. *Guelphs and Ghibellines.* 1894.

Jacob Burckhardt. *The Civilization of the Renaissance in Italy.* 1878.

J. Carcopino. *Daily Life in Ancient Rome.* 1941.

M. Cary (ed.). *A History of the Roman World.* 1935-1944.

G. and C. Charles-Picard. *Daily Life in Carthage.* 1961.

F. R. Cowell. *Cicero and the Roman Republic.* 1948.
   Everyday Life in Ancient Rome. 1961.

E. G. Gardner (ed.). *Italy: A Companion to Italian Studies.* 1934.

T. Hodgkin. *Italy and Her Invaders.* 1892-1899.

J. Lucas-Dubreton. *Daily Life in Florence.* 1960.

Sir J. A. R. Marriott. *The Makers of Modern Italy.* 1931.

C. W. C. Oman. *Seven Roman Statesmen of the Later Republic.* 1902.

D. Pettoello. *An Outline of Italian Civilization.* 1932.

J. H. Plumb (ed.). *The Renaissance.* 1961.

T. G. E. Powell. *The Celts.* 1959.

C. W. Previté-Orton. *The Shorter Cambridge Medieval History.* 1952.

Sir Steven Runciman. *The Sicilian Vespers.* 1958.

E. Sichel. *The Renaissance.* 1914.

G. M. Trevelyan. *Garibaldi's Defence of the Roman Republic.* 1907.
   Garibaldi and the Thousand. 1909.
   Garibaldi and the Making of Italy. 1911.

J. P. Trevelyan. *A Short History of the Italian People.* 1956.

A. A. M. van der Heyden and H. H. Scullard. *Atlas of the Classical World.* 1959.

F. van der Meer and C. Mohrmann. *Atlas of the Early Christian World.* 1958.

S. von Cles-Reden. *The Buried People.* 1955.

A. J. Whyte. *The Evolution of Modern Italy.* 1944.

Index